D1265621

French Colonial Archaeology

F
543
.F74
1991

FRENCH COLONIAL ARCHAEOLOGY

THE ILLINOIS COUNTRY AND THE WESTERN GREAT LAKES

Edited by

JOHN A. WALTHALL

UNIVERSITY OF ILLINOIS PRESS

Urbana and Chicago

SAUK VALLEY COLLEGE
L.R.C.
112027

© 1991 by the Board of Trustees of the University of Illinois
Manufactured in the United States of America
C 5 4 3 2 1

This book is printed on acid-free paper.

Library of Congress Cataloging-in-Publication Data

French colonial archaeology : the Illinois country and the western
  Great Lakes / edited by John A. Walthall.
      p.   cm.
    Papers from the Conference on French Colonial Archaeology in the
Illinois Country, held April 1988, in Springfield, Ill., and
organized by the Illinois Historic Preservation Agency.
  Includes bibliographical references.
  ISBN 0-252-01797-8
    1. Illinois—Antiquities—Congresses. 2. French—Illinois—
Antiquities—Congresses. 3. Great Lakes Region—Antiquities—
Congresses. 4. French—Great Lakes Region—Antiquities—
Congresses. 5. Excavations (Archaeology)—Illinois—Congresses.
6. Excavations (Archaeology)—Great Lakes Region—Congresses.
I. Walthall, John A. II. Illinois Historic Preservation Agency.
III. Conference on French Colonial Archaeology in the Illinois
Country (1988 : Springfield, Ill.)
F543.F74 1991
977.3′01—dc20   90-20292
                                                          CIP

To Paul J. Maynard

Contents

1. French Colonial Archaeology
    John A. Walthall and Thomas E. Emerson   1

2. The Archaeology of La Salle's Fort St. Louis on
    Starved Rock and the Problem of the Newell
    Fort   *Robert L. Hall*   14

3. Fort de Chartres: Archaeology in the Illinois
    Country   *David Keene*   29

4. French Colonial Fort Massac: Architecture and
    Ceramic Patterning   *John A. Walthall*   42

5. Ouiatenon on the Ouabache: Archaeological
    Investigations at a Fur Trading Post on the
    Wabash River   *Vergil E. Noble*   65

6. Documents and Archaeology in French Illinois
    Margaret Kimball-Brown   78

7. The French Colonial Villages of Cahokia and
    Prairie du Pont, Illinois
    *Bonnie L. Gums, William R. Iseminger, Molly E.
    McKenzie, and Dennis D. Nichols*   85

8. The Louvier Site at Prairie du Rocher
    Edward T. Safiran   123

9. Ste. Genevieve, a French Colonial Village in the
    Illinois Country   *F. Terry Norris*   133

10. The Search for French Peoria
    Thomas E. Emerson and Floyd Mansberger   149

11. Frontier Colonization of the Saline Creek Valley
    *Michael K. Trimble, Teresita Majewski, Michael J.
    O'Brien, and Anna L. Price*   165

12. An Archaeological Perspective on Animal
    Exploitation Patterns at French Colonial Sites in
    the Illinois Country *Terrance J. Martin*   189

13. The French in Michigan and Beyond: An
    Archaeological View from Fort Michilimackinac
    Toward the West *Donald P. Heldman*   201

14. Variability in Trade at Eighteenth-Century French
    Outposts *Dean L. Anderson*   218

15. French Presence in Minnesota: The View from Site
    Mo20 near Little Falls *Douglas A. Birk*   237

Bibliography   267

Notes on the Contributors   288

Figures

1-1   Map of French Colonial Sites in the Mississippi Valley Region
1-2   Map of French Colonial Sites in the American Bottom Region
3-1   Archaeological Plan Map of Fort de Chartres
3-2   Plan of the Fortress of Louisbourg
3-3   Plan of Port Royal
4-1   Plan for Fort Massac (1745)
4-2   Archaeological Plan of Fort Massac
4-3   Typical Cross Section of Moat
4-4   Cross Section of the Palisade
4-5   Plan of the Northwest Bastion
4-6   Structure Complex One
4-7   Structure Complex Two
4-8   Structure Complex Three
4-9   Faience Rim Border Designs
4-10 Faience Vessels
5-1   Aerial Photograph of Fort Ouiatenon Location
5-2   Excavation at Fort Ouiatenon
5-3   Remains of the Storehouse at Fort Ouiatenon
5-4   Reconstructed Plan of Fort Ouiatenon
7-1   Map of the Illinois Country by Thomas Hutchins (ca. 1766)
7-2   Map of Cahokia by Thomas Hutchins (ca. 1766)
7-3   1898 Photograph of the Cahokia Courthouse
7-4   1938–39 WPA Excavation Map of the Cahokia Courthouse
7-5   Reconstructed Cahokia Courthouse (1940)

7-6   Church of the Holy Family

7-7   Nicholas Jarrot Mansion (ca. 1894)

7-8   Locations of Areas A–F at the Cahokia Wedge Site

7-9   WPA-reconstructed Map of Cahokia for 1790–1826

7-10   1841 Lithograph of Cahokia

7-11   Ca. 1927 Aerial Photograph of Cahokia

7-12   Excavation Trench at the Cahokia Wedge Site

7-13   Pierre Martin/Nicholas Boismenue House

7-14   Map of Excavations at the Martin/Boismenue House

7-15   WPA-drawn Plan of the LePage House

9-1   Relationship of Historic (1881) to Present Mississippi River Channel

9-2   23-SG-124 Feature Distributions

9-3   "Standard" Illinois Country Village Lot

9-4   Old Town Ste. Genevieve (ca. 1766)

9-5   Old Town Ste. Genevieve (1793)

9-6   Old Town Ste. Genevieve (Collet, ca. 1796)

9-7   Old Town Ste. Genevieve (Anonymous, ca. 1796)

9-8   Old Town Ste. Genevieve (ca.1797–98)

9-9   Old Town Ste. Genevieve (ca. 1777)

9-10   Plan Views of Kaskaskia

10-1   Plat of the Old Village of Peoria

10-2   Coles's 1834 Plat Map of La Ville de Maillet/New Village of Peoria

10-3   Map Showing the Relationship of the Old and New French Villages of Peoria

10-4   Drawings of Apparent Earthworks of Probable Fort Crevecoeur

10-5   Modern Topographic Map of the Area

11-1   Map of the Lower Saline Creek Locality

11-2   Detail of the De Finiels Map

11-3   Locations of Archaeological Work at the Kreilich Site

11-4   Plan View of Furnace Walls at 23-SG-5

11-5   Profile of South Wall of Furnace at 23-SG-5

11-6   Profile of East Wall of Furnace at 23-SG-5

11-7   Surface Artifact Concentrations in Area V, 23-SG-5

11-8   Plan View of Palisade at 23-SG-5

11-9   Plan View of *Poteaux en Terre* Structure at 23-SG-5

11-10   Plan View of Cedar Logs in Cellar of *Poteaux en Terre* Structure at 23-SG-5

11-11   Ceramic Sherds from 1985–86 Excavations at 23-SG-5

13-1   French and Indian Sites in Michigan

13-2   Expansion of the Palisaded Curtains

13-3   Straits of Mackinac

13-4   Archaeological Map of the Mission/Fort

13-5   Map of Fort Michilimackinac in 1749

13-6   Map of Fort Michilimackinac in 1766

13-7   Map of Fort Pontchartrain

13-8   Archaeological Map of the Southeast Quadrant of Fort Michilimackinac

13-9   Archaeological Master Map of Fort Michilimackinac

15-1   Selected French Sites in the Western Great Lakes Region

15-2   Major Vegetation Features in the Little Falls Area of Central Minnesota

15-3   Site Mo20 Surface Feature Map

15-4   Selected Artifacts Found at Mo20

15-5   Additional Mo20 Artifacts

15-6   The Central Structure at Mo20

15-7   Drawn Glass Seed Bead Distribution

Tables

4-1 Brittany Blue on White Vessels at French Colonial Sites in the Illinois Country

4-2 Evidence of Vessel Mending at Sites in the Illinois Country

4-3 Minimal Vessel Counts, Fort Massac

8-1 Artifact Groups Represented at the Louvier and Cahokia Wedge Sites

9-1 Artifact Concentrations at 23-SG-124

14-1 Outfits by Year for Each Post

14-2 Variety of Goods

14-3 Expenditure for Trade Goods by Year

14-4 Ranked Order of Trade Goods

14-5 Number of Years Each Item Was Taken to Forts

French Colonial Archaeology   1

John A. Walthall and Thomas E. Emerson

The Illinois Country was a major theater of French colonial economic and territorial expansion during the seventeenth and eighteenth centuries. That early presence left an indelible mark on the historical and cultural heritage of what was to become the state of Illinois. This period was kept alive in the early writings of such famous historians as Francis Parkman in his *LaSalle and the Discovery of the Great West,* in Reuben Thwaites's masterful translations of the *Jesuit Relations and Allied Documents,* and in the extensive body of early French manuscript translations and historical studies from the mid-nineteenth century to the present.

Twenty-five years ago, a gathering of researchers and scholars focused on the French in the Mississippi Valley. The first of these meetings was held in 1964 to celebrate the bicentennial of the founding of St. Louis. Because of that conference's success, it was followed by another in 1967. Both were organized by John Francis McDermott, who stressed their eclectic nature, shunning the more typical thematic or summary approach. The resulting books, published by the University of Illinois Press, contained a wide spectrum of chapters on "political, military, architectural, social, scientific, and cultural" topics (McDermott 1965, 1969:iv). There can be no doubt that these conferences fullfilled their goals of "adding something to the total score of knowledge . . . each offer(ing) evidence and interpretation which aided in the understanding of that area and time" (McDermott 1969:iv). Yet from an overall perspective much was missing.

A major topic unaddressed in those conferences was the potential of the archaeological record. While historical research into the French period has been both intensive and extensive, published archaeological research has been limited and narrowly focused. This situation, however, was not due to a lack of archaeological resources. Many of the structures and sites from this era have been preserved and serve as a visible reminder of those times when the Illinois Country was part of a greater empire reaching from Canada to Louisiana. Most of these sites are now part of the French Colonial Historic District, which stretches from near St. Louis at the village of Cahokia with its Jarrot Mansion, courthouse, and Church of the Holy Family south to Fort de Chartres, Fort Kaskaskia, and the Pierre Menard home. In recent years increasing attention has been placed on the archaeological investigation of many of these publicly owned sites but there was no attempt to summarize this new information.

In the spring of 1987 it seemed that, given the expanding database, it would be useful to provide a forum for interaction among researchers concentrating on the early French period. Even though the primary attention would be the Illinois Country, it was apparent that that region could only be understood in the broader context of French North America. Consequently, in April 1988 the Conference on French Colonial Archaeology in the Illinois Country, including scholars from the length of the Mississippi River Valley and the Great Lakes, was organized by the Illinois Historic Preservation Agency in Springfield, Illinois.

The conference format, which included a theme orientation and an attendance limited primarily to active researchers, was specifically chosen because of the previous success of such conferences in Illinois. In the past few years a number of scholars doing archaeology in Illinois have become increasingly dissatisfied with national and regional archaeology conferences. The sheer numbers of people and concurrent paper sessions have created an atmosphere that obstructs interaction with colleagues doing similar research. It was this dissatisfaction that prompted Kenneth B. Farnsworth and Thomas E. Emerson to organize the Kampsville Early Woodland Conference in 1982 and Emerson and R. Barry Lewis to hold the Middle Mississippian Conference at the 1983 annual meeting of the Society for American Archaeology, followed by the Mississippian Roundtable at the Midwest Archaeological Conference. These efforts resulted in published volumes (Farnsworth and Emerson 1986; Emerson and Lewis 1991). The French Colonial Conference was organized within the same framework as well as to provide a cultural and chronological context for ongoing studies within the Illinois State Historic Preservation Office.

French Colonial Archaeological Research

Archaeological interest in French colonial sites in the United States was inextricably linked to the rise of the historic preservation movement in this country nearly a century ago. As the ethnographic study of rapidly vanishing Native American cultures had been encouraged in the early decades of the nineteenth century, the preservation of historic sites was largely a product of the developing conservation ethic of the early twentieth century.

By the close of the first decade, organizations such as the Mount Vernon Ladies Association, the Association for the Preservation of Virginia Antiquities, and the Daughters of the American Revolution had begun the acquisition of historically important sites such as Mount Vernon and Jamestown. The interest exhibited by such influential groups toward the preservation of historical and archaeological sites led to the passage of the conservation-oriented Antiquities Act signed by Theodore Roosevelt in June 1906.

As a direct result of this conservation movement, French colonial sites in Illinois and other states began to be preserved in the public domain. For example, largely through the efforts of the Daughters of the American Revolution, Fort Massac (see Walthall, chap. 4) became the first state park in Illinois. The purchase of Massac in 1903 and of Fort de Chartres in 1914 signaled the beginning of an aquisition process leading to public ownership of many major sites. In fact, most of the sites discussed in this book are state parks or historical monuments.

The depression era of the 1930s produced not only major public works projects but also the first scientific archaeological investigations of historical sites in the United States. The modern discipline of historical archaeology in this country traces its beginnings to the initiation of the excavation program at Jamestown by the National Park Service in 1934 (Cotter 1958). Four years later, Paul Maynard, a University of Chicago archaeologist working with the Illinois Department of Public Works, began excavations at the eighteenth-century Saucier house in Cahokia, better known as the Cahokia Courthouse (see Gums et al., chap. 7). The next year, in 1939, Maynard directed large-scale excavations at Fort Massac on the banks of the Ohio River. Maynard's investigations at these Illinois sites were the first archaeological excavations at former French colonial outposts in the United States.

It is significant that Maynard's work was conducted as an adjunct activity to proposed historic reconstruction programs. His excavations, and many of those to follow, even to the present (see Keene, chap. 3, for example), were directed toward providing information concerning architectural detail. Information on the precise location of structures, structural configurations, and original building materials often could only be provided by archaeological techniques. Archaeology at French colonial sites over the past four decades has largely been viewed as a method of providing interpretive information and display materials for on-site architectural programs and museums. This adjunct role has limited much of the archaeological work at French colonial localities to those large and impressive sites, such as fortifications, that generate public attention and have development potential.

The chapters in this book on archaeological research at village and domestic sites containing no standing period architecture are based on very recent efforts. The surveys at Ste. Genevieve (see Norris, chap. 9) began in 1979, excavations at the Cahokia Wedge site in 1986 (see Gums et al., chap. 7), at Prairie du Rocher in 1986 (see Safiran, chap. 8), in the Saline Creek Valley in 1985 (see Trimble et al., chap. 11), and in Peoria in 1978 (see Emerson and Mansberger, chap. 10). While it was somewhat fortuitous that these field projects began within a very short, recent period of time, it is significant that research-oriented archaeology is now being applied at these important, and often endangered, domestic sites.

Another encouraging facet of recent French colonial studies has been the interest of scholars in more thoroughly utilizing the available data sources. For instance, the written record has too often been viewed merely as a chronological and geographical guide for archaeological investigations. However, Margaret Kimball Brown (chap. 6) has demonstrated the value of the documentary record as a tool to produce testable hypothesis on cultural behavior. Another example of important new avenues of research is presented by Terrance J. Martin in chapter 12. His numerous studies of French faunal exploitation provide an alternative and supplementary information source to the scant written record on the subject. Perhaps one of the major values of work such as Brown's and Martin's is the identification of alternative databases that allow for the independent formulation and testing of hypotheses.

French Colonial Chronology

Three periods, beginning with Jean Nicollet's landing at Green Bay in 1634 and ending with the Louisiana Purchase in 1803, have been formulated in order to accommodate the major events that occurred during the roughly century and a half of occupation in the geographical area encompassed by this book. Spatially, the French colonial sites discussed in this book are scattered over a vast region spanning the midcontinent from the western Great Lakes south to the Gulf Coast (fig. 1-1). The distribution of these sites was largely predicated on proximity to major navigable watercourses. The historian William Eccles has noted that "New France was . . . a riverine empire. Its main bases, Canada and Louisiana, dominated the two great rivers [the St. Lawrence and the Mississippi] giving access into the interior" (1972:147). After 1700 French foreign policy in North America centered around the construction of forts at strategic points along these waterways. In this way, a small number of French troops and their numerically superior Indian allies could hold back the westward expansion of the British colonies along the eastern seaboard. This policy was largely successful until the Seven Years' War (1756–63) when New France, with a total population of some seventy thousand Europeans, was finally overwhelmed by the British colonies, whose population by 1760 had reached 1.25 million (Eccles 1969, 1972).

The placement of forts and settlements along major river systems allowed the French a means of travel and a relatively rapid communication network. Concerning travel between the Gulf Coast, the Illinois Country, and Quebec, it has been noted that "the frequency with which the Canadians, both civilian and military, made this voyage . . . and thought nothing of it was astonishing to visitors from France" (Eccles 1972:147). The Illinois Country was strategically located along major water routes. Its northern border was Lake Michigan, its western boundary was the Mississippi River, its eastern borders reached the Wabash River, and along its southern border was the Ohio River, which provided access to the eastern interior.

Exploration Period (1634–1717)

Exploration of the western Great Lakes and the Mississippi Basin, the vaguely defined region referred to by the French as the Western Country, began in 1634 when Jean Nicollet landed at Green Bay. Within the next half-century, expeditions, most notably those of Marquette and Jolliet (1673) and La Salle (1679), entered the Illinois Country and explored southward to the mouth of the Mississippi River.

During this period, the Western Country was considered a part of Canada. The European presence in this region was dominated by three distinct social classes: explorers/soldiers, priests, and independent traders or *coureurs de bois*. Settlers, or *habitants,* did not reach

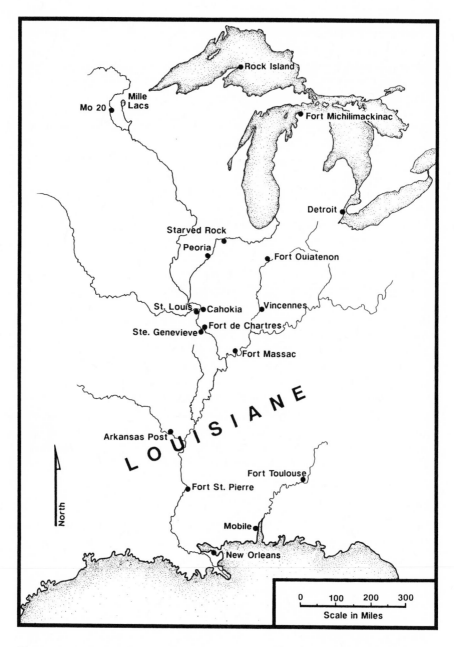

Figure 1-1. Map of French Colonial Sites in the Mississippi Valley Region

the Mississippi Valley until after 1718. Only a single French woman was recorded to have visited this wilderness during this time. Pierre-Charles DeLiette (Quaife 1947) recorded that around 1695 the explorer Charles Le Sueur brought his wife and small children with him into the Illinois Country: "when Madame La Sueur, who is very tall and slender, very blonde, and who has a well-shaped face, came among the Illinois she was much admired and was oblidged to pass two entire days outside the fort. Otherwise my house would not have been left standing because of the number of people bent on seeing her."

The introduction of European trade goods and weapons allowed a small number of French to gain the loyalty of thousands of indigenous aboriginal people. Priests, both Jesuits and those from the Seminary of Foreign Missions, established themselves in Indian villages. Whereas some of these missions were short-lived, as were some of the missionaries themselves, others, most notably those at Cahokia (1699) and Kaskaskia (1703), continued until the end of the French colonial era. These priests and the coureurs de bois lived during this time in aboriginal dwellings among the Indians. Their activities in these villages were often at odds. For example, in 1703 and later in 1711 the Jesuit Father Marest at Kaskaskia asked Jean-Baptiste Le Moyne, sieur de Bienville, the governor of Louisiane, for soldiers to control the Canadian traders. According to Marest, these coureurs de bois were inciting the Illinois to raid western tribes to obtain slaves to trade with the English and "were debauching the Indian women and preventing them from being converted" (Belting 1948:12).

By 1711 the total French population of the Mississippi Valley region numbered less than two hundred. Most of this colonial population consisted of soldiers and workmen stationed along the Gulf Coast around the newly established bases at Biloxi and Mobile. The Europeans in the interior were confined to a few locations. Archaeological sites dating to this period with any type of European architecture are therefore rare and are limited to fortified outposts and mission churches.

Robert Hall, in chapter 2, discusses the archaeological investigations at La Salle's Fort St. Louis atop Starved Rock. The only recognizable European architectural feature found at this site was a cellar or subterranean powder magazine. Period descriptions of these early outposts indicate that they only vaguely followed European precepts of fortification. Most were palisaded compounds containing a few timber structures, as exemplified by Fort Crevecoeur and Fort St. Louis II near Lake Pimitoui (see Emerson and Mansberger, chap. 11). The vertical log enclosures surrounding two rectangular buildings discovered by Ronald Mason (1986) at the Rock Island site near Green Bay date to this period and are likely typical of the nature of early interior outposts.

Colonization Period (1717–65)

In 1717 a charter was granted by the king of France, Louis XV, to John Law and his *Compagnie des Indes*. This agreement provided the Company with an economic monopoly over the colony of Louisiane which, from this time on, was to include the Illinois Country (Belting 1948:16–17; Eccles 1972). Louisiane is used in this volume as the name of the eighteenth-century French colony, to distinguish it from the modern state of Louisiana. The signing of this charter and a renewed concern to impede English expansion led to a florescence of French activity in the Mississippi Valley. Fortifications constructed between 1717 and the outbreak of the Seven Years' War in 1756 include Forts de Chartres, Kaskaskia, Ouiatenon, and Massac in the Illinois Country (Jelks et al., 1989; Keene, chap. 3; Noble, chap. 5; Walthall, chap. 4). In the western Great Lakes, which remained a part of Canada, fortifications at Michilimackinac, Detroit, and St. Joseph were rebuilt and strengthened (Helman, chap. 13; Hulse 1977). The northwestern frontier was pushed into the area now encompassed by the present state of Minnesota, where several fortified outposts were founded (Birk, chap. 15).

Although the major expansion of the French military presence in Louisiane was significant, so too was the provision of the Company's charter that provided for the transportation of settlers to the Mississippi Valley. Convoys, beginning in 1718, brought groups of farmers and craftsmen up the Mississippi River to the newly founded colonial capital at New Orleans, and further upstream to Arkansas and Illinois. In the fertile floodplain of the American Bottom in southwestern Illinois, villages of French *habitants* were established at Cahokia and Kaskaskia (fig. 1-2). Agricultural settlements were also founded around the newly constructed forts at Chartres, at Arkansas Post, in Alabama at Forts Conde and Toulouse, and in Louisiana near Fort St. Pierre. By the end of the French colonial era, the Illinois villages were producing large quantities of wheat and other foodstuffs that were shipped downstream in annual convoys to New Orleans and beyond, as far as the French sugar plantations in the West Indies. Population growth at the original villages of Kaskaskia and Chartres resulted in the establishment of new settlements at St. Philippe, Prairie du Rocher (Safiran, chap. 8), Peoria (Emerson and Mansberger, chap. 11), Ste. Genevieve (Norris, chap. 9), and Vincennes in the lower Wabash

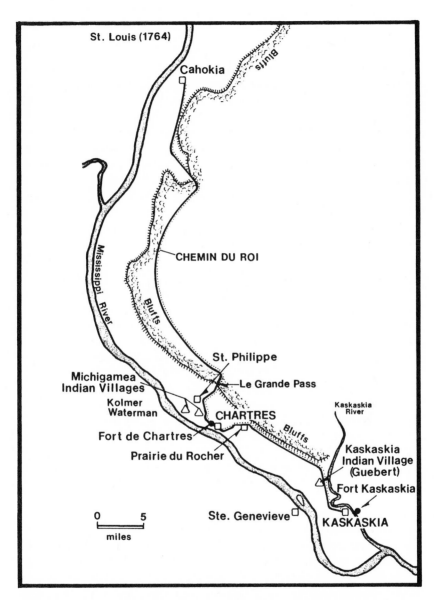

Figure 1-2. Map of French Colonial Sites in the American Bottom Region

Valley. Salt was produced from springs in the Saline Creek Valley (Trimble et al., chap. 10), and lead was mined in the eastern Missouri uplands (Walthall 1981). By 1752 the Louisiane colony had a population of some fifteen hundred settlers and nearly a thousand African slaves (Eccles 1972).

Even though agricultural and mineral products contributed to the success of the French colonial effort, the fur trade remained the most vital part of the overall economy (Anderson, chap. 14). During this period French officials used the fur trade as a diplomatic tool to maintain Indian alliances and to cement new ones. However, for a variety of reasons, from English intrigue to intertribal rivalry for territory and access to trading posts, the French military in Louisiane was involved in an almost constant state of warfare against regional native populations such as the Fox and the Chickasaw. Even among their aboriginal allies, relations were often strained due to competition with French settlers for arable lands. Such conflicts led to near warfare between the French and the Illinois tribes (Walthall and Benchley 1987) and to outright rebellion among the Natchez in the lower Mississippi Valley.

The Louisiane colony was never a profitable enterprise for the French monarchy. However, by the outbreak of the Seven Years' War in 1756 these French holdings were firmly established and were moderately successful. This final confrontation between the English and French colonies, called the French and Indian War in North America, was decided wholly in eastern Canada (Eccles 1969). The fortifications of Louisiane were never tested by British troops. Although the French crown might have retained the Mississippi Valley, it chose, for diplomatic expediencies, to relinquish this vast interior region to the English victors. In 1765, two years after the cessation of hostilities, British troops entered Fort de Chartres, and the *Fleur-de-lys* was lowered for the last time.

Creole Period (1765–1803)

While the French colonial era ended with the formal surrender of Fort de Chartres in 1765, French creoles remained the dominant European population in the Mississippi Valley until a flood of Anglo-American settlers entered the region after the Louisiana Purchase in 1803. The terms of the treaty that ended the Seven Years' War divided the Mississippi Valley between the English and the Spanish crowns. England received the lands on the eastern side of the Mississippi River and Spain the lands to the west. However, both countries maintained only token military forces in their Mississippi Valley holdings (Ekberg 1985; McDermott 1974).

The arrival of British troops did, however, create major changes in French creole life. British firms entered former French trading territories and, over time, began to dominate the fur trade. In the Illinois Country, fear of the British military caused the creole settlers at Chartres and St. Philippe to abandon their villages. Large-scale outmigration took place westward across the Mississippi River to Ste. Genevieve and to the new settlement at St. Louis, founded in 1764.

This final period of French colonial life in the Mississippi Valley has attracted the attention of historians interested in the American Revolution and the campaigns of George Rogers Clark. The French inhabitants are generally viewed in such studies as of secondary importance to the events of American expansion. French domestic and industrial sites dating to this period are now beginning to receive archaeological attention (Emerson and Mansberger, chap. 11; Trimble et al., chap. 10; Norris, chap. 9; Gums et al., chap. 7). Such sites have the potential to produce important new information concerning frontier adaptation and patterns of acculturation.

Future Directions

One of the primary goals of synthetic works such as this book is to clarify avenues for future research as well as to define the current state of knowledge. One aspect of French colonial archaeology that has been made obvious is the extensive amount of early twentieth-century excavations and their resultant collections that have never been adequately described or analyzed. In Illinois early work at such critical sites as Fort Massac and Fort de Chartres was long neglected. To some extent this problem has been alleviated by the active interest of the Illinois Historic Preservation Agency in promoting and funding French period research. This effort has resulted in test excavations at, analysis of, and publication about Fort de Chartres I (Jelks et al. 1989); analysis and publication of the long unrecognized River L'Abbe Mission site at Cahokia (Walthall and Benchley 1987); testing, analysis, and publication of French domestic sites at Cahokia (Gums 1988; Gums et al., chap. 7); and the new excavations, analysis of all existing collections, and planned publication of the massive Fort de Chartres III site by David Keene (chap. 3 and work in progress). Continued efforts in funding, analysis, and publication are a necessary ingredient for future success of French colonial studies.

French colonial archaeological research has been, to a great degree, directed toward publicly owned sites by access to state funding. This has led to the neglect of some very important site types, such as the French villages, farmsteads, and industrial sites. Archaeological evidence of the life of the French *habitants* is virtually unknown and no industrial sites have been intensively excavated. The potential of such sites is tremendous. Field surveys and collections made by an amateur, Irving Peithman, in the Fort de Chartres and Prairie du Rocher area identified several villages as well as suggested the presence of many isolated French farmsteads. In addition, there are sites such as the quarries and lime kilns from which materials used for construction were obtained, numerous mills, granaries, mines, shipping sites, and sites associated with other accoutrements of production that have yet to be located. Specific, systematic, and comprehensive surveys are of the highest research priority for all the areas of French occupation, especially in localities that have been relatively little affected by modern disturbance.

Equally important is the formulation of more sophisticated models to explain the French presence, exploitation, and settlement of the Mississippi Valley. Presently, only Tordoff (1983) has attempted to develop a model of French settlement relating to the colonial archaeological assemblage. Her model creates a hierarchical classification of sites relating to their importance in the fur trade. As Keene (chap. 3) demonstrates, the model has little use in explaining Fort de Chartres or the large-scale agriculturally based establishment that developed in that locality. It can be argued that Tordoff's fur trade model may well be applicable to the Exploration period sites in Illinois such as Fort St. Louis I and II or Fort Crevecoeur. These sites were clearly functional segments of the western fur trade. However, the Colonization period sites such as Cahokia, Kaskaskia, or Chartres cannot be understood in this framework. The shifting position of the Illinois Country relative to Canada and Louisiane clearly illustrates the limitations of synchronic, unitary explanatory models such as Tordoff's.

French colonial archaeology also has great potential to contribute to the growing body of knowledge on frontiers and their associated artifact assemblages. Despite the importance of pattern recognition in historic archaeology (South 1977, 1988), little effort has been made to define a French colonial pattern. Nor has there been any study of the French cultural transformations that resulted from adaptations to the environment or later political and economic changes. The potential of late French or creole cultures for providing a rich database seems excellent given the success of such studies as Lewis's (1984) on American frontier life. The late French sites may provide a unique laboratory to evaluate such complex factors as Euro-American ethnicity and acculturation in the Mississippi Valley.

The Archaeology of La Salle's Fort St. Louis on Starved Rock and the Problem of the Newell Fort

2

Robert L. Hall

In 1678 René-Robert Cavelier received from his sovereign Louis XIV a patent giving him a monopoly in the trade of buffalo hides in the vast reaches of New France that lay south of the commerce with Montreal. With it went the right to build and garrison forts and to gather about these posts settlements of Indians. After this date history knows Robert Cavelier as the sieur de La Salle.

Historical Background

The story of La Salle's venture has been widely known since the publishing of Francis Parkman's *Discovery of the Great West* in 1869, a book ten years later retitled *La Salle and the Discovery of the Great West.* La Salle was able to capitalize on Indian desire for trade and fear of Iroquois raids to assemble about him at one time a would-be empire of perhaps twenty thousand Indians in an area centering on what is now La Salle County, Illinois. At its heart was the village of the Kaskaskias or Kaskaskia-Illinois tribe, which Louis Jolliet and Father Jacques Marquette had visited in 1673, and the fort La Salle dedicated to his king when it was completed in the spring of 1683. La Salle was murdered in Texas in 1687 and the fort location was abandoned in 1692, but as late as 1760 a band of the Peoria-Illinois tribe still living in the area of the old fort retained in their possession a document affirming an alliance between France and the Indians of the Illinois nation, a document signed by La Salle himself (Kellogg 1935).

On his map of 1684 the French cartographer Jean-Baptist Franquelin depicts in some detail the deployment of La Salle's Indian allies around Fort St. Louis. The Illinois nation is shown to be assembled in a village of twelve hundred warriors (*hommes*) on the north side of the Illinois River opposite the fort. The Shawnee (*Chaouenon*) occupy a village of two hundred warriors nearly south of the fort. Elsewhere in the vicinity are villages of the Wea (*Ouiatenon*), *Ouabona*, *Kilatica*, *Pepikokia*, Miami (*Miamy*), and Piankesha (*Peanghichia*). To the north on the map and separated from La Salle's would-be colony by a dotted line lies the Kickapoo (*Kikapou*) and other tribes or bands obviously meant by Franquelin to be identified by the group name Mascoutin (*Mascoutins*) or Fire Nation (*Nation de feu*).

If this unnatural gathering could have been kept intact it would have been a singular achievement for La Salle and his successors, Henry de Tonti and François Dauphin de la Forest. As it was, the tribes gradually drifted away until there remained only the Peorias, Kaskaskias, and others making up the Grand Village of the Illinois nation, and soon most of these, too, were gone. By 1692 both French and Indians alike had removed to a location on Lake Peoria where Tonti had constructed a new and larger fort, most properly called St. Louis but more familiarly known as Fort Pimitoui (Emerson and Mansberger, chap. 11). For several generations bands of Peorias returned to the upper Illinois Valley where they settled near *le Rocher* (the rock) and the abandoned, original Fort St. Louis.

The fate of Fort St. Louis after its abandonment is not recorded. It undoubtedly fell rapidly into decay and by 1721, when its location was visited by Charlevoix, he did not recognize there the labor of his countrymen (Charlevoix 1761). Despite this, the memory of Fort St. Louis must have survived in French tradition and on maps preserved from an earlier day. We can assume this because in 1760 a young French officer, Captain Passerat de la Chapelle, left Detroit with a force of French and Indians with La Salle's Fort St. Louis as their immediate destination. His ultimate objective was to reach Louisiana and avoid surrendering to the British, who had just won a decisive victory over the French at Montreal and were receiving the surrender of all French forces in Canada. After a forced march in the face of approaching winter Captain Passerat de la Chapelle arrived to find that La Salle's fort had long before been reduced to burned ruins. This and other considerations caused him to return to the location now known as Buffalo Rock west of present-day Ottawa, Illinois, where he built winter quarters named Fort Ottawa (Kellogg 1935).

Captain Passerat de la Chapelle chose not to reconstruct Fort St. Louis, in part because the location "did not offer any natural means of defense against a possible attack of the English from the east" (Kellogg 1935:66–67). It is clear, however, that what this French officer saw as a natural defense was something on the order of a major body of water, since he chose a location that put both the Fox and Illinois rivers between himself and the British, explaining that "the two rivers made natural obstacles against an attack." It would, in any case, have been difficult to garrison 200 royal troops and 110 Canadian and *metis* (French-Ottawa) militia on the summit of Starved Rock together with the horses and mules that they brought with them. He chose instead to fortify Buffalo Rock. This was a geological outlier of larger size, which was the location during the 1930s of the Civilian Conservation Corps camp that the University of Chicago used as a field headquarters for its archaeological projects in the Starved Rock area in the postwar 1940s.

The burning of Fort St. Louis at *le Rocher* is confirmed by archaeology. If this burning was not accidental, then the decaying remains of the fort may have been intentionally burned by Indians or traders to salvage the forged iron nails and the iron prongs that once tipped the palisade poles to discourage scaling.

The location of *le Rocher* and La Salle's Fort St. Louis was a matter of keen personal interest to Francis Parkman as he was writing *The Discovery of the Great West.* It was principally Parkman who attracted attention to Starved Rock as the probable location of this citadel and the only one fitting the description provided by early documents. From his correspondence we know that he toured La Salle County in 1867 seeking out geographical features he might recognize from his historical sources. Col. Daniel Hitt's recollections of this visit are recorded in a newspaper feature written about twenty years after the event: "Parkman came down to Utica [Illinois] and after seeing the meadow and 'Starved Rock', just described all the country around and beyond as if he had been a surveyor of it. He said he got that description from the papers of Marquette, La Salle, and Tonti written 200 years ago. Mr. James Clark of Utica, now dead, and I took the historian all over the place, and it's curious, but he told us what we should see every time before we got there."

Two years later, when the first edition of *Discovery* was published, Parkman was able to add this note:

> Starved Rock perfectly answers in every respect, to the indications of the contemporary maps and documents concerning "Le Rocher," the site of La Salle's fort of St. Louis. It is laid down on several contemporary maps, besides the great map of La Salle's discoveries made in 1684. They all place it on the south side of the river; whereas Buffalo Rock, three miles above, which has been supposed to be the site of the fort, is on the north. The latter is crowned by a plateau of great extent, is but sixty feet high, is accessible at many points, and would require a

large force to defend it; whereas La Salle chose "Le Rocher," because a few men could hold it against a multitude. Charlevoix, in 1721, describes both rocks, and says that the top of Buffalo Rock had been occupied by the Miami village, so that it was known as *Le Fort des Miamis*. This is confirmed by Henri Joutel, who found the Miamis here in 1687. Charlevoix then speaks of "Le Rocher," calling it by that name; says that it is about a league below, on the left or south side, forming a sheer cliff, very high, and looking like a fortress on the border of the river. He saw remains of palisades at the top, which he thinks were made by the Illinois (*Journal Historique*, Let. xxvii.), though his countrymen had occupied it only three years before. "The French reside on the rock (Le Rocher), which is very lofty and impregnable" (*Memoir on Western Indians*, 1718, in *N.Y. Col. Docs.* [*New York Colonial Documents*], IX. 890). St. Cosme, passing this way in 1699, mentions it as "Le Vieux Fort," and says that it is a "rock about a hundred feet high at the edge of the river, where M. de la Salle built a fort, since abandoned."

As attention turned to Starved Rock, the French curios found there became objects of more than personal interest to the finder, some being described in newspaper accounts or placed on display at the county seat. In *Pioneers of Illinois* (1882:175–76), Nehemiah Matson reports that on the summit of Starved Rock a rusted gun barrel was found imbedded in the trunk of an old cedar when the tree was cut down, and that two bronze medallions had been found, one with a representation of Louis XIV, king of France in La Salle's day, the other with a "head of Pope Leo X" (Giovanni de Medici, pope in 1513–21).

Matson also mentions some curious stone structures below Starved Rock, of which there may be more detail in some overlooked letter or newspaper story. In "the vicinity of Starved Rock" he says are found "many underground furnaces consisting of a large flue built of stone and mortar." Matson believed them to be devices used by the French in warming their houses, a practice he says was still in use in some parts of Canada in his time. As he describes them, these "flues" are a puzzle. Nothing similar has been reported for the area since Matson's account, although silting of the Illinois River floodplain may have buried the evidence.

Many people have speculated on the location of Fort St. Louis, thinking it to be elsewhere than on the top of Starved Rock, but the only combination of location and physical evidence that meets the requirement is Starved Rock. People who have considered other locations either were not actually familiar with or have had to ignore historical descriptions of the site of the fort. La Salle describes the fort in these words:

[The fort] is situated half a league below the [Kaskaskia] village, on the left side, descending the river, on the top of a rock which is steep on almost all sides, which it [the river] washes at the foot, so that one can draw water there from the top of the rock, which has about a six-hundred foot circumference. It is accessible from only one side, where the ascent is quite steep even so. This side is closed by a palisade of white oak stakes eight to ten inches in diameter, and twenty-two feet in height, flanked by three redoubts made of squared beams, [placed] one on the other to the same height, and situated so that they all defend each other. The rest of the circumference of the rock is surrounded by a similar palisade, only fifteen feet high, since it is not accessible, and is defended by four others like the redoubts behind the palisade. There is a parapet of large trees laid lengthwise one on the other to the height of two men, the whole being covered with earth and at the top of the palisade there is a sort of *cheval de frise*, the points of which are tipped with iron in order to prevent a scaling. The neighboring rocks are all lower than that one, and the nearest one is two hundred paces away, the other ones being further. Between them and the fort Saint-Louis there is a great valley on two side, which a brook cuts in the middle, and inundates when it rains. On the other side, there is a field [*prairie*] which borders the river, in which, at the foot of the fort, there is a beautiful island cleared at a former time by the Illinois, and where I and my inhabitants have done our sowing within musket-range of the fort, so that one can defend the workers from inside the fort and prevent enemies from landing on the island. The edge of the rocks which surround the fort, as I have just said, is covered with oaks for a space of three or four *arpents* in area, after which there are vast fields [*campagnes*] of quite good soils [*terres*] (translated by Tucker 1941).

Henri Joutel (1962:157, 159) adds that there was a spacious *esplanade* or "place of arms" on the rock, several huts occupied by Indians, a warehouse or magazine, and a chapel. The location of the fort at the very edge of the Illinois River, so close that water could be drawn from the river to the fort, eliminates as the site of La Salle's fort an "old fort" long known to exist at the head of French Canyon, the canyon which separates Starved Rock from Lovers Leap. Lovers Leap does not satisfy the physical description of the fort site and has never produced any evidence of French occupation. Buffalo Rock is on the wrong side of the river and the wrong side of the Kaskaskia village. The additional evidence of a French occupation on the summit of Starved Rock during the last quarter of the seventeenth century fairly well clinches the identification.

The place-name "Starved Rock" dates no earlier than the late eighteenth century. The name refers to the tradition that a village of

Illinois Indians took refuge on this rock and suffered starvation while besieged by Potawatomis allied to the Ottawas. Circumstances suggest that the siege can be dated to sometime just after the murder of the Ottawa chief Pontiac in 1769 at the hands of an Illinois Indian. One of the first published descriptions of Starved Rock in English was that of Henry R. Schoolcraft (1825, 1918:105–10), included in a description of a journey up the Illinois River in 1821. In this narrative Schoolcraft called Starved Rock the location of a former French fort and referred to it as *Le Rocher*, as did the French of La Salle's day, and he went on to detail the contours of the top: "On gaining the top of this rock we found a regular entrenchment, corresponding to the edge of the precipice, and within this other excavations, which from the thick growth of brush and trees, could not be satisfactorily examined. The labor of many hands was manifest and a degree of industry not usually bestowed upon works of defense. We found upon this elevation broken mussel shells, fragments of antique pottery, and stones which have been subjected to the action of heat, resembling certain lavas" (Schoolcraft 1825, 1918:106–7).

The lavalike rock mentioned by Schoolcraft is possibly the material described in excavation records of Starved Rock as "slag" or "clinker," the product of an intense heat such as that which might be found in a blacksmith's forge. Schoolcraft was accompanied by a Potawatomi Indian guide who was well acquainted with the Starved Rock legend. Schoolcraft was apparently also familiar with Charlevoix's *History of New France*. Schoolcraft does not mention Starved Rock by name in this work, calling it *Le Rocher* and the Rock Fort, but he summarizes the story that gave Starved Rock the name by which this geological feature came to be known.

Controlled Excavations on Starved Rock

Scientific excavation on Starved Rock began in 1947 as part of a program of cooperative research in the upper Illinois Valley between the Illinois State Museum and the Department of Anthropology of the University of Chicago. This program attempted to identify the archaeological expression of the cultures of Illinois's historic Indian tribes. Searching historical records, Sarah Tucker of the University of Chicago had by 1941 concluded that the village of the Kaskaskia-Illinois tribe visited by Jolliet, La Salle, and others was located just upstream from the Starved Rock dam and not down farther downstream as Francis Parkman had believed. The same location had been identified independently as the site of the Kaskaskia village by Charles

W. Paape (1938), a student technician and historian working for the National Park Service.

The existence of an extensive Indian occupation on the presumed location of Kaskaskia was confirmed in the field by Richard MacNeish in 1945, and the presence of a historic component was confirmed by the finding of burials accompanied by historic trade goods eroding from the banks of the Illinois River. An excavation was conducted at the Kaskaskia village location in the summer of 1947 as part of a field project codirected by John McGregor of the Illinois State Museum and Kenneth Orr of the University of Chicago Department of Anthropology. During the summer several days were spent exploring the potential for excavation of the summit of Starved Rock itself. Five-foot-square test pits were dug and enough prehistoric and historic material found to justify moving the entire operation from the Kaskaskia village to Starved Rock for the 1948 season. The excavations continued in 1949, which was the last season for the University of Chicago-Illinois State Museum team on Starved Rock, but the excavation was joined in 1949 by Richard Hagen working for the State Department of Public Works and Buildings Division of Architecture and Engineering, and Hagen's project continued in 1950. Testing was resumed for a season in 1974 by the University of Illinois at Chicago and later by Illinois State University under contracts let to Robert L. Hall and Edward Jelks, respectively, but the greater part of the knowledge of the archaeology of Starved Rock comes from the excavations of 1947–50.

The largest single structure on Starved Rock attributable to the French occupation is that dubbed the "dugout," perhaps a *caveau* or cellar beneath a powder magazine or warehouse. This was a square excavation sixteen feet on a side extending to a depth of almost five feet beneath the surface, with evidence of interior support posts and posts on the sides. This is most evident along one wall where there were four large postmolds spaced at five-foot intervals. The stratigraphic profile within the fill of this structure shows that the building above the cellar was destroyed by fire, the burning timbers falling into the cellar, where extensive strata of charcoal, ashes, burned earth, and building hardware were found in lower levels of the fill. Above this destruction debris about two feet of loam had accumulated when a pit intruded into the fill, into which was placed the body of an Indian accompanied by a triple string of glass and shell beads, twelve brass Jesuit rings, and a stone ball. About the same time or slightly later a second aboriginal burial intruded into the fill of the cellar. This burial was that of a small infant nestled beneath an overturned brass kettle found at a depth of eighteen inches. Fill continued to accumulate, which, in its upper levels, included modern debris.

Four of the Jesuit rings were heart-shaped and one octagonal. Brass rings of these shapes are placed by Charles Cleland (1972) in the period of A.D. 1700–1780. This dating agrees with the known date for the abandonment of Fort St. Louis in 1692 as a headquarters for the trading operations of La Salle's successors. In and below the charcoal and ash level of the cellar were found four Dutch white clay pipe fragments, of which H. G. Omwake expresses his expert opinion that they date closer to the period of construction of Fort St. Louis in 1682–83 than to its abandonment in 1692 (personal communication, 1964).

Within the fill of the cellar there was a sequence of artifact categories that also supports the suggested dating of the cellar. Modern wire nails were limited to the top foot of fill. Hand-forged nails were found in all levels but were concentrated in the lower levels with the charcoal, ash, and burned earth lenses. Gun cartridges, ironstone whiteware, bottle caps, and other modern artifacts were found only in the upper foot of the fill. Within the fill of the cellar/dugout were found forty-four nails, forty-one of them handwrought and only three machine-made. During the excavations of 1947, 1948, 1949, and 1950 a total of 122 handwrought nails were found on the rock.

Interestingly, there was one abundant kind of artifact that was not recovered in the early fill levels of the cellar. This was the category of brass and copper patches from metal kettles. Seventeen such items were found during the excavations of 1947 to 1950, but only one of these was found in the fill of the cellar, and that was found in an upper level. Metal kettle patches may thus relate only to a postfort Indian occupation and probably represent elements discarded during the scavenging by Indians of sheet metal from old brass and copper kettles.

The structure described as a "cellar" resembles no known aboriginal construction but does correspond to some known French architecture. It lay below a building that was destroyed by fire, a fact which agrees with the observation of Capt. Pierre Passerat de la Chapelle, who in 1760 found Fort St. Louis in ashes: "There was no fort; it had been burned a long time ago" (quoted in Kellogg 1935:66). The building above the cellar was destroyed early enough that several feet of fill accumulated before two Indian burials were placed in graves excavated into the location of the former cellar.

La Salle's description of Fort St. Louis indicates that it included seven redoubts constructed of squared timbers extending to the edge of the rock, between which were palisade walls of vertical timbers. If no convincing evidence of this construction has been found, it need not be for the original absence of this evidence. During the 1930s the Civilian Conservation Corps (CCC) was employed to landscape the top of Starved Rock. The activities of the CCC included the clearing and burning of brush and the filling of many depressions scattered over the summit of the rock. The archaeological stratigraphy clearly shows the evidence of twentieth-century rubbish burning in some depressions and the subsequent covering of this burned rubbish with artifact-filled clay excavated from the edge of the rock, where evidence of the fortifications might have been present. This resulted in a locally reversed stratigraphy with seven to nine thousand-year-old, early Archaic flint artifacts placed over materials dating to the depression era.

The earth at the edge of the summit was removed to bedrock around much of the perimeter beginning sometime at the beginning of the century. Plans for landscaping drawn in 1939 show that masonry retaining walls were planned to replace decayed, aging, wooden re-taining walls. This landscaping produced a pleasing appearance for visitors to Starved Rock but undoubtedly destroyed much buried evidence of the fortifications that originally rimmed the rock. The evidence of this rubbish burning is clearly distinguishable from the burning of the fort buildings during the French regime both for reasons of stratigraphic position and because of the twentieth-century artifacts abundantly mixed with the charcoal and ashes left by the landscaping crews.

Objects bearing actual dates were found only among the artifacts obviously modern in age. Being modern, they are important to the archaeologist at this site only for the information they provide on the degree of mixing, or lack of it, between recent and earlier historic and prehistoric materials. Twenty-six recent coins were found, all but two of them in the top (0–6″) level excavated. One exception was a 1919 Lincoln penny from the 6–12″ level of a square dug in 1949 partially over a test pit excavated in 1947. The other was an 1889 Indian head penny found in the second 6–12″ level of a square ex-cavated in arbitrary horizontal levels in a sloping deposit over an early historic ditch. This coin could belong legitimately in its second-level provenience, but its location might also have been within the topmost six-inch level if levels had been measured from the sloping surface rather than from an arbitrary horizontal level. The coins with dates ranged in age from 1886 to 1940.

The only coin that might belong to the French occupation at Starved

Rock is a thin (0.35 mm) silver coin found in the 12–18″ level of the fill of feature 13, the presumed cellar of the fort. This level is too high to make the deposit contemporaneous with the occupation or destruction of the fort. The coin itself is actually older than the fort, but it came to rest in its find spot after the destruction of the fort. The coin bears no date, but it has been placed within narrow limits by Jefferson T. Warren, director of the John Woodman Higgins Armory, Worcester, Massachusetts (personal communication, 1964). Warren noted its similarity to a silver *douzaine* struck by Francis I of France (reigned A.D. 1515–47). There is little resemblance to the coinage of Louis XIV or later French kings. The edges of the coin were trimmed at one time to the extent that the only letters legible are several that appear to spell *Dni,* presumably part of the wording *Sit Nomen Dni [Domini] benedictum.*

A lead bailing seal also found in the fill of feature 13 is of special value in determining the age of this cellar and the surface structure associated with it. The embossing on this seal reads "·F·L·14·RE," presumably the greater part of an abbreviation for the Latin text "·FRANCORUM·LUDOVICUS·14·REX·" (Louis 14 King of the French). This clearly dates the making of this seal to the long reign (1643–1715) of Louis XIV. Unlike coins, which remain in circulation for many years, bailing seals were intended for one-time use. This one was found with other early historic material—hand-forged nails, iron and brass scraps, gun parts, ash, clinker, and building hardware—within the 30–42″ level of feature 13, a zone including the greatest concentration of debris left by the fire that destroyed Fort St. Louis. Part of another lead seal was found in 1949 in feature 3, a refuse-filled pit dating from the period of the French occupation, but this item bore no writing.

The quantity of historic material of European manufacture found on Starved Rock is impressive, but only a fraction may date to the period of occupation of Fort St. Louis. For example, of approximately twenty-eight hundred glass trade beads only twenty were found in the cellar fill (feature 13), and of these twenty only half may predate the destruction of the fort.

The distribution of gunflints suggests that the spall type made of tan French flint antedates the blade type of honey-colored French flint. This is indicated by the sequence in feature 13 as well as by the sequence represented in superimposed features 32 and 31. Pit F32 contained one gunflint of the blade type made of honey-colored flint and underlying pit F31 produced three gunflints of the spall type made of tan flint.

The Newell Fort

As the site of Fort St. Louis, the only competition to Starved Rock given serious thought in this century has been the Lovers Leap/Eagle Cliff bluff location and that of the Newell fort at the head of French Canyon. The Lovers Leap/Eagle Bluff location was proposed by Allan Westover (1984) and the French Canyon location by two residents of nearby Utica, Jack Newell and his son John. Both suggested alternative sites lack important requirements of the physical descriptions given us by La Salle himself and others (see above), requirements which only Starved Rock in the area satisfies (Hall 1986), but the Newell fort was obviously either a fortified Indian village or a stockaded trading post of the early French period and has never been accounted for by existing historical documents nor eliminated as a possible adjunct of Fort St. Louis itself.

The Newell or French Canyon fort was surveyed by Col. Daniel Hitt a century ago and its plan published in a history of La Salle County (Baldwin 1877). About sixty years ago purchase of the site was included in recommendations to the state, because the location lies just yards outside the boundaries of Starved Rock State Park.

During the 1930s John ("Jack") Newell of Utica obtained for ten dollars per year a lease to excavate the fort site, and he proceeded to do so, excavating two-thirds of the entire site, which covered a fairly large area. The enclosure mapped by Colonel Hitt was about 390 feet from east to west and 185 feet from north to south but was irregular in form and covered only about an acre.

I interviewed Jack Newell in June of 1962 when he was eighty-two years old, examined a small cabinet of historic artifacts from the fort site, and visited the site with Newell himself. He said that he began testing around Utica, looking for a location to find arrowheads to sell for a profit during the depression. In looking for places to dig he eventually went to the Lovers Leap bluff next to Starved Rock, to the "Gorbet" farm (Corbin farm), and then to the enclosure at the head of French Canyon, which was owned by James Mitchell, whose son Edwin married Elizabeth Newell. Jack Newell's son John laid out the site in squares and excavation proceeded using pointing trowels, whisk brooms, ice picks, and tiling shovels, techniques they had apparently learned from working with Dr. A. R. Kelly, then of the University of Illinois at Urbana-Champaign, who conducted excavations on nearby Plum Island and in the Utica Mound Group in 1930. A hat was placed next to the Newells' dig for donations because these were depression years, but no artifacts were actually sold.

The entire outline of the enclosure was excavated by the Newells. Below the surface this outline was represented by a trench whose fill was three to four feet deep and about three feet wide but said to have been without evidence of individual postholes. Newell said there was a gap in the enclosure trench at the east end, an "entrance," which he remembered to be about fourteen feet wide; Colonel Hitt's plan records a ten-foot gap in the surface indications of the enclosure at the same point. Newell said that one-quarter of the whole stockade line, the part on the northwest, was double with the walls "3 rods" (49.5 feet) apart. I would interpret this as an enlargement of the stockade. The stockade could only be enlarged on the northwest and northeast because the southwest and southeast sides border on French Canyon and a tributary ravine.

Newell said that he excavated twenty-one houses within the stockade, each rectangular in outline, formed into a "circle" and set apart from the stockade line "a short distance." Twenty-one houses, each, say, twelve by eighteen feet in dimensions, would occupy only 4,536 square feet, about one-tenth of an acre. Jack Newell's son John showed me the distribution of houses within the enclosure by placing eight marks on a copy of Colonel Hitt's plan in a pattern roughly concentric with the outline of the stockade line. The houses were said to have been destroyed by fire. In the center of the stockaded enclosure was a round feature three feet across and fourteen feet deep, called by the Newells a "well."

John McGregor, Kenneth Orr, and others of the Old Kaskaskia dig group also talked with the Newells at the time of their 1947 excavation and their report on file at the Illinois State Museum contains a list of the following materials:

1	whole gun barrel (bore 1.2 cm) and 3 partial barrels
5	"flint holders" (hammers)
5	triggers
10	flintlock hammers (batteries)
2	gunstock butt plates
15	flintlock springs
4	trigger guards
3	powder pans
1	lock plant with "flint holder" (hammer) attached
10	ornamental pieces from gun "butts" (stocks)
	Several hundred musket-balls (lead) of various calibers
30	iron knife fragments
8	iron axes, 1 whole
1	iron nails 13-mm wide and 7-mm thick

SAUK VALLEY COLLEGE
L.R.C.

   14   fragments of brass or copper kettles, some with rivets and lugs
  100   copper "tinkling cones"
        copper bracelets of both rolled and drawn wire
    6   copper or brass rings with designs, 2 marked "IHS"
   50   "white, globular glass beads ('bristol' beads)"
    2   "black, octagonal 'rosary' beads"
   30   elliptical white porcelain beads, varying sizes
   15   "blue glass beads with star and half-moon designs inlaid in white
        (Orchard's 'beads made for the Moorish trade')"
   25   octagonal blue glass beads
    5   elliptical polychrome beads
    1   raspberry-shaped blue glass beads

A second report of the visit adds to the above list the following:

    1   copper triangular projectile point
        buckles
        scissors
        thimbles
        rings with religious symbols, "IHS, TY, small hearts, arrows, etc."

This latter report in the files of the Illinois State Museum conveys the erroneous impression that the Newells' historic materials were excavated at a site on the Lovers Leap/Eagle Rock bluff. I know this not to be true because I visited the location of the dig with Jack Newell himself, but the Newells' old fort would have been in a direct line behind Lovers Leap/Eagle Cliff if one were pointing out the location of the fort and dig from the south end of the Old Kaskaskia village at the Starved Rock dam.

I saw less of the Newell artifacts than McGregor, Orr, and the others, but I was able to measure the lead musket balls and take notes on the gunflints. I saw thirty-five spall-type gunflints of gray and tan French flint, mostly badly used, twenty-six fragments of gunflints of the same material, and two blade-type gunflints of honey-colored French flint. This distribution would be consistent with an occupation during the French or early British regime in Illinois and would argue against a dating within the American period, by which time some blade-form gunflints of gray-black English flint should have been present.

Twelve lead balls ranged between about 0.54 inch and 0.59 inch, averaging 0.56 inch, with two balls well out of this range at 0.63 inch and another at 0.44 inch. These diameters were based upon the average of three measurements taken on each ball with a micrometer; obviously impacted balls were not measured. The central range of 0.54 to 0.59 inches can be compared to a range of 0.53 to 0.62 inches for thirteen balls I measured among some found in and around the Fox Fort at Arrowsmith, McClean County, Illinois, besieged by the French and their Indian allies in 1730, and to a range of 0.50 to 0.60 inches for fifteen measurable musket balls found in the Starved Rock excavations of 1947–50.

The best clue to the age of the French Canyon fort may be a black oak tree with 160 years of growth identified by Colonel Hitt within the stockade line ditch (Baldwin 1877). Hitt was a surveyor and an engineer and presumably well aware of the significance of the tree for the history of the fort; tree growth was commonly used at the time to estimate the minimum ages of earth mounds. Since the plan was published in 1877 this would seem to place the burning of the fort in a year some time before 1717.

Depending in part upon whether the engraving by Rand McNally took into consideration the delay between the gathering of the data and its publication by Elmer Baldwin (1877), the Newells' fort could actually have been contemporary with Fort St. Louis, as was once suspected—perhaps a village of refugee Shawnees, Delawares, or Mahicans associated with La Salle—or it could have been a village of the Peorias. Even though the Kaskaskias had left for their new village in southern Illinois by the beginning of the eighteenth century, their kinsmen the Peorias and Moingwenas moved into the Starved Rock vicinity sometime between 1703 and 1713, and by 1718 about one hundred cabins of Indians were living in the vicinity of Starved Rock. In 1722 the Fox attacked the Illinois living in the area, and the latter were forced to retreat for protection to the top of Starved Rock, as would their descendants again around 1769, the era of the legendary Starved Rock massacre.

The plan of the stockade line and distribution of the houses in the Newell fort bear little resemblance to any European establishment but are perfectly conformable with a stockaded Indian village of, say, 126 inhabitants (figuring six to a house), and this would account for the mention of only a single iron nail among the metal objects recovered. The date of the burning of the Newell fort (pre-1717) is close to the date of the routing of the Illinois at Starved Rock by the Fox in 1722, assuming an error of five or so years in counting the rings on the stump.

Conclusions

The nature and pattern of remains on the summit of Starved Rock are consistent with the identification of Starved Rock as *le Rocher* of the French and the location of the first Fort St. Louis constructed in Illinois—that built for La Salle by his lieutenant Henry de Tonti in the winter of 1682–83. The enclosure mapped by Col. Daniel Hitt near the head of French Canyon in the last century, and excavated by the Newell family around 1932, does not satisfy the requirements for identification as Fort St. Louis itself but does conform to what one might expect of a fortified village occupied by the non-Illinoisan Indian allies of the French at Fort St. Louis during the period 1683–92 or by the Peoria-Illinois in the latter part of the period 1692–1722.

The Newell fort can now, almost too late, be recognized as having been an important archaeological site that would have merited inclusion within the bounds of Starved Rock Park, as was recommended to the state in 1929. The extent of the excavations by the Newells was limited enough to suggest that much probably remains for scientific investigation, enough certainly for a surer identification of the site's inhabitants.

Acknowledgments

This paper was based upon the author's analysis of plans, profiles, field notes, photographs, and collections produced by field projects at the Starved Rock site directed from 1947 to 1950 by John McGregor, Kenneth Orr, and Richard Hagen, representing the Illinois State Museum, the University of Chicago Department of Anthropology, and the Illinois State Department of Public Works and Buildings Division of Architecture and Engineering, respectively, and upon study of analyses and reports based upon the same materials by the investigators and their students and collaborators. The author gratefully acknowledges the support provided for this analysis by the National Science Foundation under grant G-18863.

Fort de Chartres: Archaeology in the Illinois Country

3

David Keene

The construction of fortifications by the French in the Upper Great Lakes region and Mississippi River basin during the eighteenth century has been seen by some as an endeavor to secure and expand fur trade activity in the midcontinent (Innis 1956; Tordoff 1983) and by others as a military tactic to divert the attention of the British from French activity in the West Indies (Eccles 1969:157–60; Eccles 1972:179). Recent archaeological investigations, however, at Fort de Chartres in the Illinois Country suggest that French intentions in the midcontinent were more sophisticated and economic activity more diversified than previously thought.

During the sixteenth, seventeenth, and eighteenth centuries western European states experienced fundamental changes in their social, political, and economic structures. The state-controlled economies of medieval Europe were transformed into a world system that operated beyond the bounds of any one state (Wallerstein 1974:7). It was during this period of transformation that the North American continent became an important element in the economic landscape of three European powers: England, France, and Spain. Each set out to develop a series of colonies in America that would supply it with the raw materials required to fuel economic development at home.

In its quest for economic domination, France began to establish a series of colonies in four distinct areas: the North Atlantic maritime region, which became known as Acadia; the Saint Lawrence River Valley and the Great Lakes region, known as New France; the lower Mississippi River Valley and Gulf Coast region, known as Louisiane; and various island holdings in the Caribbean, commonly referred to as the West Indies (see fig. 1-1).

One region that became important to the French in the mid-eighteenth century was the Illinois Country. It was, as Eccles (1972:179) suggests, a strategic location for the French. The structure and local economy of these settlements, however, suggest that the function of these communities was more than simply defense of the expanding French Empire. In fact, when archaeological evidence is compared with settlement pattern data, a more sophisticated colonial economic system emerges. This chapter presents some background information on research at Fort de Chartres and offers a new model for structuring French colonial archaeological research.

One Hundred Years a Colony: The Development of Illinois

From the perspective of eighteenth-century Europe, Fort de Chartres and the Illinois Country were at the edge of the world. Unlike New Orleans and most of New France, the Illinois Country was not easily accessible by water (shipping merchandise and traveling from the Illinois Country downriver to New Orleans took only a few days; however, even in good weather it took two to three months to travel upriver from New Orleans to the fort). But even at this point far from civilization, the French decided to build a stone fortification that took three hundred soldiers and an undetermined number of local craftsmen almost two years to construct. Only the last of the three forts at that location was built of stone, however. The two predecessors were constructed of wooden pickets and rotted in the humidity of the Mississippi bottom. But even these first two forts were markedly different from other forts built by the French in the middle of the American continent.

Jesuit Father Jacques Marquette and his companion Louis Jolliet are credited with being the first Europeans to enter the Illinois Country in 1673. In subsequent years explorers, missionaries, and fur traders arrived to seek their fortunes in the American wilderness. So many Europeans began to settle in Illinois that by 1718 the governor of Louisiane sent a detachment of soldiers under the command of Pierre Duque, sieur de Boisbriant, to the Illinois Country to build a fort, organize the population, and "to get for his employers [the Company of the West] the largest profits from the mines and the fur trade; at the same time, by promoting agriculture, he was to establish the region as the granary of Louisiana" (Belting 1948:17).

This first fort, completed in 1721, was located approximately ten miles north of the village of Kaskaskia on the banks of the Mississippi River. In a tour of inspection in 1723 Diron d'Artaquiette wrote of the fort: "Fort de Chartres is a fort of piles the size of one's leg, square in shape, having two bastions, which command all of the curtains. There are two companies in garrison commanded by M. de Boisbriant. . . . There is a church outside the fort and some dwellings a half league lower down on the same side as well as half a league above as far as the little village of the Illinois where there are two Jesuit fathers who have a dwelling and a church" (Mereness 1916:69).

By 1726 this square fort with two bastions was almost completely destroyed by floodwaters (Belting 1948:18). After this, documentary sources are unclear about what actually took place. An inventory of the property belonging to the Company of the Indies taken in 1732 described the fort as "falling to pieces, was 160 feet square with four bastions in which there are five cannons. On each of the scaffolds was hung a bell. Inside the palisade was the house of the commandant and garde magazin, a frame building 50′ by 30′. Another building of the same size housed the garrison and the armorer's forge: there was a third house of posts in the ground, 30′ by 20′. In one of the bastions was the prison, in one the hen house, and in another, a stable" (Belting 1948:18)

The documentary sources do not clarify whether the first fort had been repaired and two bastions added or an entirely new fort built immediately after the destruction by floodwaters. A land description dating to 1726 (Brown and Dean 1977:355; Price 1980:2–3) suggests that there already was an "old Fort" distinct from that occupied at the time of the land transaction.

By the mid-1730s this fort too was falling into disrepair, and in 1748 the commandant, a M. de Bertet, moved all the troops from the fort and the surrounding area to the village of Kaskaskia (Pease and Jenison 1940:77). By this time the Illinois Country had become a major supplier of grain to French settlements on the lower Mississippi and in the West Indies. In fact in 1748 over eight hundred thousand pounds of grain along with other agricultural products were shipped from the Illinois Country to New Orleans (Surrey 1916:293).

As early as 1733, Bienville, then governor of Louisiane, had plans drawn to construct a stone fortification in the Illinois Country (Rowland and Sanders 1932:616). Such a costly undertaking on the edge of the frontier required input from a number of sources, including the royal court. After a war in Europe and much debate over the cost and location of this new fort, construction began, fully two decades after Bienville first commissioned the plans.

By this time Pierre Rigaud de Vaudreuil de Cavagnal governed Louisiane and a new commandant, the sieur de Macarty, executed government policy in the Illinois Country. They disagreed vehemently about the best location for the new stone Fort de Chartres. Vaudreuil insisted that the fort be constructed near the village of Kaskaskia (Pease and Jenison 1940:297–98), whereas Macarty favored building the fort near the location of the first two (Pease and Jenison 1940:440). Macarty eventually won.

Macarty favored the past location of the fort over the village of Kaskaskia for a very important reason. It appears that the Kaskaskia River as it passed by the village of Kaskaskia was too shallow for the passage of boats. The site of the first two forts and subsequently the third was on the Mississippi, which was deep enough for boat traffic. In a letter to Vaudreuil, Macarty writes:

> All that I can tell you of the Kaskaskia River since I have been here, is that it has not been possible to take an empty boat up it until a few days ago, and that a loaded boat could not have been sent off for New Orleans without risk since the month of August. The experience of M. Girardeau proves it. This river is not a resource for wood which will be scarce at this post in a few years, as it has neither current nor water three-quarters of the year. Its environs are nothing but a marsh, and its water much complained of as causing frequent sickness. I have even observed the frequent colics it occasions in the troops (Pease and Jenison 1940:557).

By 1754 the new four-bastioned stone fort was nearly complete (Pease and Jenison 1940:881), just in time for the French and Indian War.

This third fort acted as a central supply center during the French and Indian War, shipping provisions, especially grain, to forts along the Mississippi and Ohio rivers. The inaccessibility of the Illinois Country and Fort de Chartres, so deep in the interior of the continent, protected it from military engagement. No battles between the French and the British were ever fought at the fort. Fort de Chartres was so far from the rest of the colonies that it took the British two years after the conclusion of the war in 1763 to take control of the Illinois Country and occupy Fort de Chartres.

Many of the French inhabitants migrated to Spanish territory on the west bank of the Mississippi, leaving the British alone in the Illinois Country with native populations long hostile to British colonial policy. Much of the correspondence between the British commandant at Fort de Chartres and Gen. Thomas Gage in New York focused on the lack of supplies and the hostility of Indian groups in the region.

Fortunately for the British troops, the Mississippi River was rapidly eroding its east bank. This provided them with an excuse to abandon the fort. In 1772 Maj. Isaac Hamilton abandoned the fort and the Illinois Country, leaving behind only a garrison of fifty in the town of Kaskaskia. Until 1848 the fort remained a ruin, with the natural vegetation of the Mississippi River Valley reclaiming the site. That year the United States government sold the fort and the property around the fort to farming interests. The fort site remained farm land until it was purchased by the state of Illinois in 1914 and established as a state park.

History of Archaeological Research

Despite efforts to reconstruct sections of the fort during its first fifty years as a state park, there was no systematic attempt at archaeological investigation on the site. Beginning in the 1970s, however, concern developed for more accurate reconstruction and interpretive programs at the fort. Consequently, the first systematic excavations were conducted in 1972 by Margaret Kimball Brown (fig. 3-1).

During this and further excavations in 1974 and 1975, Brown

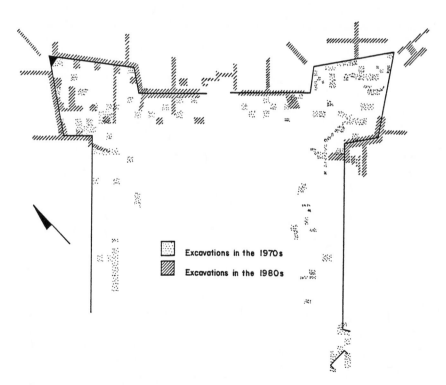

Excavations in the 1970s

Excavations in the 1980s

Figure 3-1. Archaeological Plan Map of Fort de Chartres

uncovered a series of previously unknown structural features at the fort. The location of the banquette retaining wall trench and its relationship to the north curtain wall, the powder magazine bastion wall, and portions of the north bastion wall were delineated. In addition, the remains of stone casement drains were uncovered. Finally, by excavating test units at various locations along the fort wall, the depth of the foundations was determined (Brown 1975, 1976).

During the 1975 field season, test excavations were conducted in one of the fort barracks and the bake house area. In addition, remote sensing equipment was employed in an area outside the fort to determine the location of outbuildings (Orser 1977).

Additional testing was conducted between 1979 and 1981 by Melborn D. Thurman of the Old Missouri Research Institute. Information and data collected during this period are fragmentary due to the fact that many of the field notes from this period were lost in a fire.

Finally, between 1985 and 1987 major excavations were conducted by this author in a number of areas scheduled for reconstruction. Structural features in the rampart element (i.e., the ditch, wall, banquette, and drains) were investigated. In addition to these structural elements, a mortar slaking pit located outside the northeast curtain wall and a new structure located in the north bastion were discovered and investigated (Keene 1988).

Models of Fur Trade Settlements

In her recent study of material recovered from Fort Ouiatenon, an eighteenth-century French fur trade outpost on the Wabash River near Lafayette, Indiana, Tordoff (1983) developed a hierarchical model to explain variation in artifact frequencies between a number of eighteenth-century French and French-related sites in North America. In this model, developed from her reading of historical sources, Tordoff ranked sites in reference to their function in the fur trade economy. She then tested this model by comparing the frequency of artifacts from a number of sites.

Tordoff's model ranks sites on five levels: ports of entry, government/economic centers, regional distribution centers, local distribution centers, and aboriginal distribution centers. Fort Ouiatenon, the focus of her study, is ranked as a local distribution center, whereas Fort Michilimackinac and Fort de Chartres are ranked as regional distribution centers.

At the time of her study an adequate sample of artifact material did not exist from Fort de Chartres. Tordoff did, however, compare artifact frequencies in a number of categories from Fort Ouiatenon and Fort Michilimackinac. Her results were inconclusive: "The thesis that evidence of this hierarchy will be archaeologically visible cannot be strongly supported, nor can it be rejected absolutely" (1983:143).

Recent work at Fort de Chartres, much of which is still underway, suggests that the hierarchical model does not adequately account for the variation in the artifact record between sites. Tordoff suggests that Fort de Chartres and Fort Michilimackinac functioned as regional distribution centers in the fur trade economy. However, unlike the Fort Michilimackinac assemblage, which contains an abundant amount of material indicative of fur trade activity, the Fort de Chartres assemblage contains no artifacts that suggest fur trade activity. In addition ongoing work by Vergil Noble comparing the ceramic assemblage at Fort de Chartres with those at Forts Ouiatenon and Michilimackinac suggests that the Fort de Chartres ceramic assemblage contained a greater variety of tin-glazed earthenware vessels than found at either Fort Michilimackinac or Ouiatenon, even though the Michilimackinac assemblage is considerably larger.

The variation between artifact assemblages at these three forts and particularly between Fort de Chartres and Fort Michilimackinac suggests that Tordoff's hierarchical model may be inadequate for explaining the variation we find in the archaeological record. Consequently, it may also be too rigid to describe the settlement and economic strategy of the eighteenth-century French colonists. As an alternative, the author suggests the following preliminary working model based on settlement and economic information from French colonial sites in North America.

Settlement Patterns

The Fortress of Louisbourg constitutes one of the most impressive colonial settlements on the North American continent (fig. 3-2). Louisbourg was first constructed in the 1740s by the French. Built in the Vauban style, it was a walled town that operated as a seaport in which ocean resources — primarily cod from the North Atlantic — were processed, packaged, and shipped to Europe. In addition to food resources, furs from the interior were also processed here. The predominate commercial activity, however, was fishing.

Two characteristics of this settlement should be noted. First, the interior of this fortress is laid out in a grid pattern, very characteristic of the Vauban style. Second, the entire settlement except for some small fishing camps and redoubts is located within the walls of the

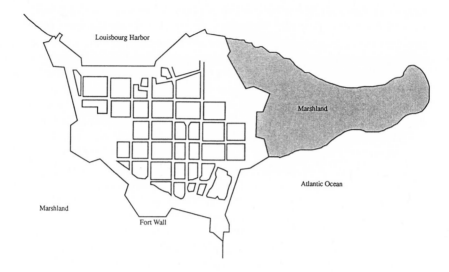

Figure 3-2. Plan of the Fortress of Louisbourg

fortress. The economic activity of processing cod, shipping, and other ancillary commercial activity is centralized.

Fort Michilimackinac was initially constructed by the French sometime between 1715 and 1717. Built of cut timber, this post was constructed to facilitate the fur trade and relations with native populations involved in fur trade activity (Stone 1974:8). Furs were brought here by various Indian groups and trappers to be processed, packaged, and shipped to Montreal or Quebec before being shipped to France for sale in the European markets.

Michilimackinac (see fig. 13-6) is a wooden stockade fort similar to a Vauban-style fort only in an analogous sense. We find in this fort as at Louisbourg a grid-pattern town layout with all of the colonial inhabitants residing inside the walls of the fort. There are some marked differences, however. Although both were fortified towns, the Fortress of Louisbourg is a massive stone fortification similar to the fortresses Vauban constructed on the French frontier in the seventeenth century. The construction of Louisbourg required thousands of men working with engineers and craftsmen. Because it was constructed with wooden pickets, Michilimackinac required only unskilled labor.

Like Louisbourg, Michilimackinac was a center of economic activity. The economic activity in both places focused on the processing of resources gathered or extracted from the environment. These sites served as centralized redistribution centers providing a link between Europe and the frontier. Manufactured goods from Europe were brought in for distribution and resources extracted from the frontier were processed for shipment to European markets. In an examination of the colonization of the twentieth-century Ecuadoran frontier, Joseph Casagrande and his colleagues defined such settlements as *entrepots*. "The entrepot provides the vital link between the area of colonization and the metropolitan area, it is the terminus of the transportation system that serves the frontier. Through it pass the goods essential to the welfare of the area of colonization. And occupying as it does a crucial position with respect to the transportation network, it usually provides the major link of the settlement within the area of colonization with the national level of socio-cultural integration" (Casagrande, Thompson, and Young 1964:312).

The settlement systems at both Louisbourg and Michilimackinac were influenced by the economic activity in which they were engaged. Louisbourg was engaged in economic activity requiring craftsmen and labor necessary to support various maritime activities such as shipbuilding and repair (carpenters, tar and pitch manufacture, blacksmiths), net makers, and labor for processing and drying fish. All of these task requiring the collective activity of a community.

Extracting furs from the frontier did not require the collective labor activity and structured social hierarchy required in a maritime-focused economy. Although based on resource extraction as at Louisbourg, the economic activity at Michilimackinac centered on the labor of individuals. Where fishing for cod required a large vessel with a team, trapping furs required the skill of a lone trapper.

The similarities and differences in the economies of both sites are reflected in the residence pattern at each site. All the colonists at Louisbourg and at Michilimackinac resided inside the walls of each fort. The processing of extracted resources was centralized and took place within the fort settlement. This residence pattern appears to indicate an extractive economy.

The settlement pattern at Fort de Chartres is somewhat different than at Louisbourg or Michilimackinac. Although structurally homologous to Louisbourg, built on the Vauban model, Fort de Chartres never housed civilian populations. In fact, the interior layout of the fort indicates a military camp and not a town as in the previously discussed forts.

The civilian population in the Illinois Country was located in a series of villages within the vicinity of Fort de Chartres. And as in the case of Louisbourg and Michilimackinac, the settlement pattern in Illinois was structured in response to economic activity. The economy of the French in Illinois did include trading furs and mining, but for the majority of the inhabitants farming was the chief occupation during most of the year. "The convoys from the Illinois country carried to the Gulf settlements, in 1748, 800,000 pounds of flour alone. Besides the flour the cargoes were made up of corn, bacon, hams from the bear as well as the hog, salt pork, buffalo meat, tallow, hides, tobacco, lead, copper, small quantities of buffalo wool, venison, bear's oil, tongues, poultry and peltry, chiefly, however, the loads were made up of pork and flour" (Surrey 1916:293). By the middle of the 1750s and well into the French and Indian War, Illinois supplied grain not only to Louisiane but also to the outposts in the Ohio River Valley. This included Fort Ouiatenon, Fort Massac, and Fort Duquesne (Pease and Jenison 1940:892–93).

An agricultural economy is an economy of production as opposed to an economy of collection, gathering, or extraction. It is labor intensive and land intensive, that is, labor input per unit of land and output per acre of land are high in comparison to an extractive economy. It implies that land be treated as a commodity and the processing and shipping of the surplus requires some central administrative authority. In a mercantile economy, that central administrative authority is the state and in a colony the arm of the state is the local government. Fort de Chartres was the seat of local government in the Illinois Country.

As with Louisbourg and Michilimachinac, the size and structure of the population in Illinois reflect economic activity. In 1752 Louisbourg was occupied by 1,500 military personnel, 674 fishermen, 437 engagés and other servants, and 1,349 residents (Clark 1968:280). The 1752 census of the Illinois Country indicates that there were 151 soldiers, 670 inhabitants or farmers, 401 black slaves, and 133 native Indian slaves (Harris 1987: pl. 41).

The substantial number of slaves—almost forty percent of the 1752 population of the Illinois Country—suggests that the demand for field labor was high. In fact, the shipment of black slaves from Louisiane to Illinois became an issue between the two colonies. In 1749 a Louisiane court put a prohibition on the shipment of black slaves to Illinois. Slaves were a scarce commodity in high demand in both colonies. At one point the governor of New France in a letter to the Minister Rouille in France noted: "that there was no other means to induce the inhabitants of that country [Illinois] to cultivate their lands. As it was, they left the land entirely to the labor of their negroes and remained in an indolence from which nothing else could draw them. . . . M. de Vaudreuil has since perceived that this prohibition was a great prejudice to the welfare of the inhabitants of the Illinois who could no longer enlarge their farms" (Pease and Jenison 1940:378). This information suggests that the production of surplus agricultural products influenced the structure of the local population as well as land use strategies and settlement.

Additional support for this hypothesis can be found by examining settlements similar to Fort de Chartres in Illinois. During the first half of the eighteenth century, French settlements in Acadia other than Louisbourg flourished. One settlement in particular—Port Royal (fig. 3-3)—served as a granary for the rest of Acadia. In other words, the primary activity of the population at Port Royal was the production of surplus agricultural products (Clark 1968:158). Inspection of figure 3-3 suggests a pattern of settlement similar to that at Fort de Chartres, with a small four-bastioned stone fort surrounded by agricultural

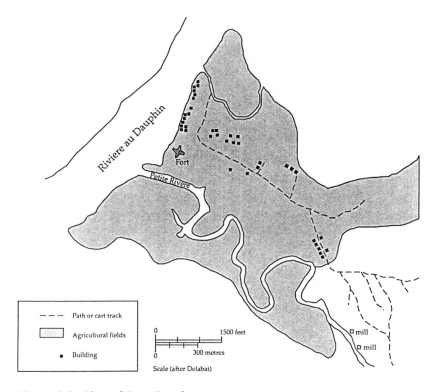

Figure 3-3. Plan of Port Royal

villages. In addition, the internal organization of structures in the fort is similar to that at Fort de Chartres.

Discussion

The French apparently established a series of entrepots throughout their North American colonial empire. Some understanding of the mercantile system is necessary to understand how each entrepot operated in a larger economic system.

Mercantilism was one of the first economic world systems (Wallerstein 1974) of the modern period. Its underlying emphasis was on building a strong national state with an economy controlled and regulated by a central state authority. Colonies served a dual purpose in this state-controlled system: they produced raw materials and surplus goods for the mother country, and they consumed goods manufactured in the mother country. To this end local economies were planned and structured by the central state authority, and manufacturing was forbidden. In addition, population growth was encouraged to increase the supply of labor, markets, and soldiers.

The entrepots in North America were primarily engaged in two basic economic pursuits: the extraction, processing, and shipping of natural resources, e.g., furs or cod; and the production, processing, and shipping of surplus agricultural goods. These two distinct economic pursuits produced two basic settlement and land use patterns (as well as population structures) in the various North American French colonies.

Conclusion

In his seminal work on historical archaeology, Stanley South (1977) insists that one of the primary objectives in historical archaeology is the recognition of patterns in artifact assemblages. Over the past decade considerable work focused upon discovering and defining such patterns; however, very little energy has gone into explaining these patterns (South 1988:25). In this chapter an attempt has been made to move beyond the pattern recognition stage of research and propose a model or system of explanation to account for the variability observed in artifact patterns between French colonial sites.

The movement away from static hierarchical models toward dynamic cultural and economic models can prove invaluable. By suggesting that the variation between artifact assemblages at French colonial settlements such as Louisbourg, Michilimackinac, and Chartres can be explained by placing them in the larger context of settlement pattern, we can successfully move away from the descriptive or particularist approach used in some historical archaeology studies toward more comprehensive approaches utilized in other fields of anthropology.

French Colonial Fort Massac: Architecture and Ceramic Patterning

4

John A. Walthall

> The Chevalier de la Salle . . . entered the Illinois area, took possession of the country in the name of Louis XIV, called it Louisiana in honor of this prince, and constructed a fort there; the Spaniards would have built a church; the English, a tavern.
>
> —*Le Voyageur François*

As the historian Samuel Wilson has observed, the building of forts was a principal objective of France in its American colonies, "forts which would maintain its domination over its vast new empire against threats from the English on the one side and the Spanish on the other" (1965:103). Following the principles of fortification expounded by the engineering genius Sébastien Le Prestre de Vauban (1633–1707), successive French colonial governments erected over a dozen forts in the territory encompassing its Louisiane colony. These ranged from temporary wooden stockades, such as La Salle's Fort Prudhomme (in 1682) to massive stone fortifications such as Fort de Chartres (Keene, chap. 3). Archaeological excavations have been conducted at a number of these French colonial forts. One of the most extensive archaeological field projects conducted at such sites was carried out nearly a half century ago in southern Illinois at Fort Massac. These excavations represent not only one of the first scientific investigations at a French fortification in North America, but also one of the earliest large-scale projects in American historical archaeology. That the research conducted at Fort Massac has had little or no impact on studies of French colonial military sites is due to the fact that this project, like many other government-sponsored public works of the depression era, was terminated by World War II and the results were never published. In this chapter, the architectural features and ceramics associated with the French occupation of Fort Massac will be described and evaluated. This endeavor will not only provide comparative data for future studies of French colonial military sites, but hopefully will also stimulate further research of the materials and records generated by this impressive archaeological project, now stored and curated at regional depositories and museums.

Historic Background

In the spring of 1757, shortly after the outbreak of the French and Indian War, an expedition was launched down the Mississippi River from Fort de Chartres in the Illinois Country. This convoy of batteaux and canoes, manned by some one hundred fifty French soldiers and one hundred Illini warriors, was placed under the command of Capt. Charles Aubry. Aubry's orders were to establish a fortification in the lower Ohio Valley, as near to the mouth of the Tennessee River as possible. This area, near the confluences of four of the largest river systems in North America, was considered strategic to the French in their attempt to protect vital supply lines from the English and their southern aboriginal allies, the Cherokee and the Chickasaw.

Captain Aubry's expedition successfully reached the Ohio and, following specified orders, established a fort of earth and wood on the high bluff along the Illinois shoreline (see fig. 1-1). This fort, known variously as Fort Ascension, Fort Massiac, and later as Fort Massac, stood as a sentinel of French colonial power until it was abandoned in 1764, after the cessation of war. The fort was burned by the Chickasaw shortly after the French garrison retreated to the Mississippi Valley. What is known from historic accounts concerning the brief French occupation of Fort Massac has been compiled by John B. Fortier (1969). The following outline of the history of Fort Massac is based on the documentation contained in Fortier's summary.

The French colonial government at New Orleans had long recognized the strategic importance of the lower Ohio River. In 1745 a fortification for this area was formally proposed by Bernard Deverges, assistant engineer for the colony of Louisiane. Deverges designed a stone fort (fig. 4-1) of standard square configuration (see Wilson 1965), to measure 20 *toises* (128 feet) on a side. It was thought that the fort would require fire only from musketry and small cannon for its defense because the most probable attacks would come from ill-equipped aboriginal raiding parties.

Deverges suggested that the fort be located atop the bluffline of

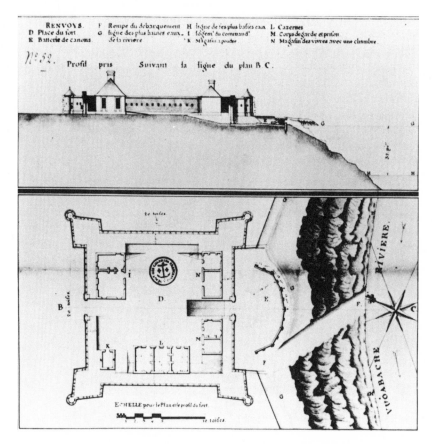

Figure 4-1. Plan for Fort Massac (1745). Courtesy of the Illinois State Historical Library

the Ohio River. A battery of small cannon would be cut into the banks, allowing artillerymen to sweep the river and control this vital river route. Deverges also submitted a second option: a wooden fort of identical size and configuration with walls of a double row of vertical stockades rising nine feet above earthen embankments could be built for half of the cost of building his proposed stone fort. Buildings to be located within the fort included a commandant's quarters, barracks, a guardhouse, a prison, a magazine, and a store house. In the end, however, neither of Deverges's forts were built due to a lack of funds and workmen.

With the initiation of hostilities with the British in 1756, the need for such a fortification became acute as news spread that hostile forces were massing to descend the Tennessee and Ohio rivers to invade the French possessions in the Mississippi Valley. In response to this threat, Aubry's expedition selected the location suggested earlier by Deverges for the proposed fort. This site, near modern Metropolis, Illinois, is elevated some seventy feet above the river's edge. The terrain to the rear of this bluff top recedes gradually to protective swamp ground dissected by deep ravines. Aubry's fort, completed "in haste," was finished by 20 June. In a report from New Orleans, Deverges described the fort as built

> in the form of a square flanked by four bastions of 26 toises, one pied, six pounces [approximately 168 feet] on each front, from the flanked angle of one bastion to the flanked angle of the other, with the wall made of two rows of stockaded tree trunks, joined together; those of the outer row being thirteen feet in length and eleven to twelve inches in diameter and those of the inner row, placed against the joints of the former, being nine feet in length and six to seven inches in diameter, the whole planted in earth to a depth of three feet, with a banquette along the interior two feet high, for firing through the loopholes which have been cut at a height of six feet in the outer walls; and with platforms raised at the flanked angles of the bastions for placing the *guerittes* and some cannon *en barbette*, with two buildings of *pied en terre;* covered with clapboards, for lodging the garrison (Fortier 1969:61–62).

Aubry's "haste" to complete the fort was soon justified. An attack on the fort took place the following autumn by a large force of Cherokee. This assault, the only large-scale action taken by the English and their allies against Fort Massac, was repulsed, and according to Aubry, the Cherokee were put "totally to flight." While no other attempts were made to capture the fort, the defenders were frequently menaced by small raiding parties. By late summer 1758, eight members of the garrison had been killed or captured at or near the fort. Nine others, including an officer and a sergeant, were killed shortly afterwards by Cherokee and Chickasaw. The following July, a force from the garrison assisted in the pursuit of Chickasaw raiders.

In that year, 1759, Commandant Macarty at Fort de Chartres ordered the fortification to be strengthened. The fort was "Terraced, fraised and fortified, piece on piece, with a good ditch." According to Fortier, this account represents "the first mention of a ditch, within which the earth had been terraced and given a row of fraises, or pickets" (1969:63).

Little is known from historic records concerning the composition of the garrison housed at Fort Massac. The staff at one point included an interpreter, a baker, a hospital attendant, and a storekeeper-surgeon. The garrison consisted of some fifty soldiers and civilian militia in 1758. This number was reduced to an officer and only fifteen men by the end of 1763, when the French settlements around Fort de Chartres were threatened.

Fort Massac served as an isolated outpost in hostile territory, and unlike Fort de Chartres, no civilian settlements were established around it. The isolation and hardships of the post created predictable problems for the military commanders. In May 1760 the Sieur Philippe de Rocheblave, *lieutenant-reforme* at Fort de Chartres, set out for Fort Massac with a supply convoy of two boats and fifty soldiers and *habitants*. De Rocheblave, who was also to take command of the fort, was given specific instructions about problems of morale he would encounter:

> We should think it an injustice to Sieur de Rocheblave to remind him of the discipline which he ought to maintain in the Fort, and of the care he must take to cultivate good feeling among the soldiers and the habitants. We will simply content ourselves with suggesting to him that drink being the only thing that could disturb the tranquility and unity so necessary in that post, we deem ourselves indispensably obliged to order him to keep his hands upon all that may be on board of every kind except that which the king is accustomed to send for the relief of the sick and wounded that may be in the garrison. . . . As to that which every good Christian owes to God his creator, we know too well the sentiments of Sieur de Rocheblave to think it necessary to recommend to him to have prayers offered every evening and morning and to put a check upon the blasphemy and oaths to which soldiers are only too much addicted (Fortier 1969:67).

After the abandonment of Fort Massac by the French military, the site remained unoccupied for thirty years. Then, in 1794, an expedition of American soldiers under the command of Maj. Thomas Dole arrived at the fort. Dole, under orders from Gen. Anthony Wayne, was to reestablish a fortification in this area, now near Spanish colonies in the Mississippi Valley. When Dole and his men reached the site they found extensive ruins, including an earthwork still rising fifteen feet from the bottom of the ditch. Dole wrote to Wayne that "The Old Fort is a Regular Fortification with four Bastions nearly of the dimensions in the Square with the one you wished me to erect. . . . This I have concluded to Fortify" (Fortier 1969:63). For twenty years, until its abandonment in 1814, the American Fort Massac served as the headquarters for an extensive customs district that controlled river traffic between New Orleans to the south and Pittsburgh to the east.

In 1903, with strong support from the Daughters of the American Revolution, the site and its surrounding grounds became the first state park in Illinois. In the mid-1970s a full-scale replica of the American fort was reconstructed in the park near the original site.

WPA Excavations

In the fall of 1939 Paul Maynard, an archaeologist with the Illinois Department of Public Works and Buildings, conducted the first scientific excavations at Fort Massac. Using a crew of twelve Works Progress Administration (WPA) laborers, Maynard, then a University of Chicago graduate student, began test excavations at the supposed location of the superimposed forts. Employing standard University of Chicago archaeological field techniques, the crew excavated two intersecting trenches, each five feet wide and 120 feet long across the site.

According to Maynard, "This excavation proved that there had been at least two occupations in the area dug. It also proved that the structures on the site were symmetrical and large enough to have been forts. Artifacts recovered included military buttons, coins, habitation debris and structural material. The artifacts dated the occupations as being within the correct historical periods. The possibilities for securing an intelligible and comprehensive body of data seemed good and it was decided to carry on the research at a later date" (1942).

Large-scale excavations were begun at Fort Massac in January 1940. Over the following months Maynard and his crew excavated nearly the entire area where the forts once stood. In his 1942 progress report, Maynard detailed the techniques used to excavate the site and outlined his methods of recording the features and cataloguing artifacts recovered. As part of the WPA project, short chemically treated posts were used to outline the French fort and some of its interior buildings. This reconstruction remains visible at the park today. American entry into World War II and the conscription of Paul Maynard into the armed forces halted further work at Fort Massac. Maynard did not continue his career in archaeology after the war. Many of the original field maps and records have been stored at the State of Illinois Archives Department in Springfield. The cultural materials recovered by Maynard, other than a small sample on display at the Fort Massac Museum, are now curated by the Illinois State Museum. A cursory examination of these materials by the author indicates that the vast bulk of the artifacts recovered date to the later, and more intensive,

American component. Features assignable to the American period component were identified by Maynard on the basis of location, content, stratigraphic position, and construction materials (stone and brick foundations, and the like). As part of a feasibility study for the reconstruction of the American fort, Margaret Brown (1970) analyzed Maynard's records and provided a summary horizontal plan of the features associated with this later component. Although preliminary studies of certain artifact types associated with the American occupation have been made (Bailey 1966), no overall analysis of this component has been undertaken. The field and laboratory records and the cultural materials from the 1794–1814 American fort constitute an important and unique data base. Hopefully, with the growing popularity of historical archaeology, these materials will be subjected to proper analysis in the future. It should be noted that subsequent archaeological investigations have been conducted within Fort Massac State Park (Bailey 1966; Penny 1981; Rackerby 1970, 1971). While several prehistoric and early nineteenth-century sites have been located, no components contemporary with the French fort have been identified. These intensive investigations support the historical interpretation of French Fort Massac as an isolated outpost surrounded by unsettled land that was only occasionally entered by supply expeditions or hostile forces.

Architecture

Maynard's excavations exposed over ninety percent of the features originally associated with French colonial Fort Massac. Post-American period erosion along the southern flanks of the fort nearest the river destroyed portions of two bastions and any evidence of an outer parapet fronting the Ohio (fig. 4-2). After the establishment of Fort Massac State Park in 1903, a sea wall was constructed along the river bank to protect the site. The fort as revealed by archaeological excavations was composed of a ditch or moat encircling a terraced earthwork upon which the wooden stockade was constructed (fig. 4-2). Gates were apparently centered in the northern and southern stockade curtains. Within the fort, each bastion contained evidence of internal structures; three had subterranean cellars and the fourth, a well. The foundations of two long buildings—one with four rooms, the other with three—paralleled the east and west stockade curtains. A third, small building was exposed near the south end of the western structure. Near the north gate was a fourth structure with a rectangular addition. According to Maynard (1942), a layer of pure, yellow

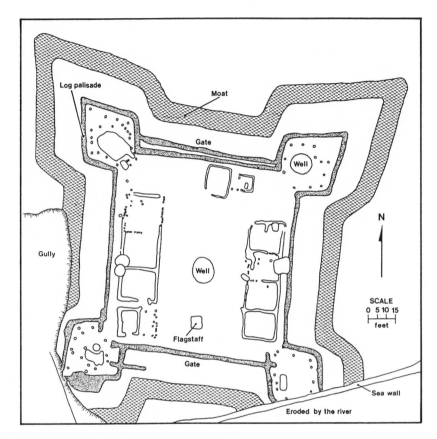

Figure 4-2. Archaeological Plan of Fort Massac

river sand covered much of the open parade ground. This sand was likely deposited by the French in order to provide better drainage and a stable surface in times of inclement weather. Two systems of shallow drainage ditches were found. One system extended under the two long structures and exited at the southern gate. The second ran east-west from the well past the northern building. Exits for this ditch were located in the northeast bastion and at the northern gate.

The Moat

The moat or ditch encircling the fort had been excavated by French construction crews to a depth of four feet. This ditch measured ten to thirteen feet wide at the top, sloping down to a width of eight feet at the base. Typical cross-section profiles of this ditch are illustrated in figure 4-3. The earth excavated from the ditch was thrown up onto the interior shoulder to form a linear rampart or elevated terrace. A line of pickets (fraise) was placed within the moat along the interior profile. These upright, pointed poles were placed side-by-side in a wall trench three feet deep. These posts measured eight to fifteen inches in diameter and many had charred basal sections.

The Palisade

Atop the earthen ramparts a log palisade was constructed in the classic square with bastions at each corner. In the palisade wall trench Maynard and his crew found post molds and log fragments. These logs

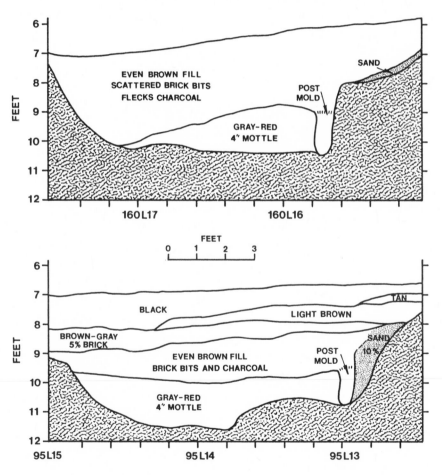

Figure 4-3. Typical Cross Section of Moat

ranged from eleven to fourteen inches in diameter and it was evident that many had charred bases. Historical accounts indicate that it was common practice for the French to char the bottom three to four feet of log palisades in order to protect the wood from insects and the elements. Frequently, old posts were dislodged and replaced upside down to extend their use (Fortier 1969:65). Vertical and horizontal cross sections of the palisade trench are shown in figure 4-4. The palisade wall trench extended three feet into the subsoil. The stockade posts would therefore have been sunk a total of six feet from the

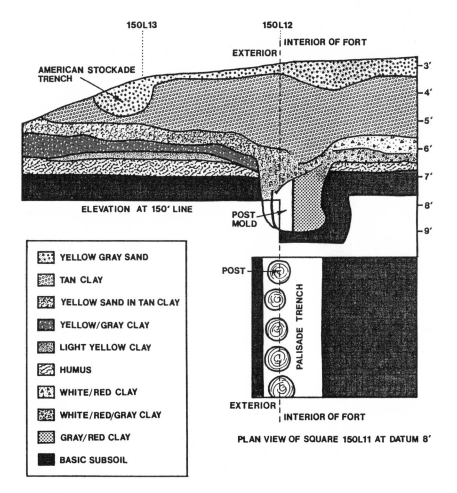

Figure 4-4. Cross Section of the Palisade

upper rampart surface. Excavation along the northern curtain revealed two parallel stockade trenches (see fig. 4-2). While it is possible that these two walls may have been contemporary, it is more likely that one was excavated as part of a rebuilding episode, perhaps during the 1759 strengthening of the fort ordered by Commandant Macarty.

Bastions

Each of the four bastions contained post patterns outlining support systems for raised artillery platforms. The flooring of these platforms, each covering some two hundred square feet, also served as roofs for structures built below them. Both the southeast and southwest bastions contained small cellars dug into the subsoil. Excavations of the northwest bastion revealed the most complex cellar system (fig. 4-5). This cellar, rectanguloid in shape, measured some twenty-five feet in length by fifteen feet in width. It had been excavated to a depth of five feet below the original ground surface. A series of log steps led down into the cellar basin, which was floored with hewn planks. An ash pit was found in one end of the cellar floor. Archaeologists found portions of a wooden keg resting on fragments of the plank flooring. Based upon the size and placement of this feature, it is probable that this cellar represents the fort's main magazine for the storage of gunpowder and other armaments (see Robinson 1977). The northeast bastion contained a well. Excavation of this feature was carried to a depth of forty-five feet before the water table was encountered. A wooden windlass was found submerged at the base of the well shaft. In profile, the well was some ten feet in diameter at its mouth. The shaft gradually sloped downward for twelve feet to a flat bench. From this point downward, the vertical shaft was four feet in diameter to its base. This well may have been cleaned out and used during the subsequent American occupation. The upper strata of well fill contained brick and other debris indicating that it was abandoned after the American period structures were razed.

Structures

The four buildings found within the fort were all of *poteaux en terre* construction (Peterson 1965). This typical French colonial construction technique involved the excavation of narrow wall trenches outlining the basic building shape. Logs, planted upright in these trenches, were joined at the top by hewn sills. Numerous pieces of rock, and fragments of lime mortar with log impressions on their surfaces, were recovered by Maynard and his crew within and around each of the structures. This indicates that rubble stone and mortar (*pierrotage*)

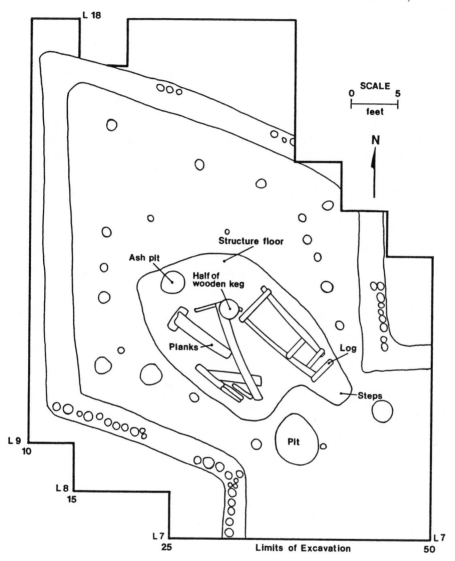

Figure 4-5. Plan of the Northwest Bastion

had been placed between the upright logs to form a solid wall. Post molds were found along the central axis of each building. These likely served as supports for a steep hip or gable roof covered with thatch or shingles.

Structure Complex One. The east barracks measured sixty feet in length by eighteen feet in width (fig. 4-6). It had been divided into four rooms of equal size. The second room from the north end, likely a kitchen or common room, contained the remains of a large hearth. Although some of the rocks used in the construction of this fireplace were found around the hearth pit, most were likely removed during the American period for reuse. A series of single posts forming a roughly rectangular pattern was discovered at the north end of this structure. These posts likely served as the supports for a lean-to or floored *galerie* or porch. Such lean-to additions were common to French colonial houses in the Illinois Country (Peterson 1965).

Structure Complex Two. The main building of the west barracks was fifty-five feet in length and eighteen feet in width (fig. 4-7). Each of its three rooms contained some three hundred square feet of living space. Two ash-filled pits, indicating the former presence of hearths, were located near the common wall of the middle and southern rooms. A second, detached building, twelve feet by ten feet, was found at the south end of the barracks. A lean-to or *galerie,* eight feet by twelve feet, of single-post construction extended from its east wall.

Structure Complex Three. Along the north curtain, just east of the gate, was located a fourth building (fig. 4-8). This rectangular structure measured fifteen feet by twelve feet. A room of similar construction was added to the east wall of the main structure. A few post molds indicated that a *galerie* may have been attached to the southern wall of this extension. Large numbers of posts were found within the

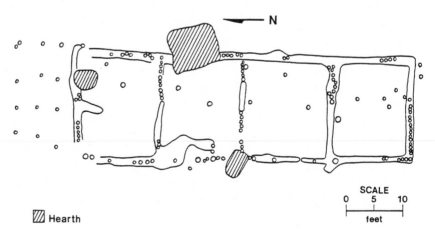

Figure 4-6. Structure Complex One

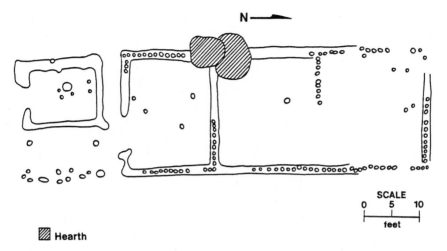

▨ Hearth

Figure 4-7. Structure Complex Two

main room of this building. While some of these were likely for roof support, others may have supported a plank floor or perhaps the shelving of a store house.

Ceramics

The excavations at Fort Massac produced a large sample of ceramic vessel fragments. The majority of these sherds were derived from the 1794–1814 American occupation. The ceramics that could be assigned to the French component are composed of tin-glazed faience and coarse earthenwares. Sherds from a single Spanish majolica plate were also attributed to this earlier component because such vessels have been recovered in French colonial contexts elsewhere in the Illinois Country. As part of a more comprehensive study of ceramics dating to the French colonial period, the author has analyzed collections from a number of Illinois sites. This ongoing study has resulted in the development of a classification system for faience (Walthall 1991). Ceramic attributes, such as finish and mode of decoration, were used to classify the faience sherds. Additionally, a number of rim border designs, each assigned an alphabetical letter designation (fig. 4-9), were delineated. This typology is used in the following discussion of the ceramic sample from Fort Massac. Because formal definitions are to be included in a future publication on the results of this multisite study, only brief descriptions of each type are provided

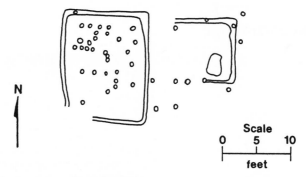

N

Scale
0   5   10
|————|————|
feet

Figure 4-8. Structure Complex Three

here. In the following pages, all references to ceramics from Illinois sites, unless otherwise noted, are based upon personal observations by the author.

Faience

Normandy Plain. Twenty-two sherds of undecorated faience were recovered. Two rim fragments are from a small ointment pot or jar. Jeffrey Brain (1979:35) illustrates two forms of such vessels from the Trudeau site (1731–64) in Louisiana. One is a jar, 9 cm in diameter and 10 cm high; the other, a bowl, is 14 cm in diameter and 7 cm high. Both forms are cylindrical with flaring, rounded rims. Such prominent rims would have allowed an oil cloth or other such cover to be tied over the vessel mouth with string or wire. The vessel from Fort Massac, which measures 7 cm in diameter, most resembles the jar form. A large fragment of an ointment jar recovered at the Laurens site in Randolph County, Illinois (Jelks, Ekberg, and Martin 1989) measures 14 cm in diameter and 6 cm in height and is, in all respects, identical in form to the bowl reported at Trudeau. According to Brain, such vessels "belong to a special functional class of containers intended for viscous substances. Depending upon their contents, they were known as *pots à onguent, confitures,* or *conserves*" (1979:35). Four sherds, two rim fragments, a body section, and a complete annular base represent a large, handleless cup. This vessel, 10 cm in diameter at the mouth, has a yellow-buff paste and an unusual crazed surface, apparently in imitation of Chinese crackle glaze. Two identical cups have been recovered from two other Illinois sites, at Fort de Chartres (1753–65) and the nearby Michigamea village at the Waterman site (1752–65). The recovery of these cups in these contemporaneous

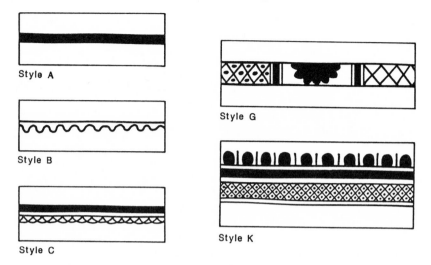

Figure 4-9. Faience Rim Border Designs

contexts strongly implies a terminal French colonial period date for vessels of this type. They may have once comprised part of a set. Although they have been classified here as faience, their origin of manufacture is unknown. The crackle glaze resembles that found on some Spanish majolicas (Deagan 1987), and at this time, such a possible derivation cannot be ruled out.

Normandy Blue on White. Four sherds with underglaze blue floral and/ or geometric decorations are in the Fort Massac collection. Three of these specimens are rim sherds, each representing a different vessel: a platter with a Style C rim border, a plate with a Style B rim border, and a plate with a blue decoration outlined in black with a Style G rim border. The fourth sherd, a basal fragment of a plate, exhibits portions of a single, centrally placed blue flower.

Brittany Blue on White. This type consists of plates with a solid blue band around the interior of the vessel rim (Style A rim border design). Double solid blue bands are known but are rare. Some plates exhibit a second, thin blue line around the interior edge of the marli. Simple geometric designs are at times painted in the center of these plates, although many examples have undecorated interiors. Plates of this type have been attributed to potteries in Brittany (Brain 1979:37; Long 1973:3). More sherds of Brittany Blue on White (n = 37) were recovered from Fort Massac than were any other faience type. A minimum of eight plates are represented by the twenty-four rim sherds. Some of these plates also had a thin blue line around the rim interior. One reconstructable plate base had a highly stylized central rosette motif consisting of two concentric circles with a centrally placed, solid blue sphere. Petal-like loops, originating at the interior design element, expanded out beyond the outer ring (fig. 4-10 *top*). Plates with this specific geometric/floral motif have been recovered from Fort Desha (Arkansas Post) in Arkansas (McClurkan 1971: fig. 1-h), Fortress Louisbourg in Nova Scotia (Long 1973), the Cahokia Courthouse site in Illinois, and at Fort Toulouse in Alabama. At this last site, thirteen Brittany Blue on White plates with this central motif were found in a pit datable to the fort's abandonment in 1763 (Brooms and Parker 1980:17). Nicole Genêt (1977) believes that plates of this type are a good temporal marker for the second half of the eighteenth century. Data from sites in Illinois (table 4-1) and from sites in Canada (Long 1973) indicate a more restricted data range for their occurrence, 1750–65. These dates bracket the period of the French and Indian War (the Seven Years' War in Europe). The frequent recovery of such plates at French fortifications dating to this period further suggests that they were a particularly popular table service among officers serving at these stations.

Seine Polychrome.   Vessels of Seine Polychrome are characterized by stylized borders and floral and geometric designs executed in combinations of blue, black, yellow, green, purple/brown, or orange-red. Four rim sherds, all from a single, large oval platter, are in the collection. This platter had a Style K rim border design (fig. 4–10 *bottom*) painted in green, red, and blue. Two of the sherds exhibit evidence of mends. These rim fragments have holes drilled from surface to surface filled with a lead plug. The flattened ends of these plugs are countersunk to fit flush with the interior vessel surface. On the exterior (underside) surface channels, also lead-filled, were cut across the break to be repaired. Apparently, a wire rivet was passed through the drilled holes and along the channels to make the mend. Molten lead was then poured to fill the drill holes and the channel. This channel system may have been employed when ferrous wire was to be used in order to impede rust. Other sites in the Illinois Country where mended faience vessel fragments have been recovered are enumerated in table 4-2.

Stanley South (1968:62–71) has discussed the mending of ceramic vessels at eighteenth-century sites of both French and British affiliation. He illustrates repairs on a faience platter (Rouen Blue on White)

Figure 4-10. Faience Vessels: *top*, Brittany Blue on White; *bottom*, Seine Polychrome Platter. Drawn by Carla Zedialis Londrigan

Table 4-1. Brittany Blue on White Vessels from French Colonial Sites in the Illinois Country

Site	Dates	No. of Sherds	No. of Vessels	Total Faience Vessels
Guebert	1719–65	1	1	26
Kolmer	1719–52	0	0	27
Waterman	1752–65	13	8	41
Cahokia Wedge	1750–1800+	10	4	20
Cahokia Courthouse	1737–1800+	2	1	5
Laurens	1721–65	6	4	30
Ste. Genevieve	1750–90	6	1	15
Fort de Chartres	1753–65	39	7	82
Arkansas Post	1750–1800+	0	0	40
Fort Massac	1757–63	37	8	14
Total		114	34	300

and plate (Brittany Blue on White) from Fortress Louisbourg. The platter has six lead-filled holes indicating a repair technique similar to the one described above. The plate has drilled holes with a wire rivet still in place. No lead is evident in the drilled holes of this specimen, indicating a simple technique in which the wire is passed through the holes and then twisted to tighten.

Majolica

Puebla Blue on White. There are six sherds in the Fort Massac collection from a single Puebla Blue on White plate. According to Deagan, "This type is the most abundant, widespread, and frequently encountered of the eighteenth century Puebla majolicas. It is found throughout the Carribean and Florida as well as in Mexico and the southwestern United States" (1987:83–84). While Puebla Blue on White is not a common type at French colonial sites in the Illinois Country, fragments of a few vessels have been observed in the collections from a number of sites, including Cahokia Courthouse, Cahokia Wedge, Laurens, Fort de Chartres, Arkansas Post, and at the Louvier site in Prairie du Rocher a few miles east of Fort de Chartres (Safiran, chap. 8).

Coarse Earthenwares

Saintonge Plain. Vessels assigned to this type have a chalky white to buff paste covered with green lead glaze. According to Kenneth Barton (1981:6), this ware, along with the related slipped type, was a

Table 4-2. Evidence of Vessel Mending at Sites in the Illinois Country

Site	Type	Vessel Form	Evidence of Mending
Cahokia Courthouse	Seine Polychrome	Platter	Drilled hole
Cahokia Wedge	Brittany B/W	Plate	2 drilled holes
Ste. Genevieve	Rouen B/W	Platter	Basal sherd with lead-filled drilled hole
Fort de Chartres	Normandy B/W	Tureen	Several drilled holes
Arkansas Post	Rouen Plain	Platter	Drilled hole
	Charente Plain	Bowl	Two rim sherds each with a lead-filled drilled hole

product of the kilns of La Chapelle-des-Pots, near Saintes, Charente Maritime, in the province of Saintonge. These potteries were located near the colonial trade center at La Rochelle and the major naval base at Rochefort. Soldiers and supplies for the American colonies frequently embarked from this area of France. Saintonge earthenware, as well as faience from nearby Brittany, were part of the cargo on the *Machault,* a French frigate sunk in Canadian waters in 1760 (Barton 1977). The nine sherds of this type found at Fort Massac are from a shallow bowl and a deep bowl or pot. Two body sherds from this latter vessel have sets of four combed or incised lines, one set straight and the other wavy, around the vessel exterior. This is a decorative treatment not seen elsewhere in the ceramic collections from Illinois.

Saintonge Slip Plain. This type is composed of coarseware vessels with a salmon-colored fabric covered with a white slip and a bright green lead glaze. It is one of the most common earthenwares found at French colonial sites in North America (Barton 1981). The eight sherds of this type from Fort Massac are derived from two shallow, flanged bowls.

Charente Plain. This earthenware type, apparently related to the Saintonge wares, is composed of vessels with a deep salmon to red paste and a clear lustrous glaze. This clear glaze takes on a brown hue against the reddish vessel fabric. Several vessels of this type were reported from Trudeau (Brain 1979) and it is one of the most common coarse earthenwares in the Illinois Country. The twenty-two sherds from the Fort Massac collection are from two deep bowls with flattened bases and rounded rims.

Discussion and Summary

The archaeological investigations conducted at Fort Massac have provided a wealth of data concerning eighteenth-century French colonial fortification systems. The nearly complete excavation of this site revealed not only the configuration of the defense works but also internal structural plans. The size, shape, and spatial distribution of the garrison buildings indicate that French engineers closely followed prescribed architectural plans. Such architectural standardization was, in part, the product of a centralized military bureaucracy situated at New Orleans, which maintained tight control over the few engineers working within the Louisiane colony. In 1751 Bernard Deverges, who had drafted the original plans for Fort Massac, was appointed engineer-in-chief for Louisiane. Deverges sent his subengineer, François Saucier, who had previously worked on the fortifications at Mobile and at Fort Tombecbe, to Fort Toulouse to design and supervise the construction of a new fort there. When this project was completed, Saucier was then dispatched to the Illinois Country, where he designed and commenced the construction of a new Fort de Chartres. In turn, Pierre de la Gautrais, who worked under Saucier at Fort de Chartres, was sent with the Aubry expedition in 1757 to supervise the building of Fort Massac. It is, therefore, of little wonder that La Gautrais's fort was very similar to the one proposed earlier by Deverges and to Fort de Chartres, then still under construction. Future analysis of the cultural materials recovered from the French component at Fort Massac may generate data concerning the specific function of the garrison buildings and their various rooms. A cursory examination of the spatial distribution of the ceramic sherds discussed in this chapter indicates that over eighty-five percent were derived from excavation units within and around the east barracks. This distribution pattern suggests that the officers' mess, if not their quarters, was located in this building. The attribution of these ceramics to the officer ranks is based upon historical records, which indicate that both French and British common soldiers during the eighteenth century used wooden trenchers and plates and cups of pewter or tin to eat food prepared in quantity in large iron pots (Ferguson 1977; South and Widmer 1977:141–42). The data concerning ceramic forms present in the Fort Massac collection (table 4-3) suggests that the equipment of French officers during the French and Indian War included a limited variety of serving vessels, mainly plates, platters, and bowls. Fragments of only a single cup were found. This functional pattern contrasts dramatically with that recorded for British officers during the same period. By the

Table 4-3. Minimal Vessel Counts, Fort Massac

Type	No. of Sherds	Vessel Form				
		Plate	Platter	Cup	Ointment Jar	Bowl
Normandy Plain	22	—	—	1	1	—
Normandy B/W	4	2	1	—	—	—
Brittany B/W	37	8	—	—	—	—
Seine Polychrome	4	—	1	—	—	—
Puebla B/W	6	1	—	—	—	—
Saintonge Plain	9	—	—	—	—	2
Saintonge Slip Plain	8	—	—	—	—	2
Charente Plain	22	—	—	—	—	2
Total	112	11	2	1	1	6

middle of the eighteenth century, tea and vessels used in its serving (cups, saucers, pots, and bowls) had become immensely popular among the English. The consumption of this beverage evolved into a social "ceremony" of great import among higher social groups (Roth 1961). Chocolate and coffee were preferred by the French, and no such widespread social custom developed around these beverages. Even at remote eighteenth-century British outposts such as Fort Michilimackinac and Fort de Chartres, archaeologists have recovered quantities of porcelain and refined earthenware tea service vessels (Stone 1974; Vergil Noble, personal communication, 1987). Lois Feister (1984), based upon her analysis of ceramics recovered from archaeological test excavations at the British fort of Crown Point (1759–73) on Lake Champlain, has proposed that by the end of the French and Indian War the tremendous production of ceramics by British potteries allowed access by soldiers of lower ranks to porcelain and refined earthenware tea services. The mass production of these high quality and inexpensive wares had an adverse effect on faience production. Many French potteries were closed during the late eighteenth century because they could not compete with the influx of these British imports. Of the 110 minimal vessels recovered during the 1976–77 excavation at Crown Point, over half functioned as tea service ware. The location of Crown Point on a major shipping route and in close proximity to a well-provisioned civilian population weakens the implications of comparisons to remote frontier posts such as Fort Massac. However, the numerous differences in ceramic patterning at these two sites serve to underscore the significant cultural variance between eighteenth-century French and British military personnel. The historical record indicates that Fort Massac was constructed in haste to impede possible encroachments into French territory. As such, this fort was viewed as only a temporary stopgap in time of war. Had the French been victorious, it is likely that these earthen and wooden fortifications would have been replaced with a more substantial structure. However, as the British won battle after battle in eastern Canada, it became clear to French authorities in Louisiane that the presence of Fort Massac did little to advance the course of its military effort. As threats were made on settlements to the north, the garrison at Fort Massac was reduced to a token force until its complete abandonment in 1764. As an isolated, short-term military outpost, Fort Massac was unique among the fortifications constructed by France in its Louisiane colony.

Ouiatenon on the Ouabache: Archaeological Investigations at a Fur Trading Post on the Wabash River

5

Vergil E. Noble

It has been a decade now since a spade of earth was last turned at the site of Fort Ouiatenon. But between the years 1968 and 1979, that particular cornfield on the banks of the Wabash River was subjected to intensive archaeological scrutiny (fig. 5-1). Indeed, only Fort Michilimackinac can boast more intensive and prolonged excavation among French colonial sites of the Great Lakes region. Furthermore, the lack of any substantial postoccupational disturbance and the remarkable state of preservation combine to make this site rather exceptional. Consequently, it is no exaggeration to count Fort Ouiatenon among the most important fur trade period archaeological sites in all of North America.

Unfortunately, findings from much of the research performed at the site are not widely available. Several popular articles have been written (e.g., Noble 1982), but only a few scholarly works are in print—and those deal with rather narrow aspects of the overall program. As a result, most of the accumulated data on Fort Ouiatenon remain in dissertation form. Indeed, data gathered in the early years of investigation have not been reported at all. Thanks to a renewed interest in the early historic occupation of the central Wabash River valley, however, as well as increasing opportunities for publication, there is ample cause to hope that the site will soon become better known in the archaeological literature.

Summing up the history and archaeology of Fort Ouiatenon comes as no mean task, considering the fact that Ouiatenon was occupied for nearly seventy-five years. Further, there were more than ten field seasons of increasingly expansive excavation at the site by various institutions. As a result, it is not possible within the limits of this

Figure 5-1. Aerial Photograph of Fort Ouiatenon Location

chapter to offer more than a cursory overview of the essential facts
and interpretations.

History of Fort Ouiatenon

The French Period

Fort Ouiatenon was one of many French fur trading posts that once
stretched across the North American interior. Established in 1717
under the command of Ensign François-Marie Picoté, it was meant
only as a temporary measure to forestall British ascendancy in the
regions south of the Great Lakes. By showing a presence in the Wabash
River valley, the French hoped to persuade the local Ouiatenon Indians—a branch of the Miami tribe better known today by their
English name, the Wea—to relocate to their former homeland near
Lake Michigan. There, in a region more securely under French control, important trading alliances might be maintained with less effort.
Nevertheless, owing in part to their staunch devotion to the memory
of a late departed friend, Jean-Baptiste Bissot de Vincennes, who died
early in 1719, the Wea remained steadfast in the valley. Accordingly,
the French had no choice but to stay with them, protecting King
Louis's economic and political interests against the rival British. It
was thus more accident than design that established Fort Ouiatenon
as the first European settlement in what is now the state of Indiana.

As time passed, Ouiatenon prospered and became a regular stopping place along the Maumee-Wabash route connecting the two great centers of French colonial power on the continent: New France (Canada) and Louisiane. According to eighteenth-century accounts, the post was but three days' journey from a nine-mile portage (at present-day Fort Wayne, Indiana) connecting the Maumee and Wabash rivers. The growing importance of this waterway is signaled by the fact that within a few years of its establishment as a trading center, Ouiatenon was accompanied by posts near either end of the Wabash River. St. Philippe des Miamis (Fort Miami) was established to guard the portage in 1722, and by 1732 the younger sieur de Vincennes, François-Marie Bissot, went south from Ouiatenon to begin building the post that would bear his name.

The commerce at Ouiatenon also drew many native peoples to the Wabash valley, including the Mascouten, the Kickapoo, and the Piankeshaw, among others. The newly arrived Indians settled in several villages about the post and carried on a lucrative trade. Indeed, by midcentury over three thousand souls were said to reside in the region.

The British Period

Events elsewhere, however, were to defeat the French cause at Ouiatenon. With the fall of Quebec bringing an end to the long-fought French and Indian Wars, most of the fortified French holdings west of the Alleghenies and east of the Mississippi River were given up to the British. Thus, late in 1761, Lt. Edward Jenkins lead a garrison of fifteen men from Detroit to take command of Fort Ouiatenon.

Unlike the French, the British did not enjoy particularly good relations with their Indian trading partners. For this reason, the widespread uprisings of 1763, collectively known in popular literature as Pontiac's Rebellion, come as no startling surprise. Ouiatenon and seven other outposts were captured that summer. In fact, among the fortifications west of Fort Niagara only Detroit remained in British hands, withstanding a long and debilitating siege of four months.

It took years before the British regained control of their western interior possessions. Indeed, some forts were never regarrisoned. Having reconsidered their North American colonial policy, the British began a period of retrenchment after hostilities ceased. Accordingly, Ouiatenon and several other remote outposts were abandoned in order to concentrate efforts at more strategic positions, such as Fort Michilimackinac and Detroit.

That episode, however, conferred upon Ouiatenon its only true claim to prominence in a major historical event. Not only was its capture remarkable, since it fell into native hands without bloodshed, but Ouiatenon also played host to negotiations that led to resolution of the conflict. It was here that George Croghan, an influential British agent captured on the Ohio River, met with Pontiac to discuss the terms of the peace.

The Passing of Fort Ouiatenon

Ouiatenon's last few decades passed rather uneventfully. According to Croghan and other observers, such as Thomas Hutchins, slightly more than a dozen French *habitant* families remained in the immediate area despite the shift of hegemony. By the century's third quarter, however, trading activities had diminished markedly. During the American Revolution, minor intrigues were played out as both sides in the struggle vied for native allegiances, but little else happened. The period does, however, contribute history's only substantive description of Fort Ouiatenon. Henry Hamilton, later lieutenant governor of the Indiana Territory, passed through the area in 1778 and recorded his impressions of the post. Hamilton (cited in Krauskopf 1955) described Ouiatenon as a "fort, which is formed of a double range of houses, enclosed with a stockade 10 feet high." He also observed that it was a "miserable stockade surrounding a dozen miserable cabins."

In its final days the decrepit stockade often served as a staging ground for Indian raids on American settlements of the Ohio Country. Indeed, by the late 1780s native unrest had forced most Europeans to forsake the Ouiatenon area for safer locales, such as Vincennes. Accordingly, an expeditionary force was sent on a punitive campaign into the Old Northwest under the command of Gen. Charles Scott. Thus in the year 1791 Fort Ouiatenon, several nearby Indian villages, and even the fields of corn were burned to the ground. To make sure that the native populace would disperse, the soldiers returned a few months later and torched the replanted crops.

Apparently by the time the city of Lafayette, Indiana, was founded in the early 1820s, no visible trace of the old fort survived. By that time periodic flooding of the Wabash had no doubt hidden any surface remains under a blanket of alluvium. Nevertheless, settlers of that era clearly were aware of the early historic occupation of the valley. Indeed, one pioneer, Sandford Cox, boasted of collecting European artifacts as a youth in 1827–28 from his family's farm on the Wea Plain and recalled his younger sister's observation: "Is not this a rich country, when even the grass and weeds bear beads?" (1970:34–35). Some accounts make specific reference to Ouiatenon, but locational information is vague and conflicting. In time, knowledge of Fort Ouiatenon became even more obscure, and only a very few historians maintained an interest in the early French colonial occupation of Indiana.

The Search for Ouiatenon

Around the turn of the century, scholars again began to make directed inquiries into the matter of Fort Ouiatenon (e.g., Craig 1893), and residents of Tippecanoe County, Indiana, began to take stock of their heritage. Owing to the imprecision of eighteenth-century maps and the ambiguity of contemporary accounts, archival researchers found little to guide them in their search for the site. Most sources, however, seemed to point to the Wabash River bottoms opposite the mouth of Wea Creek as Ouiatenon's most likely location. Accordingly, a roadside commemorative marker was erected there by the Daughters of the American Revolution in 1907, and a historical park complete with replica blockhouse was created in the late 1920s. Still, the physical evidence for a large fortification and satellite villages was strangely absent, fostering doubt that this low-lying stretch of floodplain could be the actual site.

As a result, the search continued for any new clue pertaining to the fort. Documents long forgotten in European and North American repositories were brought to light, translated, and published (e.g., Krauskopf 1955), while others combed the fields of Tippecanoe County for artifacts that might indicate the site's location. Records relating to Ouiatenon, however, proved to be woefully sparse. Despite the considerable number of commercial records, relatively few pieces of official correspondence were found, and to this day no map or drawing of the post is known to exist. Further, the hoped-for physical evidence of Fort Ouiatenon remained elusive.

Then, in 1967 local enthusiasts discovered large numbers of what appeared to be eighteenth-century European artifacts on the surface of a plowed field about a mile downriver from the historical park. Interestingly, the cultural materials seemed to be concentrated on a small rise rarely inundated by floodwaters. Subsequent testing of the field in 1968 and 1969, jointly sponsored by Indiana University and the Indiana Historical Society, demonstrated to the satisfaction of all that this was indeed the site of Fort Ouiatenon (Kellar 1970). It then became possible to enter the archaeological site into the National Register of Historic Places in 1970. Moreover, with Fort Ouiatenon's true location at last confirmed, it became possible for research on the early French occupation of this region to enter a new phase.

Archaeology of Fort Ouiatenon

Early Efforts

Directed by James H. Kellar of Indiana University, the initial investigations at Fort Ouiatenon focused upon what appeared to be the very center of the site, which was then still under cultivation. A large block excavation was opened up, revealing numerous cultural features, and a large sample of artifacts was collected. The archaeologists involved in those excavations, however, had only a passing familiarity with eighteenth-century material culture and colonial fortifications. For that matter, little comparative literature was then available to assist the researchers in their endeavor. Accordingly, the artifact inventories compiled at that time are superficial by today's standards, and interpretations were not extended beyond simple identification of the site. Nor was any formal report of the investigations ever written.

If the late 1960s added little to our knowledge of Fort Ouiatenon other than its location, investigations of the early 1970s must be considered even less informative. There were no excavations at all in 1970, but efforts were resumed the next year with local volunteers led by a Purdue University undergraduate, Larry Chowning. Owing to the admitted limitations of their expertise, that crew confined itself to collection of artifacts by sifting the plowzone. A 1972 team lead by Claude White similarly restricted all efforts to the upper layer of disturbed soil. The year 1973 saw the return of Chowning as fieldwork supervisor, and on that occasion he ventured a small-scale excavation below plowzone in the southwestern reaches of the site. There they encountered a set of wall trenches, which were interpreted by the excavators as evidence of the fort's southwest corner.

Although records and collections survive from the early 1970s, no field report was published or filed. Indeed, most of the artifacts were not even washed and catalogued, merely boxed and stored in their field bags. As a result, the data gathered in those years have not yet contributed to our interpretation of the post. Nevertheless, the limited investigations of 1971–73 served the important purpose of keeping local interest in the site of Fort Ouiatenon high despite constrained resources and circumscribed expertise. Indeed, largely because of this public involvement, concerned citizens of the Lafayette community initiated a fund-raising drive that enabled the Tippecanoe County Historical Association to purchase the site in 1972.

Michigan State University Investigations

In 1974 the Tippecanoe County Historical Association approached staff of the Museum at Michigan State University about undertaking a more intensive examination of the archaeological site. Having been involved with the initial investigations at Fort Michilimackinac and other eighteenth-century sites of the upper Great Lakes, museum personnel welcomed the invitation to begin work at Fort Ouiatenon. Accordingly, Curator Charles E. Cleland outlined a three-year program of exploratory research, with Judith Tordoff implementing the plan. Under her direction, student crews assisted by local volunteers excavated several exploratory trenches aligned on the cardinal directions with the intent of delineating the stockade (fig. 5-2). Block excavations were also laid out in areas of particular interest, some of which were designed to make "ground truth" comparisons with soil resistivity and proton magnetometer surveys conducted by students from the geology department at nearby Purdue University. Among the more important features examined under Tordoff's supervision were a forging area, a well, and a semisubterranean trader's storehouse

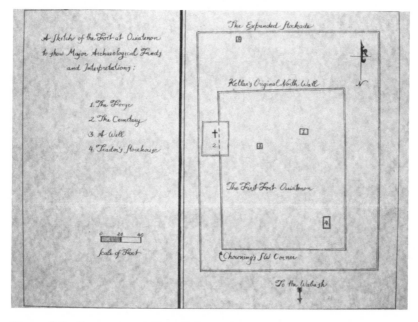

Figure 5-2. Excavation at Fort Ouiatenon

(fig. 5-3). Through those efforts, a basic understanding of the fort's size, structural arrangement, and complexity was achieved (Tordoff 1983).

Owing to the success of the 1974–76 field seasons, the historical association sponsored a second three-year program that would expand upon the first. The task of directing the 1977–79 field crews fell to me, and I began the implementation of a systematic site sampling strategy designed to gather information on the entire range of archaeological deposits present in the northern half of the site. In addition to pinpointing the locations of numerous structures and refuse deposits both in and around the post, it was discovered that an earlier stockade was enclosed within the perimeter defined by Tordoff; a second well was also identified (fig. 5-4). Moreover, the location of Fort Ouiatenon's cemetery was evidenced by several graves exposed in two separate test units, resulting in the recovery of two European burials for subsequent analysis (Noble 1982, 1983).

Analytical Progress and Prospects

Recent Research

The six summers of Michigan State University fieldwork at Fort Ouiatenon produced a tremendous amount of data, which has formed the

Figure 5-3. Remains of the Storehouse at Fort Ouiatenon

Figure 5-4. Reconstructed Plan of Fort Ouiatenon

basis of several doctoral dissertations. Those studies have addressed broad issues in historical archaeology while reporting empirical data on site features and artifacts.

Tordoff's (1983) study, for example, employed Ouiatenon artifact assemblage frequencies in a comparative analysis of eighteenth-century French colonial sites. Her approach entailed the formulation and testing of a hierarchical model describing the dynamics of fur trade redistribution in terms of site functional complexity as reflected by material culture. The model has proved seminal insofar as it has helped organize the research of other students of the fur trade period (compare Martin, chap. 12, and Anderson, chap. 14).

My own research (Noble 1983), on the other hand, assessed the usefulness of certain statistical methods and computer modeling programs in the delineation of activity areas. That intrasite spatial analysis employed artifact frequency distribution data derived from forty-eight excavated sample units. Factor analyses performed with those data first sought to define functionally related artifact sets through the correlation of depositional associations. Critical artifact types were then subjected to trend surface analysis toward the identification of discrete activity areas within the site.

In combination, the Tordoff and Noble dissertations on Ouiatenon present a comprehensive catalogue of the artifacts recovered from the site by Michigan State University field crews between 1974 and 1979, including many types previously unreported in North America. They do not, however, contribute much data useful to the interpretation of specific structures within the fort, because only one such feature, the semisubterranean storehouse described by Tordoff, was excavated in its entirety. Nevertheless, the Fort Ouiatenon collections summarized in those two dissertations should prove valuable to scholars dealing with comparable archaeological sites.

Several specialized studies have also derived from the 1974–79 excavations. Martin (1986), for instance, has contributed a major study of the more than one hundred thousand faunal elements collected at Fort Ouiatenon as his doctoral dissertation. In his analysis of some eleven thousand bone fragments identifiable to the specific level, he addresses the differences that obtain among fur trade sites in terms of the exploitation of wild and domestic species. Further, Martin's examination of the modified animal remains provides insights into European interaction with the local native population.

In the realm of physical anthropology, a recently published study of one human skeleton collected in 1977 from the Fort Ouiatenon graveyard sheds new light on a genuine mystery (Sauer, Dunlap, and Simson 1988). Although the postcranial skeleton was in an excellent state of preservation, the skull had been shattered by a large morning glory root that had grown through it. Subsequent laboratory reconstruction of the skull revealed that this unidentified adult male had suffered several perimortem wounds, likely inflicted with a trade axe. Historiographic sources do not mention any such fatality at the post. It is possible, however, that the unfortunate victim suffered his injuries in a skirmish of the so-called Chickasaw Wars, which extended into this region during the 1730s. Not only did the physical remains give testimony to the probable circumstances surrounding an unrecorded violent death, but the successful application of modern forensic techniques in the examination of a 200-year-old body also provides further support for their utility in current police investigations.

One other major area of research, geophysics, has played an important role in the interpretation of Fort Ouiatenon. The magnetometer survey conducted at the site in 1974 and 1975 was one of the very first such studies performed on an archaeological site of the Historic period. Moreover, it represents one of the few instances in archaeology when a remote sensing technique has been followed with continuing excavations, many designed expressly to investigate apparent magnetic anomalies. Thus the study served to evaluate the use of magnetometry in archaeological research, while it established correlations between distinctive anomaly signatures and certain cultural features. Further, certain data enhancement techniques designed to clarify raw magnetometer readings proved successful, indicating their potential for application at other sites (von Frese 1978, 1984; von Frese and Noble 1984).

Current Research Directions

In recent years a number of other researchers have turned their attention to Fort Ouiatenon and its immediate environs. Neal Trubowitz, formerly of Indiana University-Indianapolis, for one, has initiated a long-term program of archaeological survey and testing in the central Wabash valley (Trubowitz 1987). Already his research teams have located and evaluated numerous historic Indian occupation sites, and there is the promise of much more new information in years to come as data are analyzed and reported. Further, Trubowitz has acquired the pre-1974 artifact collections from Fort Ouiatenon on loan for study. The long overdue description and analysis of this data set will be a valuable addition to the literature and complete the site assemblage inventory to date.

Jack Waddell, an ethnologist at Purdue University, also has embarked on several avenues of research relating to Ouiatenon. A few years ago he began preliminary ethnohistorical research on the Wea and their relationships with the French (Waddell 1985), which he hopes to elaborate in the future. At this writing, he is pursuing the topic of eighteenth-century French popular culture. Indeed, Waddell recently returned from a year's sabbatical in France, where he performed archival research on the subject.

When Dean Anderson's (chap. 14) research on documents relating to fur trade shipments is complete, it will place Fort Ouiatenon in a much broader regional context. Furthermore, his comparative examination of trading inventories from several contemporary sites in the Great Lakes region should help explain the processes of eighteenth-century commerce and commodity flow. Doubtless the study will have significant archaeological implications, as well, particularly with regard to the relative importance of perishable goods in the fur trade economic system.

Finally, many archaeologists working at other sites are now employing Fort Ouiatenon data to illuminate their own research. Indeed, most of the contributors to this book have compared their artifact finds with those reported from Ouiatenon, and Terrance Martin continues to apply his own dissertation data to the interpretation of other faunal assemblages. No doubt as the data from Fort Ouiatenon become more accessible through continued publication, they will gain even wider currency.

Conclusion

Excluding the interim period of volunteer activity at Fort Ouiatenon (1970–73), archaeological excavations carried out at the site from 1968 through 1979 can be characterized in three major phases: identification (1968–69), exploration (1974–76), and evaluation (1977–79). In the first phase, the site of Fort Ouiatenon was located and its identity confirmed. In the second, information on site size and composition was accumulated, while excavators collected a large sample of eighteenth-century artifacts for comparative analysis. With critical site parameters established and a basic grasp of the site's depositional complexity in hand, a third phase of testing could be planned and executed. That most recent phase of excavation produced data on a wide range of cultural features present in the northern half of the site, demarcating areas of interest for future investigation.

It should be clear, in conclusion, that much has been learned at Fort Ouiatenon, but there is much more that can yet be ascertained. With the exception of Fort Michilimackinac, and perhaps the last Fort de Chartres, no other eighteenth-century French colonial site in the Midwest has been subject to as much archaeological investigation as Fort Ouiatenon. Still, less than one-tenth of the site has been excavated and only one structure examined completely. It is hoped, therefore, that excavations will one day be resumed at this important site, filling the gaps in our present knowledge. But even without additional field research, new insights can be gained through additional analyses and comparative studies using the volumes of data already collected. Accordingly, the history of Fort Ouiatenon is far from being a closed book. Indeed, it may be that only the introductory chapter has been written.

Acknowledgments

I would like to acknowledge the Tippecanoe County Historical Association of Lafayette, Indiana, for its generous support of the archaeological research at Fort Ouiatenon. In addition, Charles E. Cleland was a critical influence on the successful realization of all Michigan State University investigations.

F. A. Calabrese, Chief of the National Park Service's Midwest Archeological Center, deserves thanks for providing release time and facilities used in connection with the presentation and production of this chapter. I also thank Carrol Moxham for assisting with the illustrations and commenting on various drafts of the manuscript.

Documents and Archaeology in French Illinois

6

Margaret Kimball-Brown

The French colonial period in Illinois lasted about one hundred years, from the exploration of Jolliet and Marquette in 1673 to the fall of 1765 when Fort de Chartres was handed over to the British. The temporal extent of French influence, of course, was longer, as the Illiniwek already were trading for European goods by the mid-1600s. In addition, the official political action in 1765 did not end the French influence. In fact, French cultural traditions were maintained into the late nineteenth century, both by descendants of the original French settlers and by later immigrants from France.

Despite this long temporal span, there is not the quantity of sites available for study that might be expected, for several reasons. Many of the early sites were in locations that later became population centers and were destroyed by construction. Natural elements have also affected sites; the movement of the Mississippi River has wiped out a number of historic Indian and French settlements. Also, the location of many early settlements is not known, and the few that are recognized have not been extensively excavated. Some Indian villages have been examined, but our archaeological knowledge of the French settlement sites is virtually nil.

Work has been done on fortifications and the development and change in these. Fortifications are a very important part of the picture, but they are only one piece of the total colonial development in the Midwest. There are other pieces. For many of those we have not yet even located sites to be examined. To list a few of the types of sites possible, and not to attempt an exhaustive list, there were for historic Indians: main village settlements, winter camps, hunting camps, and burial areas. For the French there were: trading centers, forts, farmsteads, villages, churches, church cemeteries, and industries. The list of our ignorance is appalling or, to take a more positive approach, challenging.

Documents can play an important part in trying to meet that challenge; they can assist us in finding some of these locations of past cultural activities. Documents also can provide data for producing anthropologically oriented hypotheses concerning cultural behavior and for suggesting areas in which it is suitable to test these hypotheses by archaeology.

Obviously, there are many different sources of documents for research for the French colonial area: governmental records from France, Canada, Spain, and Britain; maps; church and notarial records from many areas; missionaries' and explorers' accounts; and, for the later periods, local, state, and federal government records.

I will discuss mainly one collection, the Kaskaskia Manuscript Collection, and its utility in providing information on the French settlements in southern Illinois in the eighteenth century. The Kaskaskia Manuscript Collection is housed in the archives at Chester, Illinois, and is composed of approximately six thousand documents dating between 1708 and 1812.

The Kaskaskia documents are all that are extant of the notarial records. The notarial records were those created and maintained by the royal notaries, officially throughout the French regime and unofficially on into the British and American periods. There were no lawyers in the Illinois Country and the royal notary took care of many different facets of community life. They drew up marriage contracts, inventories of community property, wills, work contracts of all types, and sales of land and other goods. As the notary was frequently also the clerk for the local judiciary body, records of court cases were included in his office. With the creation of the county government, the records assembled by the notaries were deposited in the county office located first in Kaskaskia and then in Chester.

These records provide a wide and varied database that can be drawn upon. Just briefly, there are data on domestic artifact assemblages, tool assemblages, subsistence activities and sequencing, and diet. Status both within the village and between villages can be studied, as can the relative status of Canadian, French, Indian, and black populations. Slavery, the status of free blacks, and the status of women can be examined, likewise land use patterns and the cultural landscape, and there are data on trades and industries.

One of the most obvious sources for information on domestic artifact assemblages is the household inventory. Inventories were drawn up upon the death of a spouse for the division of community property or sometimes for lease of a property. The inventory listed most items of size or value within the household, the house itself, the land holdings, outbuildings, slaves, animals, and outstanding debts to or against the estate.

Some items were not recorded in the listings, such as personal possessions and ordinary items of daily household use. It should not be assumed that these items were not part of the cultural assemblage just because of their omission from the inventory. This error was made by one writer who claimed that the French women did no sewing because needles, pins, and thimbles were not in the inventory, and that the French were not clean and neat because soap and combs were not listed! Although only a small amount of archaeological work has been carried out in the area, pins, combs, and thimbles have been found, thus supplementing the information from the inventories. But can soap be identified archaeologically? Here is where documentation is of great assistance; for example, in a box that contained the possessions of a deceased voyager, soap and a comb are listed. If the voyager had taken those with him on his last voyage, for the unglamorous activity of paddling up the Mississippi, probably we can be confident that the settlers were not the great unwashed, or at least not more unwashed than the rest of the eighteenth-century population.

Having dispensed with this cautionary statement, what is in the inventories and how can they be used? The inventories list the household furnishings, frequently room by room. This may be only by the main living/cooking area and the bedchamber, or it may include a number of different rooms. Although it is rare that the enumerators explicitly mention going from room to room, the movement can be recognized from the shift in material description, for example, the bed and its furnishing versus a table with folding leaves and armchairs. One inventory does list the main room, another room (which was a bedchamber), a cellar, a kitchen (perhaps a detached or summer kitchen), the granary and a courtyard, all containing items.

Groups of items occurring together suggest usage areas and functional associations. Some obvious ones are kitchen utensils, blacksmithing tools, and farming tools, but there are other more subtle assemblages that can be extracted from the data showing occupation or activities. Perhaps the man who had a dozen uniforms at his house was storing these for the government and acting as a supplier. Several persons who had large supplies of trade beads, trade axes, packets of furs, and such most likely were those who had a prominent role in the tripart economy of the area, that of trade with the Indians, production of foodstuffs, and trade with lower Louisiane for imported goods. But without the documents, we would not be able to interpret trade beads in a house in this fashion. Here is the significance of the documents, for although the presence of trade beads would suggest a trader, the complete list of materials in the inventory allows us to place the person in his role in the complex economic pattern.

No detailed comparison of the content of inventories has been done, yet these are very important for understanding both the archaeological artifact assemblage and the status of individuals. Of course, not all materials in the inventory will turn up archaeologically. Clothing, furniture, bed linens, and the like cannot be expected, although buttons, hooks, and hardware may survive. We are dependent upon the documents for the descriptions of perishable or curated items.

Ceramics, though, are one of the best sources for archaeology, yet unfortunately, the inventories were written by men, who did not, except on rare occasions, give any description of plates, platters, cups, and cutlery. One does say "earthenware plates glazed in white" and they could distinguish between pewter plates and plates (for example, "18 plates, a platter, 16 plates of pewter"), but that is all. Were the plates faience, wood, or coarse earthenware? Archaeology will have to answer this question and supplement the inventory. On the question of whether any of the coarse earthenware could be Spanish, "two Spanish jars" are listed in an inventory.

Do we expect to find archaeologically fragments of some of the more costly items, such as silver goblets, crystal goblets, and mirrors? Silver was most likely reused, but broken fragments of crystal could occur. Without recourse to the inventory, mirror fragments might be expected only from small trade mirrors rather than possibly from "the large mirror with a curved frame."

Inventories have been used successfully in social history to develop quantitative statements about social status and material goods, and the change in these through time. This itself has not been done for the French area, and could be. The inventories between 1720 and 1762 number about 110 and are for most groups of society except for the soldiers in the garrison and slaves (who were not supposed to have material goods, although they did). For comparisons of the relative status of individuals, the inventories can be extremely useful. The crystal and silver goblets mentioned are not items that everyone would have; however, extremes of wealth and poverty do not occur in French colonial Illinois. The lack of a currency or industries to invest in prevented the accumulation of great wealth, and the fact that land was cheap, even free, meant that anyone could own land and provide for himself.

It appears that the higher-status individuals had a larger quantity of certain types of items and larger variety of goods. As a brief example, a voyager/farmer had for some of his personal clothing three coats, a vest, and three pairs of breeches. A more prosperous trader/farmer had three frockcoats, two hooded greatcoats, four vests, and three pairs of breeches listed. Distinctions did exist and a more thorough examination of all inventories would reward the researcher with a greatly needed outline of the statuses in French colonial Illinois. With such status definitions in mind, one then could proceed with archaeological work to see how these are reflected in the disposal patterns at domestic locations.

Another artifact grouping is that of tools, those amorphous decayed "iron objects" that one encounters too frequently in excavations. There were many specialized trades in the French colonial area, and tool designation in the inventory can help in identification of items, as the men were much more conscientious in distinguishing these. We have inventoried such things as a vine dressing pick and a nail maker; what do those look like? Fortunately, Diderot probably made drawings of them.

Indian and native materials occur in the inventories also; buffalo robes, mitasses and moccasins are not uncommon. Also, interestingly enough, a "calumet or pipe of red stone" and a "lump of calumet stone" are enumerated, as are "two pottery jars of the Natchez, full of bear oil."

A little about the individual household and its contents has been considered, but what of the house and its relation to the house lot? The inventories describe the house, its lot, and other buildings: for example, a house twenty-five feet by eighteen feet of post in the ground, shingled, floored above and below, with a double chimney, on a lot thirty by twenty-five *toises*, fenced with pickets on all sides, with a stable, half a well (in other words, shared), and a garden. The property was bounded by Hennet, the street, on the other side by Finet and another street.

This is the basic spatial layout of a French village lot. But archaeologically we have not yet identified a single one. What is the correspondence between these descriptions and the actual lot? Is there a particular consistent relationship between the placement of gardens and house, stable and house, and hopefully, the well and other facilities? Are there other facilities, such as latrines? Or were there just chamberpots and use of night soil on the garden? Obviously, there is a great lack in our knowledge of disposal patterns.

The cultural landscape included these house lots, the roads along which they were situated, the barn lots (often some distance from the houses), levees, bridges, gates, fenced common fields, a church, a cemetery, a calvary, and a fort with governmental buildings.

Details of the construction of the houses, barns, stables, and such are often given, and building contracts exist for these, which can help to interpret the archaeological remains when they are found. Besides the relationship of the elements of the house and home lot, within the village there are many houses and lots in some consistent spatial relationship to each other. What is this relationship? Both maps and documents indicate that the favored village layout was linear, a few lots deep and many long. The land sale records consistently describe the plots of land as square or rectangular. Such rectilinearity is not suited to the natural landscape, which is curved and shaped by the river. Did the French impose rectilinear lots upon the land, or are these measurements ideals, or ideals perceived as reality?

Turning now from artifacts and landscapes to people, let us take a brief example from one of the poorly documented ethnic groups, the blacks. What was life like for the blacks in Illinois, and is there hope of finding some information about them? Although most blacks came as slaves, there were always free blacks in the communities as well. Despite their economic value to their masters, it was possible for slaves to obtain freedom, and in the Kaskaskia manuscripts there remain records of eleven emancipations of fifteen persons.

Free blacks had the right to make contracts, bear arms, and to buy and sell land. For example, a black voyager, Jacques Duverger, purchased a house and lot in Kaskaskia in 1739 for 800 *livres*. Several documents remain concerning Duverger; most of these are contracts that he made with other voyagers. In one contract he hired a Frenchman for the winter hunt and also to go to New Orleans to sell the meat. In other agreements he contracted strictly for the transportation of goods to and from New Orleans. Duverger appears to have also had medical training, for he is referred to as a surgeon in some records and received payment from a Frenchman for medical treatment.

Although there are a few records for free blacks, there is very little for slaves. We do know that slaves often did have personal property and apparently could earn money at trades. The slave cabins are another important missing link in our knowledge of the French colonial period.

Sufficient data exist to study change and development from the primary "pioneered" settlements to the successfully settled third-generation communities. And there was change. Even in the census data of 1726, contrasts can be seen between the older community of Kaskaskia (1703) and the recently settled Fort de Chartres village (1720). For example, the Fort de Chartres village with newer families statistically had less than one child per family, whereas Kaskaskia averaged nearly two per family. The Fort de Chartres village had 89 cattle and 47 horses, whereas Kaskaskians had 273 cattle and 74 horses. By the next census in 1732, however, these distinctions between the communities had become less noticeable.

How are these changes reflected in the archaeological record? Unfortunately, there is no hope of being able to compare archaeologically Kaskaskia and Fort de Chartres because Kaskaskia is gone, wiped out by the river. But with the records and archaeological data from Fort de Chartres, and the changes that occurred there through time, contrasts can be made between the earlier and later establishments, which can be extrapolated to relate to Kaskaskia also.

Only excavation can resolve many of the questions suggested here, but the documents also have much to offer. Rigorous analysis of the documents as anthropological data is needed to produce hypotheses that can be tested by future archaeological work.

The French Colonial Villages of Cahokia and Prairie du Pont, Illinois

7

Bonnie L. Gums, William R. Iseminger,
Molly E. McKenzie, and Dennis D. Nichols

Research and fieldwork conducted in 1938–40 by the Works Progress Administration (WPA) included documentation of historic buildings in Cahokia and archaeological investigations and restoration of the Cahokia Courthouse, originally built in ca. 1740. In 1949 the major project coinciding with the 250th year anniversary of the founding of Cahokia involved the restoration of the vertical log Church of the Holy Family, which dates to ca. 1799. Recent archaeological investigations at the Cahokia Wedge site uncovered the remains of a French colonial domestic structure. Nine miles to the north, at the Cahokia Mounds State Historic Site, are several historical and archaeological sites relating to French Cahokia, including the archaeological remains of a French colonial chapel and a Cahokia Illini cemetery dating from ca. 1735 to 1752. Located one mile south of Cahokia is the village of Prairie du Pont, which was initially settled as a dependency of Cahokia in the second half of the eighteenth century. Only a few historical and archaeological sites remain in Prairie du Pont, including the Pierre Martin/Nicholas Boismenue House constructed in ca. 1790. Several other French colonial-style houses in Prairie du Pont were recorded by WPA researchers in the late 1930s; however, these have since been demolished.

Historical Background

In 1699 missionaries from the Seminary of Foreign Missions in Quebec settled among a village of nearly ninety cabins of the Tamaroa and Cahokia Illini Indians (Fortier 1909:236–37). A chapel was built and the raising of the cross was celebrated during the third week of May (Fortier 1909:233). An estimated two thousand Indians attended the ceremony, including Cahokia, Tamaroa, Michigamea, and Peoria (McDermott 1949:9).

This settlement, which became known as Cahokia, was the first of several French forts and villages in the American Bottom region of the Illinois Country (fig. 7-1). The other French settlements located on the eastern side of the Mississippi River included Kaskaskia (1703), Fort de Chartres (ca. 1719), Prairie du Rocher (ca. 1721), and St. Philippe (ca. 1723). Across the Mississippi River in Missouri were the historic French settlements of Ste. Genevieve (ca. 1750) and St. Louis (1764).

A 1723 census of Cahokia, although incomplete, recorded seven *habitants,* one white laborer, one married woman, and three children living at the settlement (Belting 1948:13). The newly erected fort was described as a "wretched fort of piles" with a garrison of six soldiers (McDermott 1949:13). In 1732 the population of Cahokia and Peoria Illini at the Indian village near French Cahokia numbered between 300 and 400 (Palm 1931:72). By 1735 the increasing French population and the need for agricultural land led to the relocation of more than half of the Cahokia Illini to the Monks Mound area, nine miles to the north (Palm 1931:70–71; Walthall and Benchley 1987:90).

The first detailed description and map of the village at Cahokia were produced in 1735 by missionaries Mercier and Courier (Tucker 1942: pl. 23). The map identifies fifteen dwellings, including the houses of two Negro families and one Indian family who served at the mission, the fort built in the previous year, the mill at St. Michael's Bluff (Falling Springs), the common fields to the east of the village, the road leading to Fort de Chartres, and the Illini village. In a letter accompanying this map, Father Mercier described the setting:

> The island of the Holy Family, which conceals the view of the Mississippi from the French settlement as well as from the Indian village of the Kaokia [*sic*], measures one league or more in length by nearly one half of a league in width [and] is completely covered with a forest of full grown trees good for building purposes or for fuel, especially quantities of cottonwoods but very few walnuts and mulberry trees. It is almost everywhere covered with rushes, which our horses seek greedily. When the waters of the Missouri and the Mississippi rise very high, the greater part of the island is flooded (Donnelly 1949b:75).

The 1735 map also illustrates a bridge over Riviere du Pont connecting with the road to Falling Springs, where the missionaries had built a water mill. The vast prairie south of this bridge had been known as Prairie du Pont several decades before the establishment of the French village of the same name.

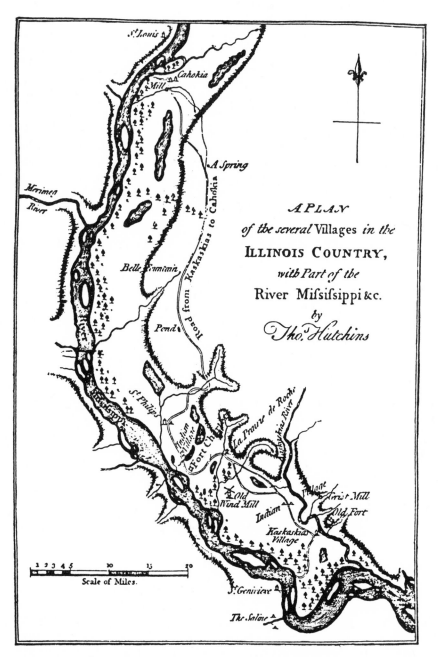

Figure 7-1. Map of the Illinois Country by Thomas Hutchins in ca. 1766.
Source: Tucker 1942: pl. 27. Reprinted with the permission of the Illinois
State Museum.

The 1752 population at Cahokia consisted of the mission priest, thirteen married couples with forty-two children, four unmarried men, one widow, and fifteen *volontaires* or landless inhabitants (Peterson 1949b:22). This population was broken down racially as eighty-nine whites, twenty-four Negroes, and four Indians. Other resources of the village comprised thirty-three arpents of land, 224 head of cattle, eighty-three horses and mules, and 100 hogs.

In 1763 with the defeat of the French by the British in the Seven Years' War, many of the Illinois French fled across the Mississippi River to Spanish-controlled territory, settling in Ste. Genevieve and the newly founded settlement of St. Louis. In October 1765 British troops arrived in the Illinois Country and peacefully occupied Fort de Chartres and Cahokia. During this occupation, the British recorded populations, wrote descriptions, and produced maps of the French villages and forts.

A map of the village at Cahokia (fig. 7-2) drawn in ca. 1766 by British army cartographer Thomas Hutchins illustrates village lots

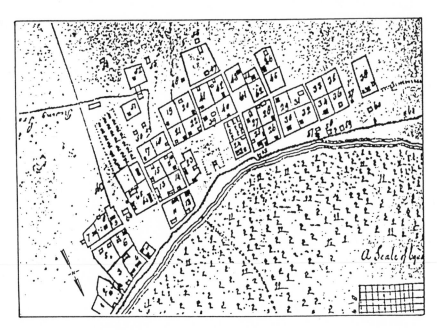

Figure 7-2. Map of Cahokia by Thomas Hutchins in ca. 1766. Source: Peterson 1949b:200-201. Reprinted with the permission of the Illinois State Historical Library.

with houses and barns and much of the street system present in the village today (Peterson 1949b:200–201). Cahokia was described as

> long and straggling, being three quarters of a mile from one end to the other; it contains forty-five dwelling-houses, and a church near its center. The situation is not well chosen, as in the floods it is generally overflowed by two or three feet. . . . What is called the fort is a small house standing in the center of the village; it differs in nothing from the other houses except in being one of the poorest; it was formerly enclosed with high palisades, but these were torn down and burnt. Indeed a fort at this place could be of little use (Pittman 1770:48).

In the same year, there were sixty-five families remaining at Kaskaskia, twelve families at Prairie du Rocher, three to four families at Fort de Chartres, and only one inhabitant at St. Philippe, although sixteen houses were still standing (Pittman 1770:43–47).

In July of 1778 George Rogers Clark and his American troops occupied Kaskaskia and Cahokia, and the Illinois French were drawn into the American Revolution. Local government was set up in Cahokia under the command of Capt. Joseph Bowman, who had occupied a stone building on the mission property that was to become known as Fort Bowman (Peterson 1949b:196). With the end of the American Revolution in 1783 and the Americanization of the region, the period of French domination was over. The remaining villages of Cahokia, Kaskaskia, and Prairie du Rocher, having survived both the British and American invasions, settled into a relatively peaceful way of life.

With the Ordinance of 1787 the Illinois Country became part of the Northwest Territory under the United States government. In 1795 Cahokia became the county seat of St. Clair County, when Kaskaskia was made the county seat for the newly formed Randolph County. In 1812 the boundaries of St. Clair County were again divided, this time to its present borders, and the county seat was officially transferred from Cahokia to Belleville. With this administrative move, Cahokia lost its prominence in the political matters of the county. Further contributing to the stagnation of the village at Cahokia was the increasing importance of St. Louis as a commercial center and the development of the town of East St. Louis, originally founded as Illinoistown in 1817. Throughout the nineteenth century, Cahokia remained a small, rural community with a mixture of French and European descendants. In 1841 the village had "a convent, courthouse, post office, catholic church, three taverns, five or six groceries, one general store, and between sixty and seventy houses" (Wild and Thomas 1841:106). One observer wrote, "the lapse of nearly two centuries has not entirely destroyed the original impress upon this people of the manners, customs and the language of Old France" (Wild and Thomas 1841:103).

The date of the first settlement of the village of Prairie du Pont is unknown. However, its location on the edge of Prairie du Pont Creek between Cahokia and Falling Springs appears to have been an excellent choice for settlement. By 1754 the Mission of St. Sulpice of Cahokia owned property along the creek and had built a water mill (Brink, McDonough, and Co. 1881:47). In 1764 Antoine Girardin of Cahokia purchased the mission property and farmed the land (McDermott 1949:49). Sixteen years later, in 1780, a petition was filed in the Cahokia court claiming that Girardin had "no right to form a village and to concede lands" that had been reserved for Cahokia inhabitants (Alvord 1907:88–89). Cahokians lost this claim and in 1783 an ordinance was issued describing the limits of Prairie du Pont and the allotment of common fields (Alvord 1907:153, 564–67). Apparently the first census of the village of Prairie du Pont was in 1791 and recorded twenty-seven heads of families, six widows, and seventeen unmarried men (Carter 1934, 2:260–61). Most of the names in this census were of French families from Cahokia.

Presently these two historic villages lie within the urban spread of the Metro East area. To the north of Cahokia is the heavily industrialized town of Sauget and the city of East St. Louis. Many of the lakes and sloughs created by the Mississippi River have been drained for agricultural use and the prairies and forests have given way to farms and urban/industrial centers.

The Village of Cahokia

The site of colonial Cahokia has not been spared from damage and destruction due to commercial and industrial development of the area. Furthermore, the lateral movement of the Mississippi River in the 1860s resulted in the destruction of the westernmost portion of the French colonial village and the remains of the "Indian Village and burying ground" as identified on the 1766 map (Norris 1984:8–9).

An assessment of the archaeological remains of the historic French village was conducted by F. Terry Norris (1984). Using common reference points, Norris was able to superimpose the 1766 map of Cahokia on a USGS map and speculate on the condition of the archaeological remains of the 1766 structures. In summarizing this research, Norris (1984:15) concludes that the archaeological remains of twenty-one structures, or twenty percent of the structures on the

1766 map, appear to have survived major alterations. Most of these potential archaeological remains lie within residential or commercial properties and the feasibility of examining these portions of the historic village for archaeological remains is limited. However, two eighteenth-century house sites have been identified as surface scatters in a plowed field adjacent to the Cahokia Courthouse State Historic Site. These house sites are identified on the 1766 map as the Boudriau Gammon residence and the Jacquet/Germain residence and represent the westernmost portion of the eighteenth-century village that survived the 1860s migration of the Mississippi River (Norris 1984:4, 16).

French Colonial Architecture in the Illinois Country

French colonial houses were typically made of handhewn logs of locally available wood such as mulberry, cedar, walnut, and oak. Buildings were vertical log structures predominantly of *poteaux en terre* (posts in the earth) or *poteaux sur sole* (posts on sill) styles. Usually the structures had whitewashed exteriors and galleries on all four sides. Several colonial-style structures are still standing in the Historic District of Ste. Genevieve, Missouri. Archaeological investigations at the Cahokia Wedge site in Cahokia (Gums 1988), at the original village site of Prairie du Rocher (Safiran 1988), and at the Kreilich site near Saline Springs south of Ste. Genevieve (Trimble et al., chap. 11) have uncovered the archaeological remains of domestic dwellings of the French colonial period.

John Reynolds, who lived at Cahokia in the 1780s, described French houses as

> generally one story high, and made of wood. . . . These house were formed of large posts or timbers; the posts being three or four feet apart in many of them. In others the posts were closer together, and the intervals filled up with mortar, made of common clay and cut straw. . . . Over the whole wall, outside and inside it was generally whitewashed with fine white lime, so that these houses presented a clean, neat appearance. . . . Some dwelling houses and the stables and barns were made of longer posts set in the ground, instead of a sill as used in other houses. These posts were of cedar or other durable wood. The small houses attached to the residences were generally set with posts in the ground. The covering of the houses, stables, &c., was generally of straw or long grass cut in the prairie. These thatched roofs looked well, and lasted longer than shingles. They were made steep and neat. All the houses, almost, had galleries all around them. The posts of the gallery were generally of cedar or mulberry. The floors of the galleries,

as well as the floors of the houses, were made of puncheons, as sawed boards were scarce (1852:50–51).

Presently, on the Illinois side of the Mississippi River, few French colonial structures remain. In 1938–39 WPA researchers recorded at least eight French colonial-style homes standing in the villages of Cahokia and Prairie du Pont; however, most of these structures have since disappeared.

Cahokia Courthouse State Historic Site

One familiar landmark in Cahokia is the "Old Courthouse." The building served as St. Clair County's first courthouse, the seat of the territorial government in the Old Northwest from 1793 to 1814. It is presently administered by the Illinois Historic Preservation Agency and is a recognized National Historic Landmark. The courthouse's remarkable history is evidence of a deep historical interest and a certain sentimentality for the structure. Always viewed as a curious specimen of early French architecture, it is considered by many to be the "granddaddy" of restored French colonial *poteaux sur sole* buildings. Today, the courthouse stands as it was restored and dedicated in 1940. The restoration of the Cahokia Courthouse helped to fuel a period of significant activity in the research and documentation of the material culture of French colonial Illinois.

The original construction date of the building remains unknown and can only be narrowed to within three decades, although it is generally considered to date to ca. 1740. The structure is probably not on the 1735 map of Cahokia, although this map is somewhat of a sketch. However, it does appear on the 1766 map by Thomas Hutchins. The earliest reference to occupancy, and probably ownership, is on the 1766 map, which lists the structure as the home of Jean La Poincet (Lapensee) (Peterson 1949b:326–27). In 1780 Angelique Lapensee became the second wife of François Saucier, son of the engineer of the stone fort of Fort de Chartres. Through some means (dowry?) Saucier assumed ownership of the commodious posts-on-sill home. Angelique died in childbirth in 1787 at age twenty-five and was buried at Holy Family Parish cemetery (Cahokia Courthouse Archives). Her daughter was interred three months later (Donnelly 1949a:259–60). Saucier's third marriage, in 1793, was to Françoise Nicolle, a widow from St. Louis with eight children. At this time, Saucier left Cahokia with his three children, adopted Françoise's eight, and later added eight more, rounding out the family at nineteen children. It was Saucier who sold the residence to the judges of the common plea court of St. Clair County in 1793 (Peterson 1949b:328).

The Northwest Ordinance of 1787 directed that a "courthouse, county jail, pillory, whipping posts and stocks" be erected in every county (Peterson 1949b:328). With Governor St. Clair's 1790 proclamation, the jurisdictional boundaries were designated and these embraced one-third of present-day Illinois (Pease 1925:521–28). Instead of erecting a new building, the county judges purchased the structure that had served as the Saucier home. Court records indicate use of the building as early as 1790, although the transfer of ownership was not legally recorded until 1793 (Peterson 1949b:328).

For twenty-four years the Cahokia Courthouse served as the administrative, judicial, and political center of the Old Northwest. The St. Clair County boundaries changed on a number of occasions as the territory moved through two reorganizations: the Indiana Territory (1800) and the Illinois Territory (1809). The county reached its most extensive size in 1801 when the court at Cahokia held jurisdiction as far as the Canadian border.

By 1814, however, the county was reduced to approximately its present size, and the newer arrivals were settling around Belleville. These newcomers were predominantly Americans who began pressuring to move the county seat to a more central location. Belleville was the geographic center of the population in 1814, it was English-speaking, and it was safe from the frequent and often devastating floods that inundated the village and courthouse at Cahokia. Primarily because of the constant threat of floods at Cahokia, the county seat was finally moved to Belleville in 1814 (Brink, McDonough, and Co. 1881:81).

The old courthouse was ordered sold and the public furniture was hauled away to the new courthouse (Brink, McDonough, and Co. 1881:186). Purchased by François Vaudry for $225 in 1816, it is believed to have become a residence once again. The Vaudry heirs passed it on to Joseph Robidoux of St. Louis in 1831 (Peterson 1949b:329–30). The building's use during the remainder of the nineteenth century is obscure, but it did function as a town hall, a warehouse, and even as a saloon (Peterson 1949b:330). The saloon was the building's most notable "adaptive use." A German family, the Lobenhofers, acquired the courthouse in 1857. They resided in several rooms and in the remaining rooms operated the "Old Court House Saloon." Local legends relate the antics of patrons questioning each other as witnesses during mock-trials in a "refurbished" courtroom. As they said, "Laughter and rowdiness replace law and order"

(Brink, McDonough, and Co. 1881:186). During their occupancy, the Lobenhofers dug a cold cellar pit under the building (Cahokia Courthouse Archives).

Photographs and sketches of the building date mainly from the late 1880s through 1900 (fig. 7-3). Clapboard siding was added to the north and west facades, apparently to contain the visibly deteriorating *pierrotage* chinking. A stone chimney was removed by the time of these photographs to accommodate a room addition made from an enclosed gallery. The added room may have been in use as a kitchen or sleeping area. A much smaller brick chimney is seen to extend just above the enclosed gallery. Exactly when these alternations were made or whose occupancy necessitated them is unknown. Judging from the wear and deterioration of the improvements themselves by the late 1890s, the siding and enclosure with the chimney were installed at a much earlier date, perhaps as early as the Lobenhofer saloon period of the 1860s.

In 1898 the old building appeared vacant, overgrown with saplings rooted in foundation cracks, and generally in a dilapidated condition. It is believed to have been used for farm storage through the 1890s, and these photographs suggest abandonment and imminent collapse. It is certain that the flooding Mississippi River reached the building many times.

Figure 7-3. 1898 Photograph of the Cahokia Courthouse. Courtesy of the Illinois Historic Preservation Agency and Illinois State Historical Library.

The old courthouse was again on the auction block in 1901. The new owner, Alexander Cella, an East St. Louis businessman, dismantled the log structure and stored the walnut timbers in his backyard. He applied for a concessionaire license at the 1904 St. Louis World's Fair (Louisiana Purchase Exposition). License granted, Cella reconstructed the building on the fairgrounds using only the timbers, placing them close together to eliminate gaps where the *pierrotage* chinking had been inserted. This had the effect of reducing the building's size to about one-third of its original dimensions. The roofline was also altered, appearing without the graceful slope and without a break for the peak over the interior trusswork. Any timbers left over after Cella's dismantling and reassembly at the fair were reportedly made into souvenir wooden cigars. Possibly to enhance the authenticity of his attraction at the fair, Cella claimed that he had "the documents from the first case that was held in the courthouse, benches, table, and the old gavel that was used at the time" (Peterson 1949b:330).

When the fair ended nearly a year later, the building was again auctioned. It was purchased on behalf of the Chicago Historical Society and the Chicago Centennial Commission, who wished "to preserve it in honor of the patriots who used it" (Peterson 1949b:330). The timbers were shipped to Chicago's Jackson Park in 1906 for reconstruction on Wooded Island. Smaller yet, it again bore no resemblance to the original building. Today, older persons still recollect its use during the 1920s as a "Japanese Tea Room."

Planning in Cahokia for the 150-year commemoration of George Rogers Clark's legendary march through southern Illinois brought public awareness of the error in allowing the historic courthouse to be taken away. Cahokians demanded the return of the former courthouse and, with much persistence, by 1927 the Chicago Park Board was persuaded to return the structure. Encouraged by this development, the diligent efforts of the community focused on enlisting the aid of the state to acquire the structure. The building was not deeded, however, until 1936, and the courthouse was not acquired until 1938.

Townspeople of Cahokia had long felt a fond sentimentality for their unique French structures and for Cahokia's prominent eighteenth-century history. Romanticized historical interest grew into a sophisticated Illinois Museum Extension Project—the Cahokia Memorial Survey. Employing as many as eighty WPA-funded workers, the Memorial Survey attempted to protect Cahokia's prominent structures and document the remainder of the eighteenth-century village. They worked with great urgency, as more of the eighteenth-century structures were doomed by lingering economic depression and rapidly encroaching industrialism.

The Cahokia Memorial Survey was enlisted to prepare for the return of the old courthouse to Cahokia. They conducted archaeological investigations, relocated historic photographs, and researched the massive collection of French documents stored in the St. Clair and Randolph county courthouses for pertinent information for the reconstruction. Not only interested in the architectural references, the Memorial Survey provided documentation on numerous aspects of the social and economic life of the eighteenth-century French.

The actual return of Cahokia's courthouse was the responsibility of the Illinois Department of Public Works and Buildings. Joseph Booton, chief of design for the Division of Architecture and Engineering, was placed in charge of the restoration. The building in Chicago was a "mere shell," leaving Booton to rely only on the archaeological evidence and a knowledge of French colonial construction methods for the reconstruction.

Archaeological work began in April of 1938 with Paul Maynard paid by the Memorial Survey to supervise the WPA workers. A brief summary and blueprint maps of these excavations were included in the Report of the Cahokia Memorial Survey from February 1, 1939 to July 31, 1939 (Maynard 1939). Features that provided crucial evidence necessary for the reconstruction of the building included the original foundations, fireplace footings, and fragments of the cedar porch columns. The Cahokia Courthouse structure was built of a combination of *poteaux sur sole* and *poteaux en terre* construction (fig. 7-4). The main structure consisted of a limestone foundation on which upright posts were set on a sill. On the eastern edge of this foundation was a smaller, rectangular structural feature consisting of wall trenches, which appeared to have been an enclosed lean-to added to the main structure. This addition measured 4.9 meters (16 feet) in width and although the exact length was not determined, it was at least 7.6 meters (25 feet long). Limited excavations on the opposite side of the structure revealed a portion of another wall-trench feature, indicating that a similar addition was present on this side of the building.

Along the eastern portion of this structural addition two pit features were also excavated. Both were superimposed upon the wall-trench feature, indicating that the addition had been dismantled before these two pits were dug. One pit feature was filled with limestone mortar and sand zones and contained very few artifacts. The fill zones provided evidence that the pit was used as a source area for sand as well as a work area for the preparation and mixing of limestone plaster

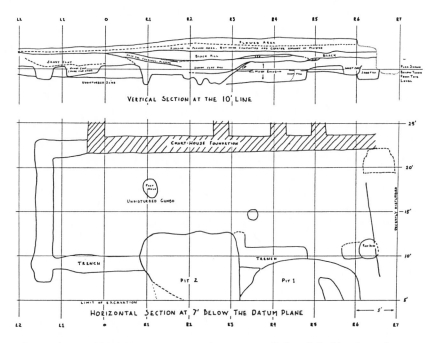

Figure 7-4. 1938-39 WPA Excavation Map of the Cahokia Courthouse. Source: Maynard 1939

or mortar. The bottom of this pit was 2.7 meters below the ground surface. It is possible that this mortar preparation pit was used immediately after the dismantling of the wall-trench addition, perhaps to repair any damage that may have occurred as a result of the disengaging of the addition walls from the main structure. While the main courthouse structure made of posts on sill construction survived for nearly 160 years prior to being dismantled for the St. Louis World's Fair, this wall-trench addition probably was only preserved for several decades: the dampness of the ground would have hastened the rotting of the logs (Peterson 1965:35). The other pit feature was superimposed upon the first pit feature as well as on the wall trench. This pit contained several ash and charcoal lenses indicating it was probably last used for refuse disposal. Artifacts recovered from this pit were reported to postdate 1850. This date was supported by an informant, "Cap" Lobenhofer, who told WPA researchers that a storage pit was located in this area during the thirty-year period in which he lived in the house in the second half of the nineteenth century (Boylan 1939:90).

With the archaeological evidence, reconstruction plans continued. Booton's assistant, Jerome Ray, was engaged in the interpretation of the documentary evidence and photographs. In addition, he interviewed early Cahokia residents, particularly "Cap" Lobenhofer. Although the archaeological and historical evidence provided important information for the reconstruction, draftsmen could not produce elevation drawings without the knowledge of the building's perspective. The Chicago logs were significantly shorter than they were originally, although how much shorter was unknown. The pitch of the roof and the height of the chimneys all required a perspective to establish the scale in order to proceed with the reconstruction drawings.

This dilemma was resolved when an 1899 photograph surfaced and Booton realized he could approximate the original dimensions of the building. In this photo, a man is standing on the courthouse porch and assuming the man's height to be approximately 5 feet 10 inches, Booton worked by means of this perspective: "Usually the perspective is made from plans and elevations but in this case we worked it backwards. That is we determined the plan and direct elevation by means of analyzing the photograph in terms of perspective" (Cahokia Courthouse Archives).

In June of 1938 Booton collaborated with National Park Service landscape architect Charles E. Peterson, an authority on French colonial construction methods. A preliminary report on the restoration project was compiled, which included an analysis of all available source material. Booton's diligence to obtain as accurate reconstruction is evident in this description: "The final restoration will no doubt shock the general public because of its excellence. The more I learn about the early French methods and the buildings erected during that period, the more it astounds me, because I cannot conceive that such fine buildings could have been constructed under the prevailing circumstances" (Cahokia Courthouse Archives).

However, the reconstruction plans, which were approximately forty-five percent complete, were temporally halted. A $25,000 Public Works Administration (PWA) grant had not been approved pending evidence that supported Booton's reconstruction. Paul Angle of the Illinois State Historical Library reviewed the evidence from the photographs and notarized statements of the former occupants. However, there was also concern about funding because the depression-era, government-funded projects were winding down. Concessions were made to cut costs, including a reduction of the archaeological investigations in other areas of the courthouse lot. However, in January of 1939, $22,000 was allotted by the state for the courthouse reconstruction.

After funding problems had been resolved, the Cahokia Courthouse was at last dismantled and shipped from Chicago. The remaining original timbers were to be incorporated into the reconstruction. As a result of the two previous reconstructions, the building required many new logs and the existing logs had to be spliced to lengthen them from eight feet to twelve feet. New walnut and oak logs were acquired from two "backwoodsmen" from southern Missouri. These new timbers were given a rough adzed finish and were seasoned for eight weeks. All the timbers, both the original and the new, were pressure-treated with zinc chloride.

Repairs to the building's original limestone foundation were completed in September of 1939 and shortly thereafter the reconstruction was begun. Through the summer and fall of 1939, Booton and Ray had consulted with Peterson on the hardware and interior finishing details. Comparing photographs of Louisiana hardware and the iron fragments of hardware recovered from the courthouse excavations, replicas of hinges, locks, and shutter parts were produced by a Springfield hardware company. The interior walls were whitewashed and the trim was given a light coat of water stain. By the spring of the following year, the reconstruction was complete. The restored courthouse (fig. 7-5), a reminder of the French heritage of Illinois, was dedicated on 30 May 1940. Nearly forty years had passed since the old courthouse was first dismantled, and its reconstruction on the original location was in good measure due to a resilient and talented community-based organization.

The Church of the Holy Family

An equally famous landmark in Cahokia is the vertical log Church of the Holy Family (fig. 7-6). The 1799 church has designation as a National Historic Landmark and is unique by nature of its continued use as a functioning Catholic church. This church can only seat a fraction of the parish's current congregation, who pray next door in a modern brick church. Use of the historic log church is restricted to holiday occasions and special events.

A similar sentimental concern prevails toward the old church building as it does regarding Cahokia's old courthouse. The parish members have great affection for this structure, which has been restored twice in this century. Behind the church in an open grassy area is the earliest

Figure 7-5. The Cahokia Courthouse State Historic Site as Reconstructed and Dedicated in 1940

of the Holy Family cemeteries, in use from the early period of Cahokia until 1820. A common cross now marks the many graves.

Little is known about civil matters in Cahokia during the 1790s, but the activities of the parish are even less familiar. Records show the names of the successive pastors and mention some of their work. For the most part, the chief concern of the parish in the 1790s was the construction of a new church. The parish had been without a suitable church since fire destroyed the previous log church in 1783. The rectory was in deplorable condition as well, after use as a barracks by British and American troops who had "defaced the walls and ruined the interior" (Donnelly 1949c:33).

Construction of the new church apparently began in 1787 or soon after a letter of intent reached the Seminary of Quebec. After describing the dilapidated condition of the existing property, the church-wardens declared: "We have decided to build a new church of the ruins of this house [the rectory] for our former wooden church had fallen and we are obliged to say Mass in a rented house. We have commenced to work on our projected church which will cost us more than fifteen or sixteen thousand livres" (Donnelly 1949b:85).

Some revenue for the new church was raised by means of fines imposed for inappropriate behavior and dedicating masses for the

Figure 7-6. Church of the Holy Family, Completed in 1799 and Restored in 1949

dead (Alvord 1907:84, 399, 449). In all likelihood, the carpentry was bid and skilled labor was probably contributed by the artisans of the village. Tradition has it that the walnut timbers were harvested from Cahokia's commons. The brothers Voudrie directed the construction project and received payment "partly in money and partly in peltries and wheat" (Donnelly 1949c:38). By the close of the parish's first century, a new church was finally completed at Holy Family.

An elaborate system of regulations was adopted to ensure the proper care of the church. Numerous policies were written pertaining to the rental of pews, maintenance of the cemetery, and the handling of secular activities at the church (Donnelly 1949c:37). However, apparently not enforced as intended, after ten years the new church had fallen into disrepair. Its condition was so poor that the Trappist Guillet refused to say mass in the church until the roof and windows were repaired (Peterson 1949b:334).

Repairs to the building prior to 1833 are not recorded. In that year, two small wings were added and, with the appointment of Pastor Loisel shortly after, money seems to have been made available for the maintenance of the church. By 1840 a wide lean-to was added to the rear, and in 1857 the building was fully repaired and freshly painted (Peterson 1949b:334–35).

After the dedication of the parish's new stone, Gothic-style church in 1891, the old log church was used as a school and parish hall. It again fell into disrepair, which prompted the congregation to agitate for the preservation of the old structure (Peterson 1949b:335). No action was taken until 1912 with the arrival of Father Hynes. He recognized his charge as a living parish and a national monument. Hynes launched a nationwide campaign to finance at least essential repairs to the century-old church building. With the collected funds Father Hynes was able to save the log church, but unable to restore the building fully. The campaign did bring to the attention of the parish the historic significance of the log structure (Donnelly 1949c:60). The 1913 "restoration" included the installation of clapboard siding to retain the *pierrotage* chinking of the *poteaux sur sole* building. Electricity was installed bringing "the interesting relic of the eighteenth century . . . into remarkable touch with the achievements of the twentieth century" (Peterson 1949b:335).

Drawings from the 1934 Historic American Buildings Survey (HABS) suggest that the church was in use as a parish hall and had been remodeled to accommodate school activities. The altar area is indicated as a stage surrounded by stage lights, and the floors were altered to include several elevations, indicating its use as an auditorium.

Elements of the Cahokia Memorial Survey were reorganized into the Cahokia Historical Society after WPA funding had been discontinued. A committee expressed concern to Bishop Althoff for the preservation of the log church and the old parish house. To their dismay the parish house was razed for safety reasons in late 1947 and the venerated old church was certain to share the same fate. From this beginning grew the Cahokia 250th Anniversary Celebration Association, which aimed to restore the old church properly and to promote Cahokia as a national shrine.

By 1948 the old church was again in ruinous condition. The 1948 restoration involved the removal of the work of the two previous restorations. The walnut logs remained in place perpendicular to the sills, but the *pierrotage* chinking was barely contained by the logs. It was clear to Charles Peterson, who served as the consulting architect, that the stonework had to be redone. The original logs remained in place except in a small area where termites had made the timbers unstable. A round-headed door that graced the main entry of the church was found buried under layers of later woodwork. The oeil-de-boeuf (bull's eye) window with frame and hinges intact was found under the modern siding. Original floor boards remained as subfloors and the removal of the metal roof revealed some hand-smoothed, nailed oak shingles still in place (Peterson 1949b:337–38).

The 1913 "restoration" of the Church of the Holy Family had the effect of sealing and preserving the original structure. With the removal of the clapboard and tin roof many of the original elements were still intact. The interior of the log church had been altered on several occasions for its various uses. It is the historic outer shell, exhibiting the original eighteenth-century materials and construction techniques, which is recognized as uniquely significant.

The Nicholas Jarrot Mansion

Another historic structure remaining in Cahokia is the Nicholas Jarrot Mansion State Historic Site (fig. 7-7) located a short distance east of the historic log Church of the Holy Family. Although not a remnant of the French colonial period, completion of the Jarrot Mansion in ca. 1810 qualifies the structure as one of the oldest masonry buildings standing in Illinois. Nicholas Jarrot arrived in Cahokia from France

Figure 7-7. Nicholas Jarrot Mansion in ca. 1894. Victorian-era porch added in the 1880s. Courtesy of the Swekosky Collection, School Sisters of Notre Dame, St. Louis.

in 1794. He occupied a log structure, probably of *poteaux sur sole* construction, to the east of the mansion site during its construction. Construction began in 1807 and Jarrot lived in the house until his death in 1820. The Jarrot Mansion served as the center of entertainment in the community until the family relocated to St. Louis in 1851. Later used as a summer retreat, a parochial school, and a convent (for the Holy Family Parish?), the Jarrot Mansion remains relatively intact. Little alteration has occurred to the mansion's interior and the exterior has only been superficially changed. Presently, the Jarrot Mansion is carefully preserved by the state under the jurisdiction of the Illinois Historic Preservation Agency.

The Monks Mound Area

Approximately nine miles to the north of French Cahokia lies the Cahokia Mounds State Historic Site. This large Mississippian mound complex originally contained over one hundred mounds, including Monks Mound, the largest prehistoric earthenwork in North America. Archaeological investigations focusing on the prehistoric occupation at the Cahokia site have been ongoing for many decades. Between 1969 and 1972 investigations were conducted on the First Terrace of Monks Mound by the University of Wisconsin-Milwaukee (Benchley 1974) and the University of Illinois at Urbana-Champaign (Bareis 1975a, 1975b). Several historic Indian burials and two historic structures were encountered during these investigations. It is only recently that the nature of this aboriginal occupation and its historic connection to the village of Cahokia has been published in detail (Walthall and Benchley 1987).

Several village sites of the Kaskaskia and Michigamea Illini Indians have been preserved and/or investigated (Good 1972; Orser 1975; Perino 1967). There is, however, limited archaeological data pertaining to the Tamaroa and Cahokia Illini villages in the vicinity of French Cahokia. Maps of the late 1600s, often merely sketches, give the relative location of the Tamaroa and Cahokia Indian villages in the present boundaries of the village of Cahokia. Although historic Indian artifacts and trade goods have been recovered in Cahokia at the Cahokia Wedge site (Gums 1988), the context of these materials (i.e., surface collection) is problematical and they cannot be clearly associated with the original Tamaroa and Cahokia Illini village. Based on a 1734 Broutin map and a 1735 map by the Cahokia missionaries, the Cahokia Illini village was located a short distance north of French Cahokia along the Rigolet in an area that now contains the heavily industrialized town of Sauget. Another Illini village and cemetery, probably of the Tamaroa, was illustrated on the 1766 map as south of French Cahokia. This Indian village site was destroyed by the meandering of the Mississippi River in the 1860s (Norris 1984:9). Therefore, the remains of the French colonial chapel and the historic Indian cemetery on the First Terrace of Monks Mound are the first documented occupations that can be associated with the Cahokia Illini.

A few historic accounts provide an approximate date for this occupation of Monks Mound by the Cahokia Illini. In 1735 Father Mercier of the Cahokia mission requested numerous items including fine cloth to furnish the retable, a crucifix, six candlesticks, six bouquets of flowers in pots, a cross to serve in processions and at burials, a banner with a picture of the Holy Family, and some packets of candles for the "new church at the Indian village" (Peterson 1949b:20). In a 1743 letter, Mercier stated that in 1731 the mission had purchased thirty arpents from the Cahokia and that "more than half of the Indians have moved about three leagues and a half from [Cahokia]" (Donnelly 1949b:79). This occupation of Monks Mound by the Cahokia Illini appears to have ended in 1752 with a devastating attack by the Fox on the Cahokia as well as the Michigamea near Fort de Chartres (Bossu 1771:77–80). Land records for the Monks Mound area in 1799 and 1804 mention the general location of the "old french church" (Walthall and Benchley 1987:81–82).

The excavations on the First Terrace of Monks Mound uncovered two historic structures, several pit features, and six burial features dating to this ca. twenty-year occupation by the Cahokia Illini (Walthall and Benchley 1987: fig. 6). The French chapel was built of a combination of *poteaux en terre* and *poteaux sur sole* construction and measures approximately 5.5 meters by 9.1 meters (18 feet by 30 feet). Postmolds along the north and south sides of the structure suggest the probable locations of galleries. The second structure, located approximately six meters from the chapel, was an oval, post structure measuring ca. 4.5 meters by 7.0 meters (15 feet by 23 feet) (Walthall and Benchley 1987:29). The structure on Monks Mound likely served as a dwelling for the Cahokia Illini or perhaps housed the priest from Cahokia during his visits (Walthall and Benchley 1987).

Six historic Indian burials dating to this occupation were excavated. The burial population consisted of adult females, juveniles, infants, and one fetus. The burial features included a bundle burial in a wooden chest and an adult female with whom a large clapper bell, possibly the chapel's bell, had been buried (Walthall and Benchley 1987:38, 40, 73). These excavations on Monks Mound were limited to a small portion of the First Terrace and it is probable that other features relating to the Cahokia Illini occupation remain preserved.

Also in the vicinity of Monks Mound, a trading post established by French merchants from Cahokia and known as La Cantine existed from 1776 to 1784. Although the exact location of this trading post has not been clearly established, it has been suggested (Walthall and Benchley 1987:87) that the site of La Cantine may be directly west of Monks Mound in the area that formerly housed the Cahokia Mounds Museum and parking lot. An 1841 description of the view from the top of Monks Mound mentions that to the north one could see "a glimpse of the cottages in the settlement of Cantine" (Wild and Thomas 1841:54). This description, however, probably refers to an 1804 settlement near the confluence of Cahokia and Cantine creeks established by French farmers from Prairie du Pont. The archaeological remains of this 1804 settlement probably lie outside of the Cahokia Mounds State Historic Site and have not been identified (Walthall and Benchley 1987:3).

The Cahokia Wedge Site (11-S-743)

In 1986 archaeological investigations were conducted at the Cahokia Wedge site, a four-acre tract of vacant land located in the village of Cahokia (Gums 1988). These investigations comprised a controlled surface collection and limited test excavations. Project funding was provided by the Cahokia French Colonial Committee and the Illinois Department of Transportation. The work was conducted by the Contract Archaeology Program of Southern Illinois University at Edwardsville.

The Cahokia Wedge site lies on a sandy ridge above Dead Creek, a former side channel of the Mississippi River known in the eighteenth century as the Rigolet. The site area represents approximately ten percent of the French colonial village. Directly across the street are the historic Church of the Holy Family and the Nicholas Jarrot Mansion. The reconstructed Cahokia Courthouse is located approximately 250 meters to the west.

Since the 1930s, the Cahokia Wedge has been vacant of structures. The historical significance of the site was first recorded by the WPA Cahokia Memorial Survey. In 1938 two of the four lots had been deeded to the county for use as a historical park by Charles and Barbara Idoux, descendants of Nicholas Jarrot. Several proposals for a historical park were considered during the following decades. It was not until 1986 that archaeological investigations substantiated the historical and archaeological significance of the Cahokia Wedge site.

The preliminary investigations comprised a controlled surface collection of 570 five-meter-square units. Nearly sixteen thousand artifacts were recovered from the site surface. Using diagnostic artifacts and artifact types, density maps were produced which identified six discrete artifact concentration, designated Areas A through F (fig. 7-8). Using historical maps and land records, five of the concentrations—Areas A, B, D, E, and F—were correlated with historic structures. The remaining concentration, Area C, contained primarily trade goods and historic Indian artifacts and appears to represent an Indian occupation.

Area A, located in the southwest corner of the site, was the only artifact concentration that contained an abundance of eighteenth-century French colonial materials, particularly faience ceramics. This concentration corresponds to the location of an eighteenth-century house illustrated on the 1766 map and a reconstructed map compiled by WPA researchers. The Area B concentration, located near the center of the site, appears to correspond to a barn associated with

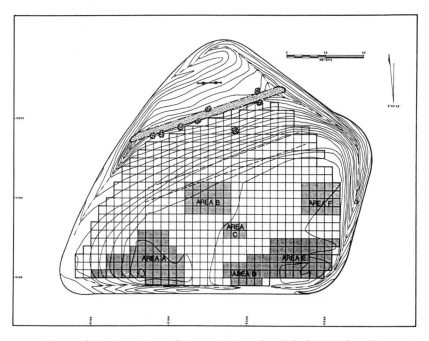

Figure 7-8. Locations of Areas A-F at the Cahokia Wedge Site

this house. In Areas D and E, on the southeast corner of the site, the remnants of three limestone foundations were plowed to the surface. The documentary evidence indicates that these structural remains may date from the early nineteenth century to the early twentieth century. Area F, located on the northeast corner of the site, correlates with a small residential dwelling dating to the late nineteenth and early twentieth centuries. The Area C concentration is located near the center of the site and may represent a habitation or activity area dating to the protohistoric/historic Indian use of the site. It is documented that during peace negotiations with George Rogers Clark in the fall of 1778, Indian groups camped for several weeks on the property of Thomas Brady (McDermott 1949:29) on the eastern side of the Cahokia Wedge site.

The 1766 map is the first document to identify French occupation on the Cahokia Wedge site; this map was rediscovered by Charles Peterson in 1949. Based on Norris's (1984:6) study, only two structures owned by Etienne Nicolle were present on the southwest corner of the Cahokia Wedge site (see fig. 7-2).

Researchers of WPA Cahokia Memorial Survey reconstructed a map of the village (fig. 7-9) as it appeared from 1790 to 1826. This map was compiled using land titles and property descriptions from Deed Books B-F. Village lot owners were identified and, when property descriptions were available, structures and other features within each lot were illustrated. WPA researchers also provided a succession of property owners for village lots, including the Cahokia Wedge site.

The WPA map has provided great detail as to the visual appearance of the village lots, illustrating palisaded lots containing domestic structures, orchards, garden plots, and numerous outbuildings, including barns, sheds, cook houses, and slave quarters. Occupation on the Cahokia Wedge can be examined from this map. The western portion of the site has the reconstructed properties of J. Meunier and J. Dehai. Most of the archaeological remains of the Dehai property has probably been impacted by the expansion and realignment of Illinois Route 3 in the last few decades. However, the Meunier property is completely within the Cahokia Wedge site. The WPA map shows a house, a barn, two sheds, a stable, a mill, and a well on the Meunier property. The location of the Meunier house corresponds to the Area A surface concentration and the records document that this is the same structure previously owned by Nicolle. The eastern portion of the Wedge is divided into three lots, two of which are identified by the owners, P. Lize Dit Mimi and L. Pinconneau. In 1809 the western properties were still owned by Meunier and Dehai, whereas the eastern portion

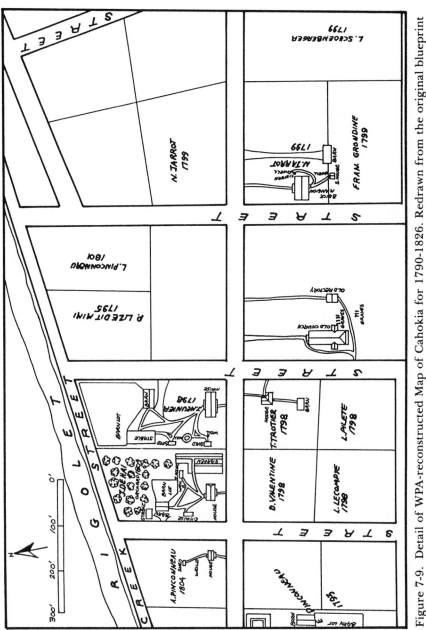

Figure 7-9. Detail of WPA-reconstructed Map of Cahokia for 1790-1826. Redrawn from the original blueprint in the Cahokia Courthouse Archives.

of the Cahokia Wedge was owned by François Bouthellier and a house was reported in this location (Boylan 1939:61–63).

A lithograph of a winter scene in Cahokia (fig. 7-10) was illustrated by J. C. Wild in the 1841 publication *The Valley of the Mississippi Illustrated* (Wild and Thomas 1841). This view, to the south-southeast, shows Rigolet Creek and a row of structures, including the Church of the Holy Family and the Nicholas Jarrot Mansion, facing the Cahokia Wedge site. The lithograph does show that the western portion of the Wedge, Areas A and B, was vacant of structures, which documents that the Nicolle/Meunier house and barn were no longer in existence. Several structures, including a two-story house and one or two outbuildings, are illustrated near the southeast corner of the site in the concentration Areas D and E. These structures could represent the house and outbuildings reported to be owned by Bouthellier in 1809.

An aerial photograph (fig. 7-11), ca. 1927, shows a view of the Cahokia Wedge and the surrounding areas to the south and southwest. Five structures are shown on the southeast corner of the site and correspond to the artifact concentrations in Areas D and E. Two of these appear to be residential dwellings; a two-story building and a one-story building of French colonial style with galleries on all four sides. The former structure, although perhaps with some alterations, is similar to the structure illustrated in the 1841 lithograph, which suggests it was at least eighty-six years old in 1927. If this is the same

Figure 7-10. 1841 Lithograph of Cahokia. Source: Wild and Thomas 1841: pl. 26

Figure 7-11. Ca. 1927 Aerial Photograph of Cahokia. Courtesy of Parks College, St. Louis University.

house recorded to be owned by Bouthellier in 1809, it would have been well over one hundred years old in 1927. The French colonial-style house was probably made of *poteaux en terre* or *poteaux sur sole* construction that appears to have been covered with a horizontal board frame. Most of the archaeological remains of this structure probably lie underneath First and Locust streets, which have been widened and realigned since 1927. A smaller structure, probably a shed, is located to the rear of these houses and is also within the Area E concentration. Two other outbuildings or sheds are shown in this photograph and correspond to the Area D concentration. In the northeastern corner of the site facing Locust Street is a small, rectangular, one-story structure of horizontal frame construction, which corresponds to concentration Area F.

Limited test excavations were conducted on the southwest corner of the site in the Area A concentration, primarily because of the abundance of eighteenth-century artifacts. The east-west test excavation trench measured about forty-five meters in length and ranged from two to four meters in width. Thirteen cultural features were identified, including four pits, portions of three wall trenches, a nineteenth-century structural foundation, two limestone concentrations, and a midden area (fig. 7-12). Of these thirteen features, six, including the wall-trench features, appear to date to the eighteenth century.

Features 7, 8, and 10 wall trenches are interpreted as a portion of an eighteenth-century French colonial *poteaux en terre* structure. The configuration of the wall trenches in relation to each other suggests that feature 7 is the main structural wall and features 8 and 10 comprised a lean-to or addition to the main structure. These structural elements are similar to those identified during the WPA excavations at the Cahokia Courthouse. Artifacts from the wall trenches include faience and creamware ceramics, dark green and blue bottle glass, a clasp knife blade, a kaolin pipe stem, a triangular iron padlock with brass plating, pieces of cut sheet copper, and rosehead nails.

The *poteaux en terre* structural remains are interpreted as representing the Nicolle/Meunier house as illustrated on the 1766 map and the WPA-reconstructed map. The structure, if originally constructed by Etienne Nicolle, dates after 1758 and before 1766, because marriage records show he was a resident of Kaskaskia in 1758 (Belting 1948:84). Nicolle lived in this house until 1779, when he and his wife were poisoned by their slaves (Alvord 1907:12–21). There were several short-term owners until 1794, when it was purchased by Jean Meunier, who lived there until at least 1809. Records show that the associated barn, located near the Area B concentration, was present during both the Nicolle and Meunier occupations. According to the 1841 lithograph of Cahokia, these two structures were no longer present at least by that date.

The opposite wall of the Nicolle/Meunier house was not identified in the test excavation trench, although based on the interpretation of the wall-trench features it should be located to the east. However, there are three features in this area dating to the colonial period that may relate to the Nicolle/Meunier house or possibly predate the structure. Feature 2 was a small, limestone concentration that possibly represents the chimney/fireplace for the Nicolle/Meunier house. If the proposed chimney was attached to the side of the feature 7 structure, it would result in this structure having a length of about twelve meters (about 39 feet), which is within the size range expected for an early French colonial home. Feature 1 was a shallow, oblong pit overlying a small, oval pit. This feature contained an abundance of wood charcoal and may represent a pit dug for refuse from feature 2. Feature 4 was a fairly large, but poorly defined, feature containing abundant faunal remains and has been interpreted as a midden area related to the activities associated with features 1 and 2. A charcoal

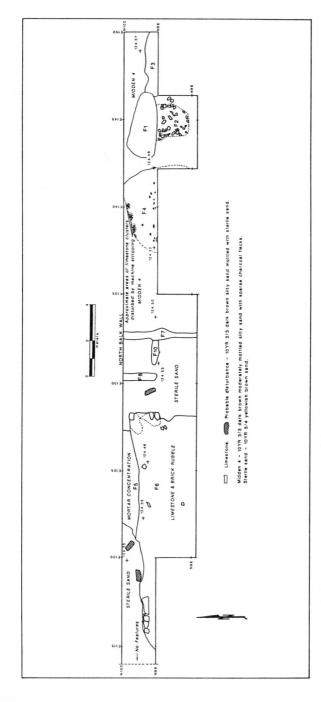

Figure 7-12. Excavation Trench at the Cahokia Wedge Site

lens associated with features 1 and 2 was also partially within feature 4, indicating the contemporaneity of these three features.

Features 5 and 6 represent nineteenth-century structural remains and were located a few meters west of the wall-trench features. Feature 6 was a structural cellar or basement excavated into the sterile sand and measured 13.54 meters in length. A limestone foundation was found at the bottom of feature 6. The abundance of brick rubble within the feature suggests that it was probably a brick structure resting on a limestone foundation. Feature 5 was probably a builder's trench or rampway for the construction of the structure. The predominance of limestone mortar in feature 5 suggests that it may also have been used to prepare mortar for the construction and was filled in with construction debris after completion of the foundation. This structure, although not illustrated on the nineteenth-century maps or referenced in the available documents, appears to have been built sometime after 1841 and was not present in 1927. The artifact assemblages of features 5 and 6 substantiate the suggested period of occupation, post-1841.

In summary, the test excavations in Area A correlated the interpretation of the controlled surface collection data and the documentary evidence with the presence of the eighteenth- and early nineteenth-century Nicolle/Meunier house. Soil stratigraphy in the excavation trench indicated that the eighteenth-century features were located at a substantial depth (40–60 cm) below the ground surface. Based on the historical documentation, the surface artifact distribution data, and the soil stratigraphy, it is assumed that other subsurface structural remains are present in Areas B, D, E, and F. In addition, there is a potential for other types of nonstructural features dating to both the colonial period and the Euro-American occupation at the site. The numerous protohistoric/historic trade items recovered from the site surface, particularly in Area C, are significant and may indicate the presence of features relating to an Indian occupation at the Cahokia Wedge site.

The Village of Prairie du Pont

As with the village of Cahokia, very few structures dating to the historic settlement of Prairie du Pont have survived. Only two structures of French colonial style are presently known: the Pierre Martin/ Nicholas Boismenue House and the LaCroix House. The WPA researchers photographed, mapped, and recorded a few other structures, including the LePage House and the Chatillion House in the late 1930s; however, these have since been destroyed.

The Pierre Martin / Nicholas Boismenue House

It was not until 1980, when the Pierre Martin/Nicholas Boismenue House was destined for demolition, that it became evident that the building was of vertical log construction. When workmen began to strip off the modern siding from the front of the structure, Dennis Nichols, who served as chief of the volunteer fire department across the street, noticed the distinctive vertical log timbers and was able to persuade the owner to stop the demolition. Within twenty-four hours, a local group of citizens, now known as the Prairie du Pont Preservation Society, was organized with the intention of saving the structure for its historical significance. The owner sold the house to the preservation group, who had secured a bank loan for the purchase.

Starting in 1981, archaeological investigations and an architectural study of the house were conducted by volunteers of the Cahokia Archaeological Society under the supervision of Bill Iseminger, site interpreter at the Cahokia Mounds State Historic Site. The structural study and comparison were done by Dennis Nichols, president of the Prairie du Pont Preservation Society, and Dennis Thomas of the Cahokia Courthouse State Historic Site.

The Martin/Boismenue House (fig. 7-13), the oldest known residence in Illinois, was listed on the National Register of Historic Places in 1990. The structure was built of *poteaux sur sole* in ca. 1790. This building was constructed by placing a heavy timber sill in top of a limestone foundation. Upright logs were seated and pegged to the sill and fastened at the top in a similar manner. The upright timbers were hewn flat on the face and back. The sides of the upright logs were concaved to hold the filling of mortar and stone called *pierrotage* or chinking. The Martin/Boismenue House may show a transition from French to English or American construction style because of the approximate date of the structure (ca. 1790) and certain building techniques including the corner angle braces placed at 45 degree angles. Earlier buildings usually had more steeply angled braces.

The original building, which measures about 6.1 meters by 10.7 meters (20 feet by 35 feet), consists of two large rooms separated by a receiving hall and a one-room, half basement finished for living quarters and with a separate entrance. All of the rooms were plastered, whitewashed, and adorned with a chair rail and base board to protect the walls. Fireplaces were located at each end of the house, including

Figure 7-13. Pierre Martin/Nicholas Boismenue House in Prairie du Pont, constructed in ca. 1790. The second story was added in 1913.

one in the half basement. A high-pitch roof supported by a Norman truss system provided sufficient space in the loft for a sleeping and storage area. Access was made to the loft by a simple ladder through an opening in the corner ceiling. A gallery stretched across the front and probably the back of the house. In the early years of the occupation, the kitchen was a separate structure.

The original house is approximately eighty percent intact. This includes most of the structural timbers of the four main walls, the foundation, the top and bottom sills, the flooring on both the first and second floors, the one-room basement and fireplace, and the fireplace foundation at the east end of the house. A few of the structural timbers of the main walls are in bad decay and need to be replaced. Approximately thirty percent of the *pierrotage* chinking is intact, but needs to be tuckpointed. The foundation and basement were tuckpointed in the fall of 1983. The original parts of the structure that have been altered and/or destroyed by renovations include the roof of the Norman truss system, the galleries, and one fireplace on the main floor.

Three renovations to this structure were done in the twentieth century. In 1913 the second story was added and a kitchen was attached to the back of the original structure on the southeast corner. In the 1950s a bedroom and bath were added to the back of the southwest corner and later the house was divided into two apartments; one upstairs and one on the ground floor with a common entrance. Although these renovations drastically changed the appearance of the house, they did little damage to the original structure.

Archaeological excavations were conducted sporadically from 1981 to 1983. Many people were instrumental in the project and it is impossible to name them all, but the Cahokia Archaeological Society, the Cahokia Mounds site staff and volunteers, several local school and scout groups, the Prairie du Pont Preservation Society, the Cahokia Mounds Museum Society field schools, the Prairie du Pont Volunteer Fire Department, and several other local groups and citizens all contributed.

A two-meter grid was laid out and excavation units were removed in 10-cm levels. Much of the yard had been subject to bulldozing and leveling and yellow loess from the bluffs had been hauled in to fill low areas. As a result, much of the surface and Level I material had been disturbed or redeposited. One of the principle objectives of these investigations was to identify features that would provide evidence for the location of porches or galleries across the front and around the side of the structure. The rear of the house was not investigated due to the presence of the later additions.

Three squarish limestone slabs at locations appropriate for a gallery on the front of the house were identified (fig. 7-14). These features were equidistant from the front of the house at approximately 1.4 meters. Two of these lined up with the corners of the house. The third feature was 3.25 meters (center to center) from the eastern feature and 6.5 meters from the western feature. The projected location of a fourth feature between the latter two was disturbed by the construction of the 1888 porch foundation. These limestone slabs appear to represent the bottommost course of a column of slabs used to support a raised gallery floor to the height of the top of the limestone house foundation. The upper courses were probably removed when the 1888 porch was built or were disturbed by bulldozer activities. Tenons and peg holes in the corner timbers of the house front correspond to expected locations for railings on the gallery. The top of the gallery would have been covered by an extension of the original roof. The angle of the notches in the upper wall plates on top of the timbers seems to confirm such a roof extension.

No limestone slabs or other features were identified on the east side of the house and the west side had been disturbed by driveways.

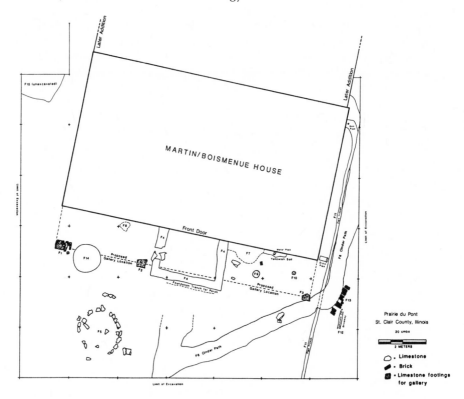

Figure 7-14. Map of excavations at the Martin/Boismenue House

Therefore, it is unlikely that this house was the type that had a full surrounding gallery. Rather it is postulated that there existed a gallery on the front and perhaps a corresponding one on the rear, which could have been obliterated by the later additions.

A smaller porch was constructed on the front of the house in 1888, replacing the gallery. This porch measures two meters by three meters and has a mortared limestone slab foundation and probably a wooden floor. Much of this porch had been removed by the bulldozing, but the lower course was relatively intact. A cinder pathway extended straight from this porch toward the street. Another path branched from this one about three meters in front of the porch and angled toward and around the west side of the house. It partially superimposed one of the gallery limestone slabs. The path appears to be curving around the rear of the original structure, but later addition truncates it. This would indicate that the path would date later than the 1888 porch and prior to the rear addition.

A circular arrangement of limestone, about two meters in diameter, was found approximately 4.3 meters north of the east corner of the house. At first it was thought that this might be a cistern or well, but it turned out to be only a single layer of stones and is more likely interpreted as a flower garden made of the remnants of construction material from the house at some unknown date.

A portion of a rectangular feature, probably a septic tank, was filled with sand and located on the east side of the house. In fact, this is the side of the house where the kitchen was added in 1913. In line with the west side of the house, a short section of concrete curbing was exposed, apparently part of a former driveway. Also uncovered was a series of bricks that may be remnants of a short, toppled wall or possibly another pathway or driveway. A waterpipe trench superimposed much of this along the west side of the house. The most recent feature was a bell-shaped pit near the east corner of the house, which contained recent debris probably dating to the last occupants in the late 1970s.

The principal objective of the archaeological investigation was achieved with the identification of a gallery on the front of the house as part of the original construction plan. This confirmed that the Martin/Boismenue House was similar in appearance to other French colonial houses. The Martin/Boismenue House is an excellent example and one of the few remaining structures of French colonial construction style and deserves continued preservation and restoration efforts.

The LaCroix House

The other known French structure remaining in Prairie du Pont is the LaCroix House, located a few blocks southeast of the Martin/Boismenue House. This structure does not appear in the WPA research; however, this may be due to the extensive alterations of several additions and modern siding. The small, originally one-room structure is built of *poteaux sur sole* construction with a Norman truss roof. This house probably also had one or more galleries, which have since been removed. The date of this structure is unknown and it is presently a private residence.

The LePage House

The WPA completed a detailed blueprint map (fig. 7-15) and description of the LePage House. The construction date of this structure

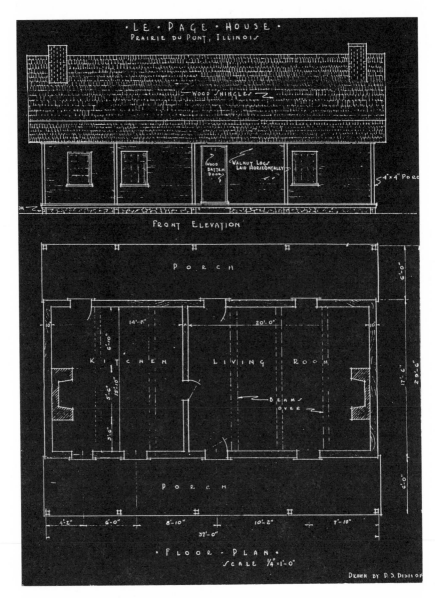

Figure 7-15. WPA-drawn Plan of the LePage House in Prairie du Pont. Courtesy of the Cahokia Courthouse Archives.

was established as ca. 1785 (Boylan 1939:89). The St. Clair County History recorded that in 1881 it was the oldest structure in Prairie du Pont (Brink, McDonough, and Co. 1881:296). This house was located across the street from the Martin/Boismenue House. The LePage House, although of French style, was made of horizontal walnut logs rather than upright logs. The structure measured ca. 5.1 meters by 11.2 meters (17 feet by 37 feet). The interior consisted of two rooms with stone fireplaces located at opposite ends and a staircase leading to a large attic. The roof was made of wooden shingles, and galleries were originally located in the front and the back of the structure. The front gallery had been removed and replaced with a modern portice and the back gallery had been enclosed and extended to form two additional rooms (Boylan 1939:88–89). The 1972 demolition of this house was documented with photographs by Dennis Nichols. At present, the lot is partially vacant.

The Chatillion House

The Chatillion House was located on the east side of the main street a few lots north of the Martin/Boismenue House. This structure, like the LaPage House, was in the French colonial style, but constructed of horizontal logs. It originally consisted of two rooms and measured 5.4 meters by 10.6 meters (18 feet by 35 feet) (Boylan 1939:88). A gallery was present on the front and modern additions had been constructed on the back. It was photographed by the WPA survey in 1939 and reported to be in reasonably good condition (Boylan 1939:88); however, it was demolished seven years later, in 1946. A small, brick structure of the Columbia Water Station now stands in this location.

Concluding Remarks

Although scattered throughout the Cahokia and Prairie du Pont areas, the remaining cultural resources attest to the importance of and the need for preservation of these remnants of the French colonial period. The potential for recovery of data relating to these two villages is not as bleak as one would expect given the conditions of the present landscape. The potential for archaeological remains dating to the French colonial period has proven significant with the investigations at the Cahokia Wedge site. The WPA documentation of historic structures in 1938–39 provides a comparison of the resources present fifty years ago with those that remain. This research may prove valuable for further archaeological investigations. Furthermore, the bulk of the WPA research has not been relocated and examined to its full potential. The example of the Pierre Martin/Nicholas Boismenue House only discovered to be a vertical log structure in 1980 emphasizes the potential, however limited, for other yet-to-be-discovered French colonial houses under modern guises. Preservation and restoration efforts beginning in the early twentieth century, with a surge of interest during the WPA years, and ongoing in Cahokia and Prairie du Pont, illustrate an enthusiastic interest on the part of the local citizens in their French heritage.

The Louvier Site
at Prairie du Rocher

8

Edward T. Safiran

Prairie du Rocher was one of the earliest settlements of the Illinois Country, which for most of the eighteenth century consisted of all French-claimed territory from the mouth of the Ohio River north to the Great Lakes, including the valleys of the Mississippi, Missouri, and Ohio rivers (Ekberg 1985:2). This small community of some five hundred people today is situated in southwestern Randolph County, Illinois.

A precise date for the founding of Prairie du Rocher has not been established. The chapel of St. Joseph at Prairie du Rocher was established as a mission to the chapel of St. Anne at Fort de Chartres (Brown and Dean 1977:2). Fort de Chartres was built about 1720 by the sieur de Boisbriant, a French Canadian who was the first commandant of the Illinois Country. Fort de Chartres represented the seat of military government in upper Louisiane. It is thought that the founding of Prairie du Rocher coincided roughly with the construction of the fort. However, a census of Louisiane of 1732 notes only two people, Gaussio and his wife, living at the "Rock Prairie" (Maduell 1972:182). Broutin's map of the Illinois from 1734 shows the location of Prairie du Rocher as "The Prairie of M. Ste. Therese" (Belting 1943:15). The American State Papers contain the following statement in reference to the early establishment of the village: "From the few fragments of ancient records which we have been able to find, it should appear that the tract containing the village and most of the present common field of Prairie du Rocher, was originally granted by the Royal India Company to Mr. Boisbriant, Lieutenant Governor of Louisiana, who transferred it to his nephew, Jean Ste. Therese Langlois, then officer of the French troops, sometime before the year 1734, in the Illinois, who appears to have divided it out in allotments to actual settlers, reserving certain seigneurial rights according to the custom of Paris" (American State Papers 1860, 2:183).

Natalia Belting (1943:21) points out that Boisbriant was only in the Illinois Country from 1719 to 1724. He also made several similar land grants to officers in 1722, which may indicate that he conveyed the one in the American State Papers at this time. Belting also notes a deed filed in New Orleans on 10 August 1737 that contains a transfer of property from Jean Ste. Therese to Augustin Langlois, "my domain of Prairie du Rocher, and I exact nothing from the other settlers on the same Prairie, they are all lords and masters." One of the best censuses of the Illinois Country is the one recorded by Jean-Jacques Macarty, the commandant of Fort de Chartres in 1752. Macarty noted fourteen heads of family at Prairie du Rocher that year (Faribault-Beauregard 1984:295).

The French lost their lands on the east side of the Mississippi to the British in the Seven Years' War, which concluded with the treaty of Paris of 1763. This meant the ceding of French lands east of the Mississippi and dwindling populations for the villages of the American Bottom. One village that did not lose population, but rather increased in size after the war, was Prairie du Rocher. A census taken in 1787 lists thirty-three heads of family residing at the village (Faribault-Beauregard 1984:296, 297). Why Prairie du Rocher was experiencing growth at a time when the other villages around it were losing population is puzzling. It may be that its location, several miles from the British garrison at the former Fort de Chartres, made it attractive to those French who had been living in the villages of St. Philippe and Chartres. Another possible explanation for the growth of the village at this time is the theory that the Seven Years' War, for all intents and purposes, was over in Canada in 1759 with the fall of Quebec. Many French Canadians fled their homes at this time. Some of them returned to France, and some of them fled to Louisiane, where they thought they would be safe from British encroachment.

The original village of Prairie du Rocher is thought to have been located just south of the present settlement and adjacent to the town cemetery. By the mid-nineteenth century frequent flooding by Prairie du Rocher Creek forced the abandonment of the original locale. The settlers moved to higher ground closer to the bluffs that separate the bottoms from the uplands.

Documentary Research on 11-R-313

Like the other early settlements of the Illinois Country, the town of Prairie du Rocher was a nucleated village with the houses of the *habitants* clustered in a village around the church. Their individually owned pieces of farmland were laid out in long strips with only a few arpents of frontage and with lateral measures that stretched from the village to the Mississippi. Around these individually owned strips of farmland was a common fence erected to keep grazing livestock out of the sown fields. Each *habitant* was responsible for the upkeep of the part of the fence that crossed his property. The commons of Prairie du Rocher was a tract of land lying east of the village. This land, as its title implies, was owned in common by the inhabitants of the town and was used for grazing livestock and as a source of firewood for the inhabitants (Alvord 1922:206). The commons of Prairie du Rocher was granted to the village on 7 May 1743 by Delaoire Flancourt, then commander of the Illinois Country (American State Papers 1860, 2:183). The settlement pattern in the Illinois Country was more closely related to the layout of villages in France at this time. French Canadians of the eighteenth century tended to live on dispersed farmsteads.

The residential lots in the villages of the Illinois Country were usually one square arpent (0.85 acres) in size. These lots were also fenced in to keep grazing animals out. In addition to the main house, these lots often contained a cow barn, a stable, a henhouse, an orchard, a vegetable garden, a bake oven, a well and sometimes slaves' quarters (Ekberg 1985:284).

The houses of the villagers were built close to the streets and their vertical log construction has become known as the Middle Mississippi Vernacular Style (Thurman 1984). The two most common types of this style are *poteaux en terre,* or posts in the ground, and *poteaux sur sole,* posts on a sill. *Poteaux en terre,* thought to be the most common type, was constructed by first digging a rectangular trench to the desired size. Then dressed logs were placed in the trench and the trench was backfilled. The spaces between the upright logs were filled with a mixture of clay and straw (or stones and mortar) and the trench was backfilled, then whitewash was smeared over the exterior to seal the walls (Ekberg 1985:285). Post-on-sill houses were built in a similar fashion except that the upright logs were fixed to a wood sill placed on a stone foundation. The investigators at Prairie du Rocher hoped that evidence of this type of construction and other remains of everyday life in a French colonial village could be examined in the archaeological record.

Unfortunately, no detailed maps of the original village of Prairie du Rocher have been found. The earliest plat maps of the town date to the 1830s. At this time the area where the archaeological testing took place is shown as lot 4 of block 7 of the original town of Prairie du Rocher. A title search at the Randolph County Courthouse in Chester, Illinois, indicates that Joseph Boutillet of Prairie du Rocher sold lot 4 of block 7 to John Kerr in 1846 for four dollars (Randolph County Courthouse Deed Book EE:228). This small sum suggests that the land may have already been inundated by the floooding of Prairie du Rocher Creek and the town may have already moved toward higher ground to the north.

Joseph Boutillet was the grandson of Jacques Boutillet who came to Prairie du Rocher sometime before 1765, the year he married Therese Gilbert at Prairie du Rocher (Faribault-Beauregard 1984:262). Jacques was the son of Jacques Boutillet and Marie Cordeau-Deloriez of l'Ange-Gardien, Canada. Perhaps Jacques came to the Illinois Country when the area where he previously lived fell to the British in 1759. Joseph is listed as head of a family residing at Prairie du Rocher in 1820. It is speculative but there is a good chance that he was living on lot 4 at that time. Speculating further, Joseph might have inherited his residential property from his eighteenth-century relatives of Prairie du Rocher.

Excavations at Prairie du Rocher

Archaeological testing at Prairie du Rocher was undertaken because the area where local lore and some documentary evidence suggested part of the original town lay is slated for destruction by the expansion of the cemetery of the Parish of St. Joseph of Prairie du Rocher, the present owners of the property. The fieldwork consisted of two weeks of testing conducted by an all-volunteer crew from Illinois State University and various other institutions in the state.

The fieldwork consisted of a controlled surface collection and excavation of several test trenches through the plowzone in a cornfield just west of the cemetery of the Parish of St. Joseph of Prairie du Rocher. We located twelve subsurface features as well as numerous artifacts that date to the eighteenth-century occupation of the village.

Time restraints did not allow the investigators to expose and sample fully the features located. However, the preliminary work did reveal what appears to be part of a post-in-ground wall trench, a possible cellar filled with small pieces of *pierrotage* chinking from a vertical log structure, artifacts dating from the abandonment of the original town, and a large pit feature containing eighteenth-century material.

Most of the cultural material recovered during the archaeological testing came from the surface and plowzone of the site. Distributional maps made from a five-meter controlled surface collection indicate that the artifacts from the eighteenth and early nineteenth centuries are concentrated within an area roughly an arpent square or 0.85 acres, which coincides with the size of an eighteenth-century residential lot. In the following paragraphs material culture from the excavations at the Louvier site is compared to material recovered at two other eighteenth-century sites in the Illinois Country, the Cahokia Wedge site and the Laurens site (Fort de Chartres I). Cahokia, the northernmost village of the Illinois Country, was established in 1699 by missionary priests from the Seminary of Foreign Missions and French fur traders interested in conducting their business in the area. In 1986 archaeologists from Southern Illinois University at Edwardsville conducted excavations in an area thought to contain remnants of the original village. The site is known as the Cahokia Wedge site (Gums 1988; Gums et al., chap. 7) and the excavations there offer some interesting similarities and differences when compared with those from Louvier.

As at the Louvier site, the investigators at the Cahokia Wedge site first conducted a controlled surface collection in order to determine the location of possible subsurface cultural remains. Gums (1988; Gums et al., chap. 7) notes six areas of artifact concentrations and labels them A–F. Excavations focused on area A, where artifacts dating to the eighteenth century were concentrated on the surface.

One method used to compare the results of the archaeology at Prairie du Rocher with the material from the Cahokia Wedge was to organize the eighteenth-century cultural material (material associated with the French occupation) from both sites into functional categories as defined by Stanley South (1977:92–96). South defined nine functional categories for artifacts recovered from eighteenth- and early nineteenth-century historic sites in South Carolina. These functional categories are: Kitchen, Bone, Architecture, Furniture, Arms, Clothing, Personal, Tobacco Pipe, and Activities. The Bone Group is not included in this study because the bone recovered from the Louvier site is limited and requires special analysis not yet completed at the time of this study. Caution must be taken in using the South artifact pattern in this study, because it was developed for use on sites on the East Coast. Furthermore, the bulk of the material recovered from the Louvier site was recovered from the plowzone and the surface, not from features to which a certain function can be attributed. Nonetheless, a large sample of eighteenth-century material was recovered during the archaeological investigations at the Louvier site, so the grouping of the material into the functional categories is an attempt to penetrate beyond mere description. It is also a convenient method to compare the assemblages of artifacts recovered from the Cahokia Wedge and Prairie du Rocher, both eighteenth-century villages of the Illinois Country.

Table 8-1 lists the number of artifacts recovered from each of the groups and the percent of the total number of artifacts associated with the French colonial occupation at both sites. An initial similarity seen when comparing the percentages of the groups represented is that in both cases the Architectural Group contains the largest percentage of artifacts (68 at Cahokia Wedge, 52 at Prairie du Rocher). The next largest group represented from Prairie du Rocher is the Kitchen Group (22%), followed by the Arms Group (14%). The same distribution is seen at the Cahokia Wedge, except that the Kitchen Group is larger than the Arms Group by ten artifacts (107 to 97). The rest of the groups represented at both sites show a striking similarity.

The validity of placing the artifacts from Louvier and the Cahokia Wedge into South's Carolina Artifact Pattern groups is limited because the size of the samples from both sites are different and were obtained in inconsistent ways. Artifacts recovered from similar features could not be compared. However, some observations can be made concerning the numbers represented in the artifact groups. The dominance of the Architecture Group on the two eighteenth-century Illinois Country sites is certainly different from the eighteenth-century South Carolina sites studied by South, where the Kitchen Group is by far the largest (South 1977:126–37). It is interesting to note that

Table 8-1. Artifact Groups Represented at the Louvier and Cahokia Wedge Sites

Artifact Group	Louvier		Cahokia Wedge	
	No. of Artifacts	% of Total	No. of Artifacts	% of Total
Kitchen	69	22	107	11
Architecture	162	52	658	68
Furniture	—	—	10	1
Arms	45	14	101	10
Clothing	15	5	35	4
Personal	2	1	9	1
Tobacco Pipe	8	3	18	2
Activities	11	3	35	3
Total	312	100	973	100

the Kitchen Group is also the largest group represented on nineteenth-century historic sites from Illinois (Walitschek and Rohrbaugh 1988). The fact that the Kitchen Group from the Cahokia Wedge and Prairie du Rocher are smaller (by percentage) than eighteenth-century sites on the East Coast and nineteenth-century sites in the Midwest may reveal the relative isolation of the Illinois Country. Settlements on the East Coast had access to ships carrying pottery and other goods directly from England. It would be much harder for the settlements of the Illinois Country to obtain goods from France via New Orleans and the Mississippi River or Canada via inland water routes. While the trip from Prairie du Rocher to New Orleans might only take a month, travel upriver could take as long as four to six months (Belting 1948:64)

Another interesting fact that emerges when comparing South Carolina artifact patterns to the assemblages from the Cahokia Wedge and Prairie du Rocher is the high percentage of Arms Group artifacts recovered from the two Illinois sites (Louvier 14%, Cahokia Wedge 10%). These figures reflect the importance of firearms to the everyday life of the people of the Illinois Country. Firearms were important for hunting, for protection from wild animals, and for protection from Indians and other enemies. So essential were firearms in the Illinois Country that it was even argued that slaves be allowed to carry guns for their own protection against hostile Indians (Ekberg 1985:349).

The grouping of the artifacts from Prairie du Rocher and Cahokia into functional categories may be a start at establishing an artifact pattern for French colonial sites in the Midwest. Although much more work needs to be done on these sites in order to have better comparative data, it seems that the Architecture, Kitchen, and the Arms groups are the artifacts that can be expected to be found on these sites.

A closer look at the cultural material recovered from the Louvier site with that of the Cahokia Wedge site leads to interesting observations. The cultural material from both sites is similar in many respects. French faience, eighteenth-century coarse earthenwares, and other artifacts commonly found on French colonial sites are present at both Cahokia and Prairie du Rocher. At Cahokia, however, trade beads, copper tinkling cones, and other ornaments associated with the eighteenth-century fur trade appear in abundance. Their presence at the Cahokia Wedge site and their absence from the Louvier site clearly reflects the original functions of the villages themselves. Cahokia was first established as a mission and fur trading site. Its location close to the Mississippi River makes it functionally different from

Prairie du Rocher, which was removed from the river and closer to the bluffs. The absence of the trade goods such as glass beads and copper and glass ornaments reveals an agriculturally based community on the colonial frontier.

Differences found when comparing the Louvier site with the Laurens site (Fort de Chartres I) are initially similar to those found when comparing Louvier and the Cahokia Wedge. Beads and other goods used in the fur trade are present at Fort de Chartres I. Fort de Chartres I and Cahokia were both established earlier than Prairie du Rocher. One of the reasons for building the first fort ca. 1720 was to establish a base of operations for the Company of the Indies, a company that was heavily invested in the fur trade (Jelks, Ekberg, and Martin 1989:7).

Another contrast that appears between the Louvier site and the Laurens site might have been expected. The Laurens site produced more military-related artifacts, including lead shot, sprue, and eighteenth-century military buttons. One would expect items like these to be more numerous at a military establishment than at a nucleated village where the bulk of the population was farmers. Prairie du Rocher was not without its firearms and militia, however, and the gun parts (twenty-six gunflints, one lead shot, and three sprue fragments) recovered show that firearms were an important part of the *habitants'* possessions.

In comparing porcelain from Prairie du Rocher and Fort de Chartres I, interesting contrasts emerge. Chinese export porcelain appears much more frequently in the collection of artifacts from the Laurens site than in that from the Louvier site. Only one fragment of Chinese export porcelain was recovered from Prairie du Rocher. Another eighteenth-century sherd seems to represent a British imitation of Chinese porcelain. Even though the porcelain sample recovered from the Laurens site is not large, it does suggest that military personnel had a higher social standing and standard of living than did the *habitants* of the Illinois Country villages. Walthall and Gums (1988) report only two fragments of Chinese porcelain from the Cahokia Wedge site. The Laurens site also produced a larger number of decorated faience vessels than did the Louvier site (Walthall 1991), which corroborates this suggestion.

Prairie du Rocher's relative isolation as seen in the archaeology is also apparent in source documents. Nicolas de Finiels, who visited the Illinois Country in 1797, noted that Prairie du Rocher, unlike the other villages on the west side of the Mississippi, remained exclusively French. The inhabitants chose not to move to the other side of the Mississippi after 1765, when the British took possession, or even after

1778, when the Americans finally arrived in the area (Ekberg and Foley 1989).

Christian Schulz, in *Travels on an Inland Voyage*, described Prairie du Rocher and its people in 1810:

> The town is constructed on a very small scale the streets [were] barely twenty feet wide. This apparent economy however was not without sufficient reason at the time these settlements were made, it being done for the purpose of consolidating the village as much as possible, that it might be near enough to assist each other in case of surprise by the savages. The people of this settlement all live by tillage, and in their outward appearances seem but a few degrees superior to their savage neighbours, yet when accosted they immediately discover their national trait of politeness (1943:36–37).

Another description of the village, from 1823, also reflects the unchanging quality of life in Prairie du Rocher: "The houses are generally built in the French style, and the inhabitants are with few exception poor and illiterate. The streets are narrow and dirty. . . . Few Americans have as yet disturbed the repose of the ancient inhabitants of this place, nor is it probable they ever will, as it possesses no advantages and is very unhealthy" (Beck 1823:149–50).

The archaeological work at Prairie du Rocher confirms that the villagers were adhering to their cultural roots. The controlled surface data indicates that the inhabitants of the site occupied the same areas or structures during the eighteenth and nineteenth centuries, which suggests that they continued much the same life-style throughout the occupation of the site. The eighteenth-century artifacts recovered also show a preference for French goods.

J. F. Snyder, a resident of Belleville in the early nineteenth century, made this observation about Prairie du Rocher in 1839, which fits nicely with our archaeological findings:

> Arrived at Prairie du Rocher early in the afternoon. Having several old-time aquaintances to visit there we remained overnight in that ancient hamlet, entertained at its only public house—or rather the private residence of Monsieur Antione Barbeau, an old native of the place, who obligingly entertained the few travelers happening to come that way. The only indellible impression I have retained of Prairie du Rocher on that occasion is of the grand rocky cliff towering over a hundred feet perpindicularly above the village. . . . I also have a lively recollection of the mosquitoes there, more numerous and more voracious than those of Kaskaskia. The Barbeaus, our host and hostess, were unalloyed specimens of the non progessive, exotic, Creole race that originally inhabited the American Bottom, dark complexion, black haired and black eyed,

slow motioned, contented, sociable and very kind and hospitable (1943:363).

Virtually every eighteenth-century *habitant* of Prairie du Rocher was illiterate. These people obviously could not leave behind a written record describing their everyday lives. Census data, estate inventories, and parish records alone are not adequate to provide a complete picture of life in colonial Illinois. The archaeologically recovered artifacts and features left behind by these people are important primary historical sources that deserve careful study, for they provide data that are not available anywhere else. The village of Prairie du Rocher has fortunately not been affected by urbanization. As this study demonstrates, the Louvier site contains portions of a lot in a nucleated settlement from the French colonial frontier. In a sense this site is a time capsule, containing information about a little-known period of Illinois history—a period before Anglo-American immigration, before railroads, and before industrialization.

Ste. Genevieve, a French Colonial Village in the Illinois Country

9

F. Terry Norris

The village of Ste. Genevieve, or Misere, as it was referred to during the late eighteenth century (Peterson 1949a:2), was the last community to be established during the French regime within the Illinois Country and the only one to be located on the west bank of the Mississippi (Ekberg 1985). Ste. Genevieve was one of six villages built on the Mississippi River floodplain between present-day St. Louis, Missouri, and Chester, Illinois, an area approximately ninety-seven kilometers (sixty miles) in length (see fig. 1-1).

Other villages in the area included Cahokia (1699), Kaskaskia (1703), St. Philippe (ca. 1723), Prairie du Rocher (ca. 1723), and "le establishment" or "Nouvelle Chartres" (post-1719) (Brown and Dean 1977). Today, the remains of these villages are collectively referred to as the French Colonial District of the middle Mississippi River Valley (see fig. 1-2).

The following narrative represents a summary of recent archival and archaeological investigations conducted by the author at a historic archaeological site (23-SG-124) located 4.5 kilometers (2.8 miles) southeast of the present-day town of Ste. Genevieve, Ste. Genevieve County, Missouri. This eighteenth-century site is believed to be the remains of the original village of colonial Ste. Genevieve (Norris 1979).

Historical Background

Although the present-day town of Ste. Genevieve was established before 1794 (Ekberg 1985:438) and is itself a National Historic Landmark, it was not the first site of this settlement. Period accounts suggest that the original village was located southeast of the present town on a wide alluvial floodplain near the Mississippi River.

Founded about 1750, Ste. Genevieve was originally considered part of the village of Kaskaskia (Ekberg 1985:27). The eighteenth-century village of Kaskaskia was approximately 6.5 kilometers (4 miles) to the east, on the opposite (east) side of the Mississippi River.

Although it has been long held that trade and, in particular, the storage and distribution of lead was the primary motivation for the establishment of Ste. Genevieve (Houck 1908:422; Alvord 1922:209–15), it has now been demonstrated that the primary impetus for the creation of this community was the increasing scarcity of tillable land on the east bank, or Kaskaskia side, of the Mississippi River (Ekberg 1985:44). Even today, the alluvial floodplain upon which the remains of the original village are located still bears the vernacular French nickname of *le grand champ* or Big Common Field, in reference to its agricultural potential (Franzwa 1967:3).

The importance of the Mississippi River to the founders of this village can be inferred by a cursory analysis of the village's proximity to the eighteenth-century river channel. Easy access to the navigation channel of the Mississippi River appears to have overridden concerns about potential flood threats when the site was chosen (Shoemaker 1927:88). This appears to have also been the case upstream at Cahokia (McDermott 1949:13). Indeed, as early as 1710 the importance of the river as a mechanism for commerce is documented by the shipment of surplus wheat from nearby Kaskaskia to lower Louisiane (Belting 1948:13).

This site was repeatedly flooded (Ekberg 1985:421; Green 1983:11) and in 1785 was inundated by what was probably the record flood on the middle Mississippi River. This event, and the prospect of similar inundations in the future, prompted residents to abandon this area in favor of higher ground. The present town of Ste. Genevieve was built on a colluvial deposit at an elevation approximately 6.5 meters (21.3 feet) above the ground surface of the original village site.

The most concise description of the village during the colonial period was provided by Philip Pittman, an English military engineer who was stationed in the Illinois Country following the Seven Years' War (Rea 1973). Pittman wrote the following description of the village based upon his observations made in the summer or fall of 1766:

> the goodness of the soil and the plentiful harvest they reaped made them perfectly satisfied with the place they had chosen. The situation of the village is very convenient, being within one league of the salt spring, which is for the general use of the French subjects, and several persons belonging to this village have works here, and make great quantities of salt for the supply of the Indians, hunters, and other

settlements. A lead mine, which supplies the whole country with shot, is about fifteen leagues distance. The communication of this village [with] Cascasquias is very short and easy, it being only to cross the Mississippi, which is about three quarters of a mile broad at this place, and then there is a portage, two miles distance, to Cascasquias. This cuts off eighteen miles by water, six down the river Cascasquias and twelve up the Mississippi. . . . The village is about one mile in length and contains about seventy families. Here is a very fine water-mill, for corn and planks, belonging to Mons. Valet (quoted in Rea 1973:50).

Although Pittman stated that seventy families were residing in Ste. Genevieve, the number of inhabitants living in the village prior to the end of the Seven Years' War (1763) cannot presently be established with any confidence (Ekberg 1985:41). During the decade following the Seven Years' War, Ste. Genevieve, as well as the fledging village of St. Louis (founded in 1764), experienced a significant increase in population. Ste. Genevieve's population is reported to have reached 691 people by 1772 (Ekberg 1985:46). This increase is attributed in part to the influx of French Catholics from the east bank of the Mississippi who feared religious and political persecution at the hands of the British, following France's loss of that territory to England at the end of the war (McDermott 1949:22).

In 1975 the United States Army Corps of Engineers, St. Louis District, conducted a series of archaeological investigations in conjunction with the congressionally authorized Kaskaskia Island flood protection study. These investigations revealed the first documented evidence of eighteenth-century artifacts being recovered from a *le grand champ* context. Two concentrations of historic debris, approximately eight meters in diameter, were identified. These concentrations were interpreted as possible refuse associated with house patterns (Linder 1975:19). These archaeological remains were discovered in close proximity to the recorded location of a United States Geological Survey benchmark, enigmatically entitled "Vieux Village" (USGS 15 Minute Quadrangle, Weingarten, Missouri, 1907). Subsequent to these investigations, the St. Louis District conducted additional studies in an attempt to determine the historical significance of these remains.

Initially, our investigations suggested that all vestiges of the original town site had been destroyed during the late nineteenth century by lateral movement of the Mississippi River channel. This belief was fostered by the well-documented destruction of the original eighteenth-century French village of Kaskaskia following an 1881 Mississippi River channel shift (Burnham 1914:107). Kaskaskia, like Ste. Genevieve, was on the alluvial floodplain near the Mississippi River channel. Furthermore, previous casual inspection of *le grand champ* had revealed no structural evidence of the former town's existence (Franzwa 1967:51).

However, two early accounts, one from the late nineteenth century and one dating to the early twentieth century, suggested that portions of the original settlement might remain intact as verifiable archaeological deposits. The first of these accounts was recorded in 1881 and reported that recent erosion caused by floodwaters of the Mississippi had exposed a well on the site of the old village (Houck 1908:338). The second was recorded during testimony documenting the destruction of Kaskaskia: "On October 26, 1913, I drove from St. Genevieve (New Town) to old Kaskaskia, passing over the site of the Old St. [*sic*] Genevieve, where nothing but a few pieces of broken crockery can now be found" (Burnham 1914:109). This information suggested that at least some portion of the original village was intact as late as 1913. What remained to be determined was the relation of the ca. 1913 right (west) bank configuration of the Mississippi (in the *le grand champ* vicinity) to that of the present-day Mississippi River channel.

Site Geomorphology

A review of existing navigation maps, hydrographic charts, and aerial photographs provided the basis for reconstructing the recent geomorphological history of *le grand champ*. This effort was structured to determine what, if any, nineteenth-century landforms might still remain intact in the vicinity of the concentrations, and whether these concentrations represented undisturbed features or redeposited artifacts (Norris 1979:10–11).

When the Mississippi River was in its post-Pleistocene valley-cutting stage, the stream slope gradient was slightly steeper than it is today and meandered over the entire width of the floodplain it was forming. As each meander loop was abandoned, a slow deposition of clayey sediments filled the oxbow lakes that evolved from the loops. These meander loops were often situated close to the new bank line and formed a portion of the bank line. These new bank line segments were much more resistant to the erosive stream flows than adjacent portions, which were comprised of relatively unstable sandy materials. These resistant clay loops acted as pivot points about which the river meandered.

In the case of the area surrounding the presumptive location of the original eighteenth-century village site of Ste. Genevieve, it appears to be just upstream of one such resistant, clay-filled meander loop. This factor may have prevented subsequent lateral river migrations from completely destroying the site subsequent to its abandonment. As referenced earlier, records indicated that at least part of the site was being actively eroded by the Mississippi River floodwaters in 1881. The close proximity of the channel to the site at this time can be seen on the 1881/1988 Mississippi River channel overlay (fig. 9-1).

In 1896–97, during the development and maintenance of a ninefoot navigation channel, the U.S. Army Corps of Engineers constructed a number of pile dikes immediately upstream from the village site on the west bank of the river. In addition to increasing channel depth and improving the navigation potential in this reach, this action formed a new land mass on the riverbank, which fortuitously insulated the site from the erosive effects of the mainstream river channel. By 1907 an earthen buffer several hundred feet wide had developed between the Mississippi River and the site. In summary, the results of this archival review indicated that the area upon which this site is situated has probably not been impacted by channel meandering in the recent past. In terms of the subsurface integrity of archaeological properties within this context, this observation is of considerable importance.

On-Site Investigations

These geomorphological data strongly suggested that a field inspection of the area surrounding the "Vieux Village" benchmark location was warranted. The purpose of this inspection was twofold: to confirm the presence and further define the concentrations identified during the 1975 survey, and to determine what, if any, additional features could be discerned on the ground surface surrounding the concentrations.

Systematic field inspections were conducted in 1979. The results of this survey were encouraging. In addition to locating the two original artifact clusters, six additional concentrations were recorded (Norris 1979:10). Surrounding these clusters was a light scatter of artifacts that extended over an area in excess of fifteen hectares (thirty-eight acres).

The written results of these investigations were forwarded to the Missouri State Historic Preservation Officer along with a recommendation for additional fieldwork (Norris 1979). In 1980 the Missouri State Department of Natural Resources funded limited fieldwork at the site. This fieldwork was conducted by the Old Missouri Research

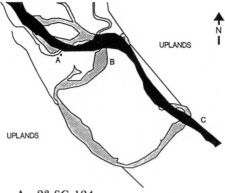

A   23-SG-124
B   Mississippi channel ca. 1881
C   Mississippi channel ca. 1988

Figure 9-1. Relation of Historic (1881) to
Present Mississippi River Channel in
Vicinity of 23-SG-124

Institute, under the direction of Dr. Melborn D. Thurman. To date, a written description of the results of these investigations has not been submitted to the State of Missouri (Michael Weichmann, personal communication, 1990). The results of these investigations are unknown to the author.

During the mid-1980s, additional investigations were conducted at the site by the Corps of Engineers in conjunction with other congressionally authorized flood control projects. This fieldwork ultimately resulted in the identification of a total of ten artifact concentrations and one stone-lined well (fig. 9-2). These concentrations range from three to eight meters in diameter and consist of metal, glass, ceramic (both tin-glazed earthenwares and creamwares), lithic, bone, brick, and limestone rubble fragments. These artifact clusters are interpreted as cultural debris associated with the remains of various types of structures.

Surface collections at the site have now yielded a total of 1,756 artifacts. Virtually *every* artifact group as identified by Stanley South (1977) is represented in these collections. A terminal date of occupation for this site may be suggested by the fine-grade English gunflints, which presumably postdate 1790 in archaeological contexts in the Mississippi River Valley (Hamilton 1980:141). Therefore, their

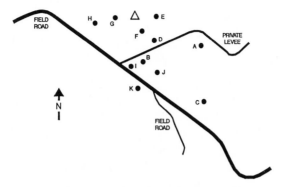

Δ   Approximate location of USGS "Vieux
       Village" benchmark
A-J   Approximate locations of artifact
       concentrations
K   Limestone-lined well

Figure 9-2. 23-SG-124 Feature Distributions

presence in at least three artifact concentrations (fig. 9-2:A, B, J) at
the site suggests an occupation extended at least into the 1790s.

The absence of pearlware ceramics is also suggestive of the relative
age of this site. Although pearlware has been recovered from archaeological contexts dating as early as ca. 1795 in Virginia (Noël
Hume 1970:179), its earliest appearance in archaeological contexts
in the Midwest is approximately 1815 (Price 1979:15). Based upon
the absence of this artifact type from the 23-SG-124 collections, a
terminal date of occupation sometime between about 1790 and 1815
is postulated. This conclusion is consistent with the written record,
which suggests that the original settlement of Ste. Genevieve was
abandoned before the end of the eighteenth century (Ekberg
1985:429).

Feature Distributions
Ten artifact concentrations have now been recorded within the general vicinity of the "Vieux Village" benchmark (fig. 9-2). When considered spatially, these concentrations exhibit an obvious regularity.
The distances between each concentration and the nearest neighbor
are intriguing (table 9-1), when compared with the settlement patterns
at other contemporary sites in the French Colonial District of the
Illinois Country (Briggs 1985).

Although an attempt was made at standardization, published de-

Table 9-1. Artifact Concentrations at 23-SG-124

	Approximate Distance to Nearest Feature	
A:D	440 feet	68.57 *toises*
B:J	160 feet	24.93 *toises*
B:I	155 feet	24.16 *toises*
C:J	500 feet	77.92 *toises*
D:F	150 feet	23.38 *toises*
E:F	165 feet	25.71 *toises*
G:H	180 feet	28.05 *toises*

scriptions of colonial period French residential patterns suggest that, in practice, considerable variation existed among house lot dimensions (Peterson 1949b:200). The most recent analysis of such practices in the Illinois Country was completed in 1985 (Briggs 1985:74–75).

Information presented in the Briggs study was gathered from property deeds of residents within the eighteenth-century parish of St. Anne, located near Fort de Chartres. As part of this study, Briggs postulated a model for standard house lots in the Illinois Country:

> A street-plus-standard lot equals one linear "*arpent*" of thirty "toises" (192 feet). The main streets were approximately 33 feet wide (5 *toises*), leaving 25 *toises* (162+ feet) for the lot. This standard lot was square, 25 *toises* by 25, equivalent to 0.58 English acres, and it accounts for 44 percent of all lots mentioned in documents (59 percent in the post-1739 period). Its existence as a standard is also proved by a reference to a "half-lot" described as being precisely 12½ x 25 *toises*. Each street in the opposite direction; thus from the far edge of one street, across the intervening block, to the far edge of the next street would have been "exactly" two linear *arpents*. . . . In practice, there must have been irregularity because 56 percent of the houselots were of a different size. These others ran through eleven different recorded sizes, the smallest (two) being just over ⅙ of an acre and the largest (two) being 3⅓ acres. The most popular non-standard size was a full square *arpent*, of which there were six. In addition to being residences, these lots were also integral parts of productive establishments. The house was up against the street, often in the corner of the lot, leaving the rest free for barn, stables, oven, orchard, etc. (1985:74–75).

In plan view, such a standard Illinois Country residential lot would appear as presented in figure 9-3.

The postulated width of the Briggs model "average" village lot (25 *toises*, 162 feet) compares favorably with the spatial configuration recorded for artifact concentrations at the Ste. Genevieve site, 23-SG-124. This similarity suggests that the ten artifact concentrations

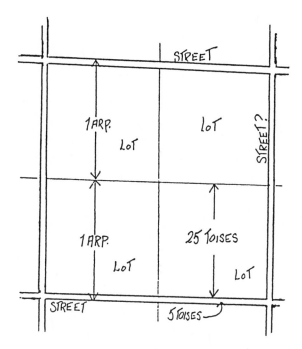

Figure 9-3. "Standard" Illinois Country Village
Lot. Source: after Briggs 1985

on *le grand champ* may not only represent the archaeological remains
of the village, but may also reflect the configuration of a portion of
the village street grid.

With these possibilities in mind, additional archival investigations
were undertaken to further clarify the extent and configuration of
the colonial village and relate this information to the distributions
present at 23-SG-124.

The Cartographic Record

Only six maps are now known to exist that depict the plan view con-
figuration of the original eighteenth-century village of Ste. Genevieve.
These maps are believed to have been drafted in 1766, 1793, 1796,
and 1797. The ca. 1766 map, originally published by Philip Pittman,
is a representation of the entire course of the Mississippi River between
Fort de Chartres (Fort Cavendish) and the Gulf of Mexico (Rea 1973).
The scale of this map is approximately one inch to three leagues (the
English league being equal to three miles). The ca. 1793 map was

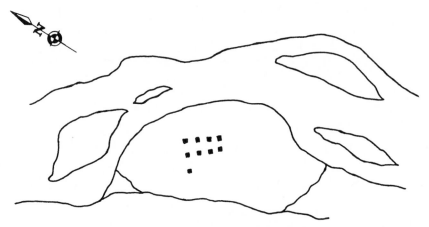

Figure 9-4. Old Town Ste. Genevieve, ca. 1766; interpretation of colonial village as published by Philip Pittman (1770)

recently discovered by Carl Ekberg in the holdings of the New World Archives in Seville, Spain (Ekberg 1987). This unsigned map was apparently created in response to a citizens' petition to incorporate the *village* commons of the original village of Ste. Genevieve into the *agricultural* commons subsequent to the abandonment of the original village (Ekberg 1987:1–3). No scale was included on the map. In 1796 a detailed map (scale: one inch = two miles) of the Illinois Country was prepared under the direction of Gen. Georges Victor Collot (Alvord 1907). Both the original and relocated villages of Ste. Genevieve appear on this map. Another Illinois Country Mississippi floodplain map, closely resembling the Collot map, has also been identified. This map is unsigned and undated but is similar to the Collot map. For the purposes of this study, this map has been labeled "Anonymous 1796." During 1797–98 Nicolas de Finiels, under the direction of Spanish authority, drafted a remarkably detailed map of the middle Mississippi River Valley (Wood 1987:395). The location of every road, structure, and noteworthy landform along a 300-mile reach of the Mississippi River floodplain was shown on this map, including internal plan view details of both the original and the relocated villages of Ste. Genevieve. The scale of the Nicolas de Finiels map is 1.75 inches to 1 league. Plan view interpretations of the village of Ste. Genevieve, as it appears on each of these maps, are presented in figures 9-4 through 9-8. In addition to these original maps, a reconstruction of the village ca. 1777 was compiled in 1982 by David Denman, of the University of Missouri, Columbia (fig. 9-9). This reconstruction is

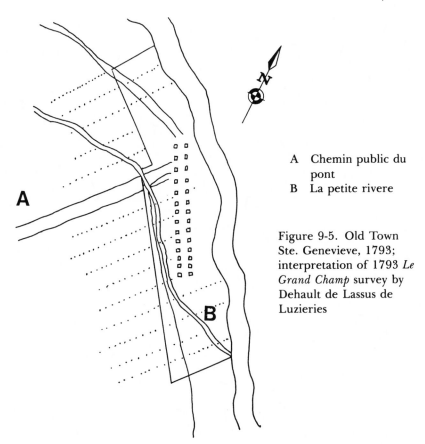

A Chemin public du
   pont
B La petite rivere

Figure 9-5. Old Town
Ste. Genevieve, 1793;
interpretation of 1793 *Le
Grand Champ* survey by
Dehault de Lassus de
Luzieries

based upon the analysis of information contained in deeds, chains of
title, and probate records in the Ste. Genevieve Archives, Ste. Genevieve County, Missouri (Denman, personal communication, 1982).

These maps, recorded over a span of more than thirty years during
the middle and late eighteenth century, represent a valuable source
of information on the changing demographics of the colonial village.
However, the value of each map must be considered in the context
of its original purpose. The image of Ste. Genevieve documented on
both the 1766 (fig. 9-4) and the 1793 survey (fig. 9-5) maps suggests
that, in these examples, the cartographer's emphasis may not have
been to reproduce an accurate record of the internal configuration
of the village, but rather to show only the village's general relation
to other geographic features in the surrounding area. On the other
hand, the Collot (fig. 9-6), Anonymous (fig. 9-7), and de Finiels (fig.
9-8) versions of the village all exhibit considerable internal detail. An

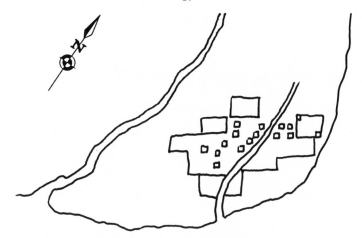

Figure 9-6: Old Town Ste. Genevieve, ca. 1796; interpretation of map prepared by Victor Collot

Figure 9-7. Old Town Ste. Genevieve, ca. 1796; interpretation of anonymous version of Victor Collot's 1796 map

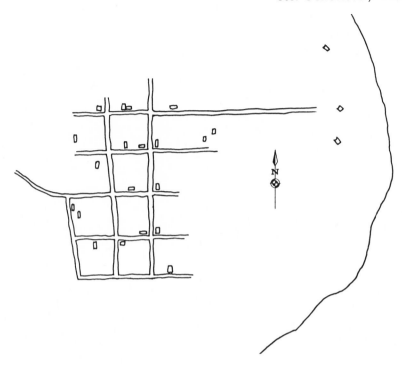

Figure 9-8. Old Town Ste. Genevieve, ca. 1797–98; interpretation of 1797–98 map of the middle Mississippi River by Nicolas de Finiels

example of such differences in intended purpose can be seen on two versions of the village of Kaskaskia (fig. 9-10) originally published in 1770 (Rea 1973:8, 41).

Interpretation of 23-SG-124

Published accounts of the eighteenth century village of Ste. Genevieve describe it as having a linear "string town" configuration (Rea 1973:50). Curiously, only the 1793 survey (fig. 9-5) map suggests such a configuration. The other four eighteenth-century examples of the village portray it as having a more clustered, gridlike configuration.

If the original (ca. 1750–60), linear settlement pattern was the result of an almost exclusively agrarian populace, as suggested by Ekberg (1985:27), then the string town descriptions of the community may be explained by the preference of each family to live on the riverside of its property. The introduction of individuals whose livelihoods were based on pursuits other than farming (e.g., craftsmen and merchants)

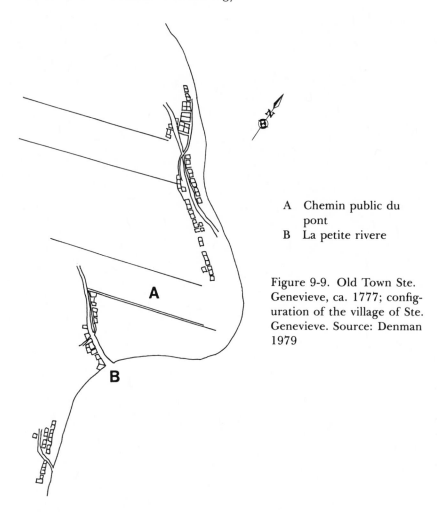

A   Chemin public du
    pont
B   La petite rivere

Figure 9-9. Old Town Ste.
Genevieve, ca. 1777; configuration of the village of Ste.
Genevieve. Source: Denman
1979

following the Seven Years' War may offer an explanation for the
nucleation depicted within the village common on the 1766, 1777
reconstruction, 1796, Anonymous 1796, and 1797–98 plan view maps
of the village.

It has been documented that the village did, in fact, grow considerably following the Seven Years' War (1763), and there is reason to
believe that the linear configuration represented on the 1793 survey
may only reflect a general sketch of the village and surrounding area
and was never intended as a detailed plan view of the village (Ekberg
1987:1–3).

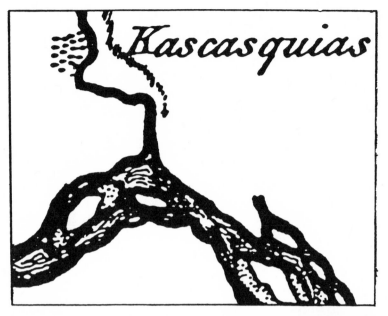

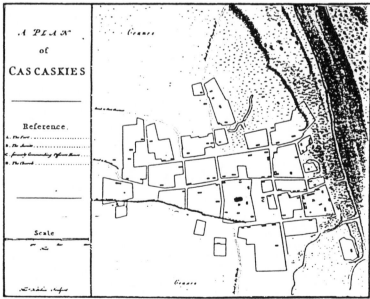

Figure 9-10. Plan Views of Kaskaskia, Illinois Country, ca. 1766; presumably drafted by Thomas Hutchins. Sources: Rea 1973: 8 (*top*), 41

Comparison of the descriptions of the eighteenth-century village of Ste. Genevieve with that of the distributions of artifacts present on the surface of 23-SG-124 is intriguing. The locations of the *arpent* (property) lines, public road (*chemin public du pont*), and *la petite rivere* recorded on both the 1793 map (fig. 9-5) and the Denman reconstruction (fig. 9-9) correlate well with existing landforms in the vicinity of archaeological site 23-SG-124. An analysis of modern and eighteenth-century maps suggests that the present-day Cotton Wood Station field road is in the same location as the *chemin public du pont* recorded on the 1793 map. The swale (linear depression) found today on the western edge of 23-SG-124 corresponds to the former location of *la petite rivere* recorded on both the Denman reconstruction and the 1793 survey map. The relation of 23-SG-124 to these features to those identified in the Denman reconstruction suggests that the site that remains today represents a portion of the south-central area of the original village.

Summary and Conclusions

The results of systematic pedestrian survey on archaeological site 23-SG-124 between 1979 and 1988 have identified ten surface concentrations of eighteenth-century artifacts. The surface area over which these artifacts have been recovered is in excess of fifteen hectares (thirty-eight acres).

Comparison of the spatial relation among these ten concentrations with the recorded dimensions of a hypothetical eighteenth-century Illinois Country residential grid suggest that the archaeological clusters on 23-SG-124 conform to that grid and reflect the original village of colonial Ste. Genevieve. Analysis of eighteenth-century maps and related documents further suggests that these clusters represent the remains of the south-central portion of the village.

The presence of fine English gunflints in three of these clusters and the complete absence of pearlware ceramics from the overall artifact assemblage suggest a post-1790, pre-1815 terminal date of occupation for this site. This date range is consistent with the archival record, which suggests a 1794 date of abandonment (Ekberg 1985:438) for the original location of the village of colonial Ste. Genevieve.

Acknowledgment

I thank Ernest E. Graf for his help and encouragement with the research leading to this chapter.

The Search for French Peoria 10

Thomas E. Emerson and Floyd Mansberger

Early French Canadian history of the sixteenth and seventeenth centuries is an intricate web of fur trade economics, European and Indian politics, and religious fervor that stretched westward along the St. Lawrence and Great Lakes corridor into the interior of North America. The topic of this chapter, the French explorers in the Illinois Country, is only a small part of that greater movement.

In the mid-seventeenth century Canada became a royal province under the government of Louis XIV of France. The final efforts of the private Company of New France and the local Communauté des Habitants to make the colony economically viable had failed. In 1663 Jean-Baptiste Colbert became responsible for the revitalization of the French colonial empire. A major underpinning of his strategies for the colonies was to create an economically diversified union that would benefit the mother country. In Canada such a plan hinged on increasing population and developing industries, agriculture, and commerce. In order to accomplish this it was imperative that the French government consolidate the small Canadian population in the eastern settlements. This, in turn, demanded stricter control of the destabilizing impact of the western fur trade.

Parenthetically, it may have been the very policies of this French colonial administration that created the strong impetus for Canadians to move into the western Great Lakes (Eccles 1969:103–31; Eccles 1972:60–89). This impetus was fueled by two factors: peace and fixed prices. In 1665 campaigns by French regular army forces against the Mohawk restrained the western aggression of the Iroquois Confederacy. This made it possible for traders to bypass the eastern Indian middlemen and deal directly with the western tribes, thereby increasing their own profits. The government later established a guaranteed fixed price for all beaver pelts. Decreased warfare and fixed prices virtually dictated the movement of fur traders and "government-sponsored" exploration parties to the West. Within five years of peace French trading posts were established in Wisconsin and three years later traders had entered the Illinois Country.

Despite the policies of the French government, the Canadian intendant Jean Talon began systematically sending exploratory parties to the western frontier. As part of this effort Louis Jolliet and Father Jacques Marquette were dispatched in 1672 to seek the Mississippi River. In the summer of 1673 the party entered that waterway from the Wisconsin River and proceeded southward to near the mouth of the Arkansas. Having demonstrated that the Mississippi flowed south into the Gulf of Mexico, they retraced their path northward. When they reached the mouth of the Illinois River they entered that stream. They passed through the three narrow lakes at Pimitoui (i.e., now Peoria, Illinois), but no mention of native inhabitants was made until, in the area of Starved Rock, Jolliet and Marquette encountered a village of Kaskaskia containing seventy-four cabins. Promising to return, the French proceeded onward to Lake Michigan. Father Marquette returned to the Kaskaskia village in 1675 to begin the Mission of the Immaculate Conception, dying later on his homeward journey. Father Allouez subsequently joined the Kaskaskia at Starved Rock to continue the mission from 1675 until 1679.

The French and Indians at Lake Pimitoui

Four years later the expedition led by René-Robert Cavelier de La Salle, with the support of the governor general Louis de Buade de Frontenac, entered the Illinois Country. La Salle had been granted the right to establish trading posts and he quickly moved down the Illinois River, past the abandoned Kaskaskia village at Starved Rock, to Lake Peoria or Pimitoui. Here he encountered an Illini village covering both sides of the river and containing several thousand inhabitants. In January 1680 at a point about a league downstream from Pimitoui, La Salle built Fort Crevecoeur. He describes the fort as follows:

> It was a little hillock about 540 feet from the bank of the river; up to the foot of the hillock the river expanded every time that there fell a heavy rain. Two wide and deep ravines shut in two other sides and one-half of the fourth, which I caused to be closed completely by a ditch joining the two ravines. I caused the outer edge of the ravines to be bordered with good chevaux-de-frise, the slopes of the hillock to be cut

down all around, and with the earth thus excavated I caused to be built on the top a parapet capable of covering a man, the whole covered from the foot of the hillock to the top of the parapet with long *madriers* (beams), the lower ends of which were in a groove between great pieces of wood which extended all around the foot of the elevation; and I caused the top of these *madriers* to be fastened by other long cross-beams held in place by tenons and mortises with other pieces of wood that projected through the parapet. In front of this work I caused to be planted, everywhere, some pointed stakes twenty-five feet in height, one foot in diameter, driven three feet in the ground, pegged to the cross-beams that fastened the top of the *madriers* and provided a *fraise* at the top 2½ feet long to prevent suprise. I did not change the shape of this plateau which, though irregular, was sufficiently well flanked against the savages. I caused two lodgments to be built for my men in two of the flanking angles in order that they be ready in case of attack; the middle was made of large pieces of musket proof timber; in the third angle the forge, made of the same material, was placed along the curtain which faced the wood. The lodging of the Recollets was in the fourth angle, and I had my tent and that of the sieur de Tonti stationed in the center of the place (Margry 1879, 2:48–49, as cited in Jelks and Unsicker 1981:4).

In March, the fort almost completed, La Salle departed with a number of men for Fort Frontenac. Shortly thereafter Tonti went upriver to explore the area about Starved Rock. While Tonti was absent the remaining men at the fort deserted, stripping the place of valuables, destroying the fort, and throwing everything they could not take into the river. However, Tonti and his companions remained in the area of the fort with the Illini until September 1680, at which time the appearance of a large war party of Iroquois forced Tonti to return upriver and the Illini to flee downstream.

When La Salle and Tonti returned to the Illinois River in 1682–83 they moved their post to the Grand Village of the Kaskaskia at Starved Rock, where they built Fort St. Louis (see Hall, chap. 2). With the increased security provided by the French the Illini returned to the village, which soon contained over three hundred cabins and members of all the Illini subdivisions. This protection also attracted the Miami and Shawnee, who occupied villages on the north side of the Illinois River near the Grand Village. By 1691–92 the Illini indicated their desire to leave the Starved Rock area due to the difficulty of obtaining firewood. Because the fort, which was perched atop the rock, would have been almost impossible to supply with wood and water during any type of hostilities, the French were amenable to such a move.

That winter the Illini moved their villages to the shores of Lake Pimitoui. At least four to perhaps as many as eleven Illini villages were established in the Peoria area, containing over three thousand people from various tribal subdivisions. Tonti began the construction of a new Fort St. Louis (II, also referred to as Fort Pimitoui or Tonti's Fort) near the Indian villages. Fort St. Louis II consisted of "1800 pickets, had two large log houses, one for lodgings and one for a warehouse, and, to shelter the soldiers, two other houses built of uprights" (Alvord 1922:100). Father Gravier, formerly at Starved Rock, followed the Illini to Pimitoui, where he built a new Mission of the Immaculate Conception near the fort.

In 1700 there was a clash between the Kaskaskia and other groups of Illini that led to the withdrawal of the Kaskaskia to near St. Louis. From that point forward Pimitoui was primarily occupied by the Peoria. Although the military importance of Fort St. Louis declined steadily from about 1700 until 1720 when it was abandoned, a number of French settlers moved into the Lake Pimitoui area. Between about 1722 and 1723 the villages along Pimitoui were temporarily abandoned due to the Fox incursions. By 1756, however, the French had rebuilt a stockade at Lake Pimitoui for protection against the Fox. In 1763 the last of the Peoria left the Illinois River valley and were subsequently replaced by southward-moving groups of Potawatomi, Miami, and Kickapoo.

The presence of Fort St. Louis II and the traders led to the establishment of a small French village along Lake Pimitoui by 1730. This "Old Village" appeared to be occupied almost continuously until the 1790s (figs. 10-1, 10-2, and 10-3), although early documentary references are scarce. The French also apparently maintained some fortifications there until at least 1773, when the fort was burned by Indians. The village was abandoned for a short time during the American Revolution (1781–83). About one hundred inhabitants are reported in the 1800 census for the Peoria vicinity (Alvord 1922:407).

During the late eighteenth century, the "Old Peoria Village" was moved approximately one and one-half miles downstream to a new location (fig. 10-3). The exact location of this new settlement is controversial. According to Coles's 1834 report on the French claims, John Baptist Maillet initiated the move sometime around the year 1788. The village that grew up around his "stockaded fort" became known as La Ville de Maillet. Maillet's fort was described as having at least two blockhouses, one for the storage of trading goods and the other for living quarters (Matson 1874:136). It was burned by

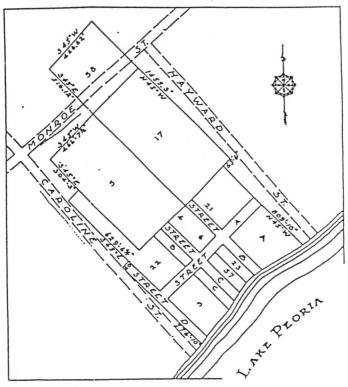

PLAT OF
OLD VILLAGE OF PEORIA
LOCATED

SECTION 3, T8N, R8E OF 4PM.

DRAWN FROM.

SURVEY APPROVED U.S. LAND OFFICE 9-20-1840
BY MAX E. WEBSTER, COUNTY SURVEYOR, PEO. CO.

Old Peorias Fort and Village
Site of Old Indian Village where
Joliet and Marquette Landed in 1673

DRAWN BY-E. BERNARD HULSEBUS-1934

Figure 10-1. Plat of the Old Village of Peoria. Source: Renwick 1934; after Barr, Moore, and Rohrbaugh 1988:9

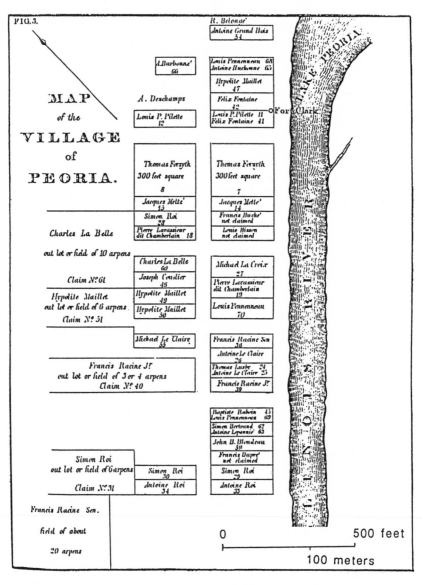

Figure 10-2. Coles's 1834 Plat Map of La Ville de Maillet/New Village of Peoria. Source: after Esarey and Dycus 1986:52

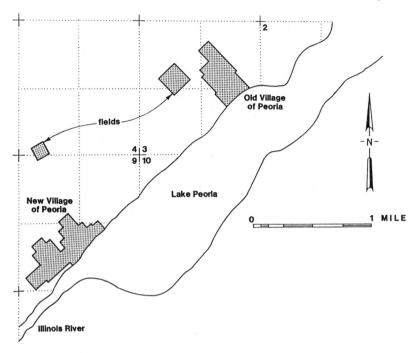

Figure 10-3. Map Showing the Relationship of Old and New Villages of Peoria. Redrawn from the U.S. Government Land Office Survey Plats of 1846.

hostile Indians in 1788. It was in La Ville de Maillet that Thomas Forsyth built a trading post for the American Fur Company in 1806.

Both the Old and New French villages appear to have been organized in the traditional patterns (fig. 10-2). In his work with the French land claims, Coles states:

> As is usual in French villages, the possessions in Peoria consisted generally of village lots, on which they erected their buildings and made their gardens, and of out-lots or fields in which they cultivated grains, etc. The village lots contained in general about one-half of an arpent of land; the out-lots or fields were of various sizes, depending upon the industry or means of the owner to cultivate more or less land. As neither the old nor the new village of Peoria were formally laid out, nor had defined limits assigned them it is impossible to have of them an accurate map (1834:477).

Other descriptions confirm that village structures also followed traditional French patterns of *poteaux en terre* and *poteaux sur sole* construction.

> I saw and examined the ground on which their houses had stood, before the ground was disturbed, and I am able to state that there was not a stone nor brick wall in the village for any purpose, nor was there a cellar. Some of the houses had a small place excavated under the floor, in front of the fire-place, for potatoes. Some of the houses had posts, in the ground; and some were framed with sills; but, in stead of being boarded up as with us, the space between the posts was filled with pieces of timber laid horizontally, with mud between them. The chimneys were made of mud and sticks (Ballance 1870:20).

Due to Indian activity and the beginning of the War of 1812 with Great Britian, several American military expeditions along the Illinois River were conducted against the French and Indians. On 4 November 1812 a group of 200 soldiers under the command of Capt. Thomas Craig arrived by keelboat in Peoria. Approximately forty French villagers were taken prisoner and the village burned. The prisoners were subsequently released near present-day Alton.

In 1813 American troops returned to the destroyed French village and established Fort Clark, named in honor of Gen. George Rogers Clark. Fort Clark was constructed by several hundred men of the First United States Infantry under the command of Lt. Col. Robert Nicholas. Work began in August 1813 and was completed by September of that year. Charles Ballance, an early Peoria resident, describes the fort as follows: "It was constructed by placing two rows of pickets, of round logs, firmly in the ground, and filling the space between them with earth. Around this was a ditch, and at two opposite corners were outworks so constructed as to defend the ditch. Within gunshot, but detached from the fort, was the powder magazine" (quoted in Drown 1844:40).

After the War of 1812 the fort was abandoned. The first Anglo-American settlers arrived in 1819 (Ballance 1870:46–47; Johnson and Co. 1880:280). In 1825 the state of Illinois established Peoria County and a year later the city of Peoria was platted and surveyed.

The Documentary Search

Within three decades of displacing the French inhabitants of La Ville de Maillet, the Anglo-American settlers began the search for their "French" roots. To some extent this effort may have been stimulated by the process of verifying the earlier French land claims. Edward Coles produced a detailed report in 1821 of the French village, which was followed two decades later by a United States Land Office survey that attempted to reconstruct a map of the village layout (figs. 10-1 and 10-2). In 1844 the Peoria town surveyor, S. Drown, produced a city directory and included "an account of the early discovery of the country with a history of the town down to the present time" (fig. 10-3). This account is probably the earliest of the attempts to relocate the first French occupation of Peoria—Fort Crevecoeur (fig. 10-4). Drown (1844:35) placed it near Wesley City on the southeastern shore of Lake Pimitoui (fig. 10-5). Both Francis Parkman (1869:157–58) and Charles Ballance, a local historian (1870:11), supported such a placement.

Near the end of the nineteenth and beginning of the twentieth centuries a new series of investigators became interested in the location of Fort Crevecoeur. In 1890 Major Wightman (Mohlenbrook 1972:23) reported locating entrenchments from the fort three miles northeast

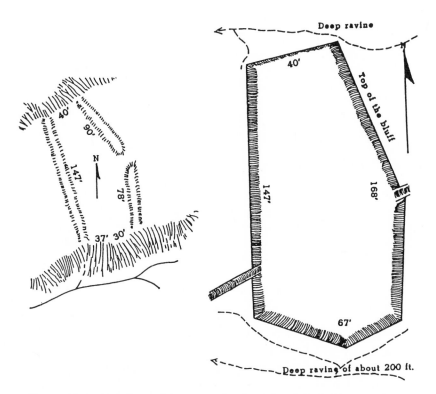

Figure 10-4. Drawings of Apparent Earthworks of Probable Fort Creve-coeur by Drown (1844). Source: after Jelks and Unsicker 1981:15

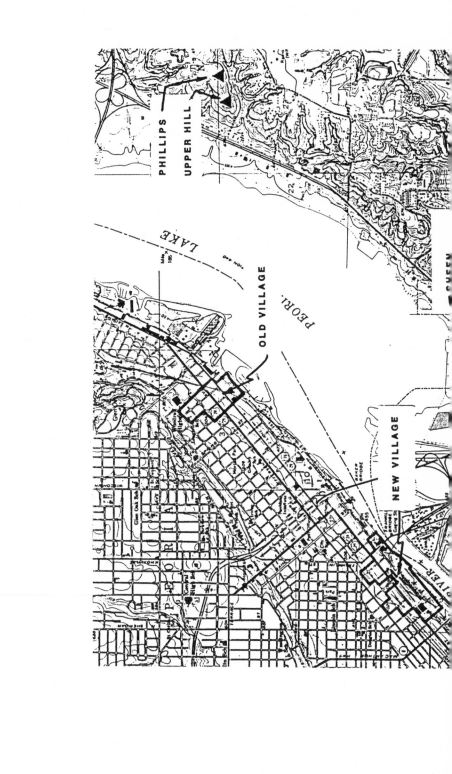

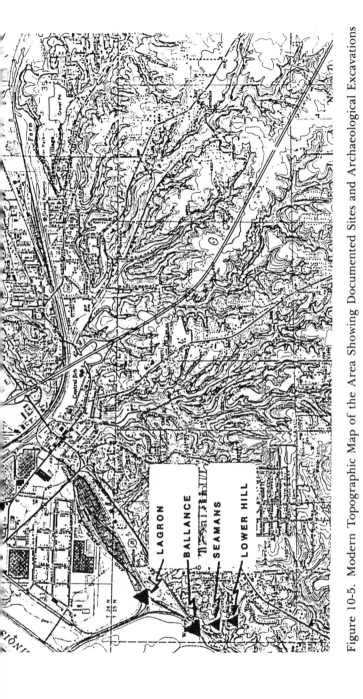

Figure 10-5. Modern Topographic Map of the Area Showing Documented Sites and Archaeological Excavations

of Wesley City (fig. 10-5). In 1902 the Daughters of the American
Revolution entered the search and the documentary research of Ada
MacLaughlin (1902:181) led the DAR to select a site about one mile
south of Wesley City. Efforts by the DAR led to the public acquisition
of this locale. In 1913 Arthur Lagron (1913:451–57) argued that the
fort had been located on land just north of Wesley now destroyed by
the Lake Erie and Western Railroad. A recent proposal by Richard
Phillips (1975:8) placed the fort on the eastern side of the river very
near the area suggested earlier by Major Wightman.

As can be seen there has been no shortage of hypotheses concerning
the location of Fort Crevecoeur, but little results. As Kevin Avery
(1988:99) notes in his review of these documentary efforts, it is clear
from the original sources that the fort was on the southeastern or
eastern shore of Lake Peoria. However, because of the three centuries
of change in the landscape and the lack of specificity in the sources,
Fort Crevecoeur will only be located by extensive archaeological reconnaissance survey of the locality.

While the search for Fort Crevecoeur has had numerous devotees,
unexplicably there has been little interest in relocating the other
French forts and occupations or the associated Indian villages in the
Peoria area. Fort St. Louis II was utilized intensively for almost ten
years and sparsely for another twenty years. Located nearby were as
many as eleven Indian villages with up to three hundred cabins. The
Old French Village and La Ville de Maillet with its structures, fort,
cemeteries, and debris have only in the last few years attracted attention.

The Archaeological Search

During the late 1970s, archaeological investigations were brought to
bear in the search for Fort Crevecoeur and the early French colonial
presence in the Peoria area. Although little has been found to date,
the search is ongoing.

During a few days in the summer and fall of 1977, an archaeological
survey of areas to be affected by the construction of a new roadway
in Fort Creve Coeur State Park was conducted by Illinois State University (ISU) (Jelks and Church 1978). The park is located along the
eastern bluff crest immediately overlooking the Illinois River valley
near the mouth of Lake Peoria and was thought by the DAR to be
the location of Fort Crevecoeur. Although no eighteenth-century
French colonial remains were found, both prehistoric and late nine-

teenth/early twentieth-century historic features were uncovered by the field investigation.

In 1978 Richard Phillips submitted to the Illinois Historic Sites Advisory Council a National Register of Historic Places (NRHP) nomination form for the Upper Hill site—a site he thought was the location of both La Salle's Fort Crevecoeur and Tonti's Fort St. Louis II (see Jelks and Unsicker 1981). Although not questioning the NRHP eligibility of either fort if indeed found, the council "was not convinced from Phillips' presentation that the Upper Hill site actually was the location of either fort" (Jelks and Unsicker 1981:2). In an attempt to validate Phillips's nomination, the Illinois State Historic Preservation Office (at that time in the Department of Conservation) contracted with ISU to investigate the Upper Hill site. After investigations at the Upper Hill site failed to discover evidence of French occupation, the field investigations were expanded to several other purported sites thought to be either Fort Crevecoeur or Fort St. Louis II. Besides the Upper Hill site, seven other locations (Richard Phillips site, Lower Hill site, Lagron site, Sheen site, Seemans site, Ballance site, and the West Bank of the Illinois River) were investigated with disappointing results (fig. 10-5). From these efforts, Jelks and Unsicker (1981:26) concluded that land modification has been excessive on both sides of the Illinois River at Peoria; there is a strong possibility that the area associated with Fort Crevecoeur has been so badly disturbed that the site will never be found; and there is more chance of locating Fort St. Louis II and the associated eighteenth-century village due to its longer occupation and more substantial nature.

In the summer of 1983, the Midwestern Archaeological Research Center (MARC) at ISU conducted a detailed archaeological, architectural, and historical investigation of the proposed Franklin Street Bridge Replacement Project located within both Peoria and East Peoria for the Illinois Department of Transportation (IDOT) (Esarey and Dycus 1986). The western terminus of the proposed bridge was to be located in the vicinity thought to contain the eighteenth-century historic Indian villages, potential burial ground, and the 1788–1812 La Ville de Maillet. As part of the investigations, ten excavation units were dug within the project area. Approximately five test units were placed near what would have been La Ville de Maillet. The excavations uncovered the remains of many mid to late nineteenth-century structural features and indicated that approximately 1–1.75 meters of nineteenth-century fill was present in the project area. In the summer of 1985, additional test excavations were dug within a second alignment for the Franklin Street Bridge Replacement Project (Robinson

1986). Two deep excavation units were placed immediately south of the present Franklin Street Bridge without results and indicated fill sequences as much as 3.8 meters in depth.

Five days of intensive field survey and testing were conducted by ISU in the area thought to be the site of Fort St. Louis II and the Old French Village (Barr, Moore, and Rohrbaugh 1988). This research was funded by a grant from the Illinois Historic Preservation Agency to the Archaeological Committee of the Peoria Historical Society. In 1837 the U.S. Government Land Office, using the testimony taken in 1820 by Governor Coles, surveyed the location of the French land claims. In 1934 Percival Rennick superimposed the 1837 U.S. Government Land Office Survey plat over a modern Peoria street map (Rennick 1934:357). Based on Rennick's work (fig. 10-1), the area bounded by present-day Caroline Street, Monroe Street, Hayward Street, and the Illinois River appears to have been the location of Fort St. Louis II and the Old French Village. Ten town lots were tested in this area. Although a wide range of nineteenth-century cultural remains were found, no eighteenth-century French colonial artifacts were recovered.

This area had been settled by Americans during the 1840s. By 1859–60 a major portion of the potential Old Village had been developed by the Peoria Pottery Company, one of the largest stoneware manufacturers in the United States between the years 1873 and 1900. According to Barr, Moore, and Rohrbaugh "the search for the old village was virtually impossible in the area of the potteries. The associated waster dumps were vast, at least a meter deep and hundreds of square meters in area" (1988:10). Consequently, the ISU investigators avoided the area of the Peoria Pottery. Mid-nineteenth-century descriptions of Fort St. Louis II (and the associated village) place it "about 150 feet above the pottery" (Ballance 1870:27). According to Ballance, the fort was situated on the land then owned by John Birket who, in 1826,

> could trace the lines of said fort by the lower end of the pickets still being there then, and by the earth being higher along the lines of the pickets than elsewhere. Back of this fort was the remains of a smithshop, and near it, in digging up a wild plum-tree, he struck into a considerable quantity of metal, mostly iron, among which were some gun-barrels, the whole having the appearance of having been the stock in trade of a gunsmith, that had long been buried there. Among the rest was some silver plate, which had probably been had to inlay gun-stocks by way of ornament.

Documentary evidence as well as the presence of eighteenth-century artifacts clearly place the site of the Old Village within the area of the Peoria Pottery Company. Future research should concentrate in the area of the Pottery.

During the winter of 1989, Fever River Research (Springfield) conducted a documentary search and architectural evaluation of five city blocks in downtown Peoria (Mansberger 1989). One of the objectives of this research was to assess the earlier occupational history of the project area. Two of the five blocks (Blocks 34 and 37) located within the project area were situated in what was once La Ville de Maillet. As such, potentially significant subsurface resources dating from the 1780s through 1810s were suspected as being within this area and testing was recommended. This project is ongoing and future archaeological testing is anticipated.

Summary and Conclusions

The French colonial and historic Indian sites on Lake Pimitoui near what is now Peoria, Illinois, represent a critical yet untapped historic and archaeological resource. This area was the location of some of the earliest French occupations in the Illinois Country with the founding of Fort Crevecoeur in 1680. Although short-lived, a new and more substantial fort, St. Louis II, was raised in 1691. This was not only a center for the French missonaries and traders but also a major concentration of Illini villages. Although the importance of the fort declined by the 1720s, within a decade there was a nucleus of *habitants* who formed the "Old French Village." This village was inhabited continuously until the early 1790s, when the majority of the population moved about one and one-half miles south to the "new" village or La Ville de Maillet. The French community at Peoria was effectively ended with the burning of the village by Americans in 1812 and the influx of Anglo-American settlers after 1819.

Few sites in Illinois have such a continuous record of occupation and utilization through the exploration, colonization, and creole periods of French history as Peoria (Walthall and Emerson, chap. 1). As the labels of these periods indicate, critical changes occurred during this century and one-half of French domination. In the written record one can perceive the transition of Peoria from a fur-trade outpost to a village and, finally, to the French as a cultural minority overwhelmed by the incoming Americans. However, beyond the broad strokes of this picture we know little. The written records are sparse or have yet to be found, and the material remains are absent. No one can doubt the importance of this encapsulated archaeological record of frontier life, multiple acculturation, and ethnic identity, if it can be found.

Also significant is the large-scale occupation of the Lake Pimitoui region by the various Illini groups. Illini sites are known from the earlier occupations at the Grand Village of the Kaskaskia associated with Fort St. Louis I at Starved Rock and from the later sites around Fort de Chartres in southern Illinois. It is clear that important changes took place in Illini society and culture during the intervening years. The Lake Pimitoui Illini sites could provide important insights into these changes. The yet-undiscovered Illini and French data sets will be important for clarifying the cultural, material, and social inter-relationships of these two societies.

What potential is there for locating these sites? Several key sites that may be found within the Peoria area include Fort Crevecoeur, Fort St. Louis II, the Lake Pimitoui Illini villages, the Old French Village, and the New Village or La Ville de Maillet. The search for Fort Crevecoeur began in the 1840s with such local citizens as S. De Witt Drown and Charles Ballance. The search has gone forward virtually unabated for almost one and one-half centuries, but we are no closer to finding Fort Crevecoeur today. The most likely sites to be found are Fort St. Louis II and the associated Old Village near the present Peoria Pottery site. La Ville de Maillet may also be present, although less likely due to extensive land modifications. There is also an extremely high probability of locating at least some of the associated Illini villages. It is clear that despite the seeming plethora of searches and searchers, there has really been little systematic or intensive attempt to find French Peoria. Such attempts should be of the highest priority for future investigators.

Acknowledgments

The Illinois State Historic Preservation Office (originally in the Department of Conservation and now in the Historic Preservation Agency) has been instrumental through the years in providing both funding and support for a number of efforts to locate French colonial remains in the Peoria area. The Peoria Historical Society, especially the Archaeological Committee of that organization, is commended for its ongoing work.

Frontier Colonization of the Saline Creek Valley

Michael K. Trimble, Teresita Majewski,
Michael J. O'Brien, and Anna L. Price

In 1985 the University of Missouri–Columbia (UMC) initiated a multidisciplinary project in the Saline Creek Valley in Ste. Genevieve County, eastern Missouri, incorporating archaeological survey and testing with archival research. The primary objective of the project was to construct a model of the land-use patterns adopted by Euro-American populations who settled in the Saline Creek Valley (fig. 11-1) from ca. 1720 to 1840 and to examine locational choices made by early settlers. Research specifically focused on settlement distribution and expansion within the Saline Valley, status and ethnicity of valley residents, and commercial organization and development in the immediate region. Discussion here primarily centers on settlement-related issues, because archaeological and documentary data pertaining to status patterning, ethnic origins, and commercial history are still under analysis.

Archival data have been drawn from substantial holdings in archives located in St. Louis and Ste. Genevieve, Missouri; Chester, Illinois; and Seville, Spain. Those holdings thoroughly document the administrative and bureaucratic history of the region during the eighteenth and nineteenth centuries, and as such shed considerable light on Euro-American land-use patterns and material culture in the Saline Creek Valley. Archaeological remains within the region are equally impressive. The Saline Creek Valley is primarily an agricultural region and has experienced little commercial or residential development since the mid-nineteenth century. As a result, numerous minimally disturbed sites and archaeological features dating to the eighteenth and early nineteenth centuries are present and can provide substantial information.

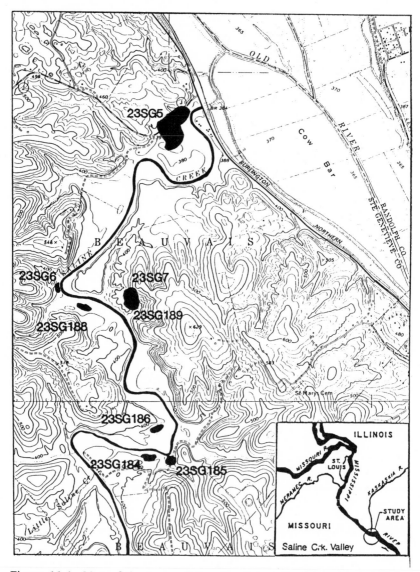

Figure 11-1. Map of the Lower Saline Creek Locality Showing Sites Mentioned in the Text

Documentary History of the Saline

During archival research connected with the Ste. Genevieve Social History Project, undertaken jointly by several departments at UMC, and with the Archaeology of the Saline Creek Valley Project, the UMC Anthropology Department, myriad documents concerning the Saline Valley were located in French, Spanish, and American archives. Records indicate the Saline was an important source of salt for Euro-Americans as early as the 1690s. Dense scatters of shell-tempered aboriginal vessels (St. Mary's Plain, Saline Fabric Impressed, and Saline Plain [Keslin 1964]), commonly referred to as salt pans or evaporation vessels, at four large sites in the Saline Valley (23-SG-5, 23-SG-6, 23-SG-7, and 23-SG-189 [Keslin's (1964) Cornucopia site, originally listed as 23-STG-112]) attest to long-term use of salt by prehistoric groups ca. A.D. 900–1300 (see fig. 11-1).

Two recently discovered maps, one dated 1686 and the other 1797–98, illustrate a Euro-American settlement at the confluence of the Mississippi River and Saline Creek. The 1686 Senex map (located in the Churchill Memorial Library in Fulton, Missouri), labeled in French but drawn in England, documents the presence of some type of Euro-American occupation seventeen years prior to the founding of Kaskaskia directly north of the Mississippi-Saline confluence (Giraud 1953:50–55). The 1797–98 map was prepared by the French cartographer Nicolas de Finiels, and the portion shown here (fig. 11-2) illustrates a sizable settlement with at least eleven structures at the confluence of Saline Creek and the Mississippi River (the Grande Saline community) and three additional structures located up the Saline Valley (the Petite Saline community). On the map, household compounds are represented by rectangles within enclosures. The latter map is of special importance, as a 200–page report was prepared by Nicolas de Finiels to accompany the map in 1803 (see Ekberg and Foley 1989). The report describes area commerce, farming, Indian trade, lead mining, and salt manufacturing associated with the Ste. Genevieve area.

Although maps represent an important data source, numerous early French colonial documents contain information pertinent to the Saline Valley and attest to its local importance in regional trade and commerce. Current research indicates that during the 1720s and 1730s, several prominent local families operated salt works on the Saline, possibly in conjunction with hog-butchering and processing operations (Price 1986).

By the 1740s (but probably earlier) there were strong ties between French exploitation of the Ozark Highland lead deposits and the Saline area. Price notes that Antoine de Gruys Verloins was granted the privilege of continued exploration for lead deposits in the Ozarks. He also held the French concession for the Saline region and in 1752

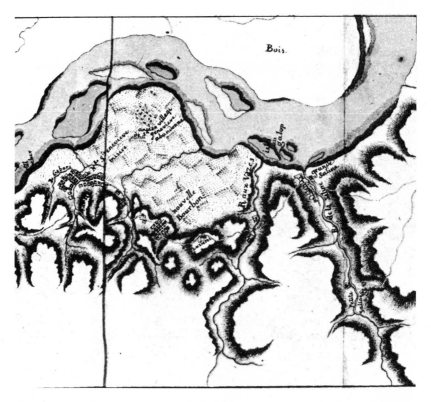

Figure 11-2. Detail of the De Finiels Map Showing the Ste. Genevieve Region: Settlements are depicted at the mouth of Saline Creek (the Grande Saline community) and upstream (Petite Saline community). Source: after Ekberg 1985:437

gained acceptance of salt as a legitimate medium of exchange (Raimond Quenel, Etienne Govreau, and Marie Louise Quenel to de Gruys Verloins, sale of property, 8 February 1752, Kaskaskia Manuscripts [KM 52:2:8:1], Office of Randolph County Clerk, Chester, Illinois). Price suggests this event marked an important change in ownership and exploitation of the salt springs in the Saline Valley. Other mediums of exchange such as flour and furs were risky, as was Louisiane's colonial currency, which was plagued by speculation, irregularities, and excesses (Pease and Jenison 1940:746–77, 858–59). Salt production, relatively unhampered by any of these factors, offered an attractive alternative. In addition, since only a limited number of individuals could exploit the resource at any one time, supply could be controlled and a steady rate of exchange maintained. Thus by controlling the concession at the Saline, de Gruys Verloins virtually acted as mint and banker in the Illinois Country, with little fear that his credit rating would drop, and capitalized on the complementary nature of seasonal lead-mining and salt-production operations (Price 1986).

Documents dating from the period 1750–90 provide significant insights into the development of the Saline and transactions that were carried out. Many documents tie landholdings or salt production to prominent residents of the area. Examples include a sale of property at the Saline by Jean Lagrange to Daniel Blouin (24 May 1766, KM 66:5:24:1); the 1782 estate inventory of François Vallé and Marianne Billeron (St. Louis Archives, Missouri Historical Society [MHS], St. Louis, and the microfilm collection of these archives — C3636 — located in the Joint Collection, Western Historical Manuscripts–State Historical Society of Missouri, University of Missouri, Columbia [hereafter SGA]); and the sale of the Saline by Datchurut to Peyroux (11 December 1787, Mines Collection, SGA 386). Information contained in the records offers insights into material wealth and ethnic identity of persons connected with salt production and agricultural pursuits. In part these documents provide information and descriptions of residential structures and other buildings along the creek and describe land sales, litigations, and contracts pertaining to the Saline locale. Importantly, documents also list and describe portions of the physical nature of the salt works (e.g., the number of employees, kettles, and pumps and furnace size and number). Illustrative examples include the sale of items related to salt making by de Grandpre to de Gruys Verloins (KM 44:2:17:1) and an agreement between François Vallé, Bernard Laulhé, Henry Carpentier, and Joseph Tellier for the operation of a pump at the Saline (21 August 1776, Mines Collection, SGA 386).

By 1786 salt from the Saline Valley was attracting commercial interest outside the region. In that year fifteen volunteers from Harrod's Company in north-central Kentucky visited the works to purchase salt (James 1912:69–70). Although ownership and control of the Saline remained in French hands throughout the colonial period, by 1780 Anglo-Americans began to dominate the labor force operating the Saline and necessary subsidiary industries. The names of Anglo-Americans abound in the SGA Litigation Collections and in the Land Petition Papers Collection, MHS (e.g., coopers, wainwrights, and carpenters). The best source, however, is the 1797 census of New Bourbon and its dependencies, which lists among the forty-one adult white males residing at the Saline three French, three Canadians, two Creoles, twenty-nine Americans, one Scot, and three Irishmen. Of those involved in salt production, eight are listed as American, and two are identified as being Irish. Other occupations listed in the census include farmer, day laborer, hunter, blacksmith, iron merchant, gunsmith, carpenter, and cooper (Papeles de Cuba, legajo 2365, folio 345, Archivo General de Indias [AGI], Seville, Spain).

By 1800 the population in the Saline community apparently was predominately Anglo-American in ethnic origin, and considerable trade had developed with the Cumberland Valley in Tennessee (Alvord 1922:359). By the late 1790s Anglo-American interests in the Saline were dominating French salt production. Anglo-American ideals of free trade and maximization of resources were at odds with the corporate French mentality, which stressed production control and the creation of monopolies to regulate the value of a commodity (see Mousnier 1970; Sewell 1982). A marked rise in litigations (see SGA) concerning the Saline from 1797 to the end of the colonial period suggests that trade and ethnic conflict were accentuated by the early nineteenth century.

To this point we have treated the Saline Valley as a single entity, although documents and cartographic sources, primary among which is the 1797–98 de Finiels map, identify two primary salt-production/occupation loci: the Grande, or Vieux, Saline, located at the Mississippi confluence, and the Petite Saline, located approximately three kilometers upstream from the confluence (see fig. 11-2). Although the Grande Saline community appears to have been the primary production area, the contribution to the production of salt by the Petite Saline community cannot be ignored. Based on archaeological survey and documentary research, two potential locations for the Petite Saline community have been identified (see below).

A considerable amount of timber was needed to fire the salt furnaces, and by 1787 salt production at the Grande Saline had increased to the point that the then-principal landowner, Henri Peyroux, petitioned Spanish officials for additional land to ensure sufficient timber for the "great consumption of the Saline" (American State Papers 1860, 7:804–5). This concession, which enclosed 7,760 arpents (one arpent is roughly equivalent to 0.85 acre), extended a considerable distance to the north and west of the Grande Saline community (surveyors' maps of Peyroux's concession, one in Amoureaux-Bolduc Papers, MHS; another in Mapas y Planos de Florida y Luisiana, no. 197, AGI; cover letter for latter map, Papeles de Cuba, legajo 2365, folio 523, AGI). As the tempo of salt production increased during the

1790s, even that vast tract of timber was depleted. Apparently Peyroux sold off small plots of land to Anglo-Americans employed at the Saline (e.g., sale of property, Henri Peyroux to Anthony Blainey and William McCan, 27 January 1798, SGA 63). Information concerning these small landholdings is limited and reveals few details about the owners and their activities. By 1787 wood had become so scarce that at least one other individual involved in salt production at the Grande Saline was forced to petition for additional land farther up the Saline. Jean Baptiste Pratte claimed a grant of 7,056 arpents from which he procured wood to fire his salt works. By the late 1790s the salt trade had become so lucrative that extraction began at a second salt spring — commonly referred to as the Petite Saline.

Results of archaeological work undertaken in 1987 indicate that Euro-American occupation along Saline Creek was tied to resource extraction (e.g., salt production). At least two sites, depicted on the de Finiels map in the Aux Vases River Valley, just north of the Saline Valley, may represent maple-sugar production locales, as documentary sources indicate the Aux Vases Valley as the predominant sugar-producing area, although some was processed in the Saline Valley as well (see fig. 11-2). Maple sugaring appears to have flourished beginning during the 1790s, possibly as a result of an increase in maple-sap production resulting from cooler temperatures associated with the Neoboreal climatic episode. Many illustrative references occur in the Missouri State Archives (Jefferson City), Land Confirmed Claims, Minute Books (e.g., Minute Book 1:315–17, 225, 318, 349).

Despite competition from other salt-production enterprises after the 1790s, production along the Saline continued unabated into the 1830s, in part because of its favorable location on a major transportation route (Denman 1979). Another factor that contributed to continued production at the Saline was that between 1804 and 1830 the Saline was controlled by Pierre Menard, a wealthy Kaskaskia merchant and Indian agent. In partnership with the influential Vallé family of Ste. Genevieve, Menard used salt as one of the cornerstones of his trade with the Shawnee and Delaware. (Correspondence between 1819 and 1833 found in the Pierre Menard Papers [Illinois State Archives, Springfield] offers abundant proof of the nature and scope of the Indian trade with regard to the partnership of Menard and Vallé. Ledgers from the same collection offer further proof of this. Additional papers that pertain to the firm of Menard and Vallé are located in the Chicago Historical Society.) Gradually, as the tribes moved west and other salt-production operations in Missouri and Illinois boomed, extraction along the Saline ceased, and the thriving community at the Grande Saline was abandoned.

An Archaeological Perspective on the Saline Creek Valley

In 1985 UMC initiated a program of archaeological field reconnaissance and testing in the Saline Valley (see fig. 11-1). Our primary goal during year one was to survey and test an area—the Kreilich site (23-SG-5)—thought to contain the remains of the earliest French occupation in the valley. The 1986 field season focused on excavation of a residential feature identified at the site the previous year. In 1987 intensive surface reconnaissance of 1,500 acres along the lower portion of the Saline Creek Valley was undertaken to develop baseline data on land-use history in the drainage. During the course of the survey, nineteen previously recorded sites were revisited, and thirty-one new sites were identified and recorded (sixteen prehistoric, eight historic, and seven multicomponent [prehistoric-historic]).

THE KREILICH SITE (23-SG-5)

Archaeological work at the Kreilich site was designed to examine three locales on the site: an area containing a series of salt furnaces and ash piles (labeled Areas I–III in figure 11-3), an area just southeast of the furnaces (labeled Area IV in figure 11-3), and an area that was thought to contain potential residential features based on configurations noted on the de Finiels map (labeled Area V in figure 11-3).

Areas I–III

Three salt furnaces were identified to the west of the salt spring depicted in figure 11-3, one of which was excavated partially in 1985 to examine its design and construction. However, it is impossible at this time to determine whether or not the three furnaces were contemporaneous, due to the paucity of diagnostic artifacts in the deposits and the fact that heavy vegetation precluded testing the other identified furnaces.

The rectangular furnace measured 8.2 meters east-west by 6.4 meters north-south. The limestone walls of the feature had collapsed and at the time of excavation averaged a little less than one meter high. The south and east walls of the furnace were exposed during the excavation (fig. 11-4); the south wall averaged 1.1 meters wide and the west wall 0.65 meters. Although the north wall was not exposed completely, the north and south walls appear to have been

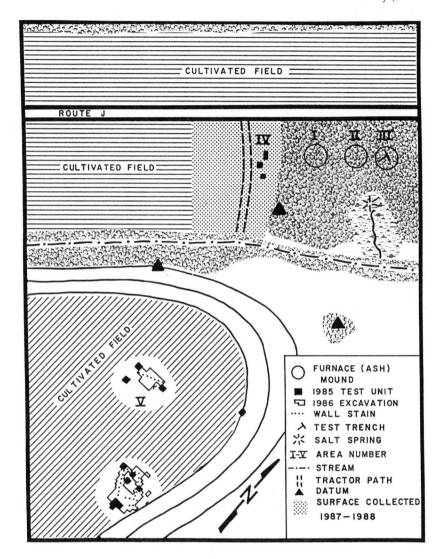

Figure 11-3. Locations of Archaeological Work at the Kreilich Site
(23-SG-5)

designed and constructed to have greater widths than the east and
west walls.

The furnace was constructed of rough-dressed limestone blocks
varying in size and shape (fig. 11-5). Decomposed mortar used to

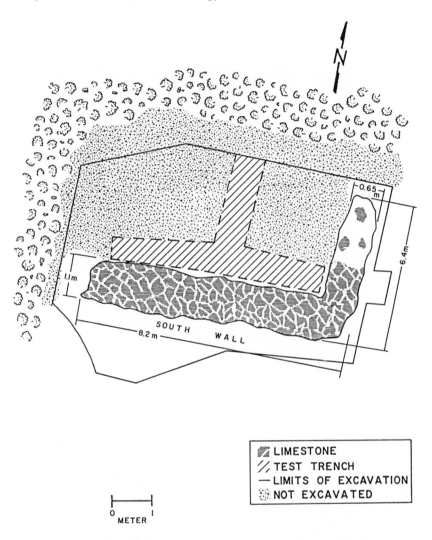

Figure 11-4. Plan View of South and East Walls of Partially Excavated Furnace (Area III) at 23-SG-5

cement the limestone blocks in place was identified in situ. After exposing the south and east walls, two trenches were placed in the interior of the furnace. One trench was oriented to parallel the south wall, and the other trench was positioned at the midline of the furnace and spanned its width (see fig. 11-4). Trenches were hand excavated

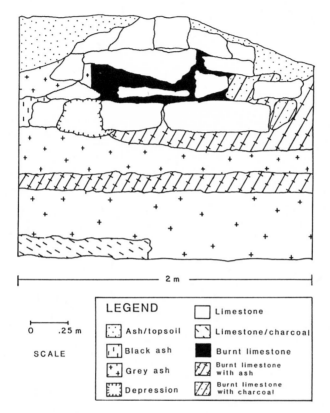

Figure 11-5. Profile of 1.5-meter Section of South Wall
of Furnace Showing Limestone Construction (23-SG-5)

to a depth of one meter, although the deposits extended deeper. Cast-iron kettle fragments recovered from the interior of the furnace were the only Euro-American-manufactured materials found. Kettles used in the furnaces no doubt experienced metal fatigue due to intense heat, resulting in metal fracture.

To understand the design and construction sequence of the furnace, a one-meter by two-meter unit was excavated to a depth of 1.8 meters—the base of the exterior of the east wall. The resulting stratigraphic profile indicates at least four episodes of rebuilding or repair in the construction history of the furnace (fig. 11-6): two along the south wall and four along the east wall. The sequence contains alternating layers of fire-cracked limestone rubble and a mixture of ash and soil.

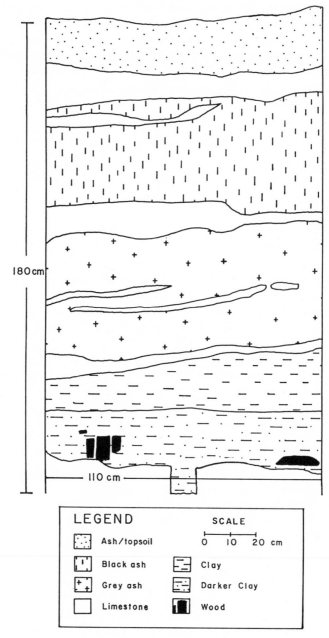

Figure 11-6. Profile of East Wall of Furnace Showing Construction Sequence (23-SG-5)

It appears that the lower courses of the limestone walls deteriorated from heat stress, as they were fractured more extensively than the upper courses were. As this deterioration proceeded, the furnace walls became structurally unsound. Then, intact blocks were removed and a cap of ash and soil mixture was placed over the fire-cracked rubble to prepare a new, level foundation. The wall then was rebuilt on top of the repaired foundation.

Area IV

Area IV (fig. 11-3) is located approximately thirty meters west of the furnace complex. Surface collection in the area yielded large quantities of musket balls, gangmolds, and lead spall. Placement of four test units was based on areas of highest surface artifact density. One unit contained a single burial with associated historic grave goods (a Micmac pipe and three silver tinklers). The remaining three units contained numerous artifacts associated with lead processing (e.g., musket balls and spall).

Analysis of recovered Euro-American cultural materials indicates that the lead-processing area was in use during the late eighteenth and early nineteenth centuries. Temporally diagnostic ceramics include creamwares and early pearlwares. However, shovel testing in Area IV in 1987 recovered four types of French faience — Normandy Plain, Normandy Blue on White, Brittany Blue on White, and Rouen Plain — indicating that occupation and use of the area may have begun as early as the first half of the eighteenth century (Walthall 1991).

Area V

Area V (fig. 11–3) is on a small knoll located approximately forty meters southwest of the salt spring and furnace complex (Areas I–III) on the south side of a wooded east-west-trending drainage. Cultural debris was scattered across a cultivated field encompassing approximately two hectares of the knoll, which rises three or four meters above the present floodplain. As mentioned earlier, the de Finiels map depicts a small community of approximately eleven structures and enclosures, some of which appear to have been on the knoll.

Initial archaeological work included piece-plotting surface materials and limited testing to identify artifact concentrations representing possible structural features related to the early settlement of the salt-spring locale. Four high-density concentrations of Euro-American artifacts (mainly ceramics and metal) were mapped (fig. 11-7). Ceramics collected included undecorated and handpainted creamwares, edge-decorated and handpainted pearlwares, salt-glaze stonewares, Chinese

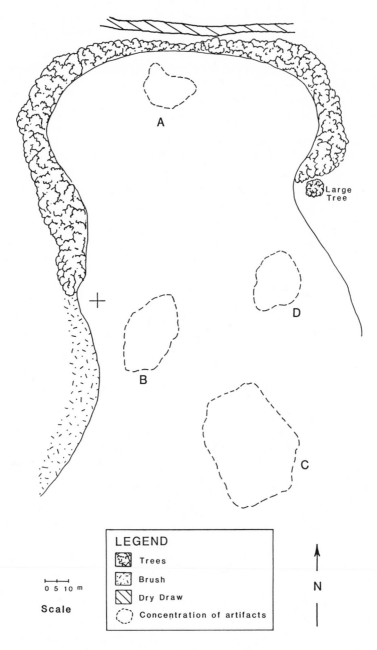

Figure 11-7. Locations of Surface Artifact Concentrations Defined in Area V (23-SG-5)

export porcelain, and small amounts of faience. The artifacts suggest that the knoll was occupied most intensively from approximately 1750 to 1820.

In 1985 four two-meter-square units were placed in Concentration B and seven in Concentration C. Two subplowzone archaeological features were identified in Concentration C: a deposit of rough-cut limestone blocks and a builder's trench/linear feature.

Concentration B. Although four units excavated in 1985 produced no evidence of structures in Concentration B, surface artifact density suggested some type of intense activity at the location. Excavations in 1986 exposed a linear, dark stain at the plowzone-subsoil interface. The dark brown to black feature was oriented roughly east-west across the knoll and a 2.9 meter segment was exposed (fig. 11-8). The U-shaped trench averaged 24 centimeters in depth and 22 centimeters in width. Along the length of the feature were postmolds spaced at uneven intervals and occurring on both sides of the trench. The one

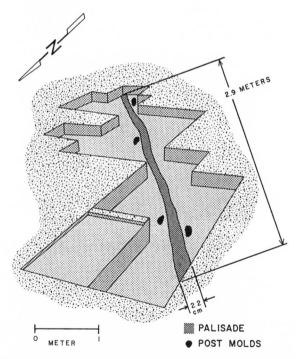

Figure 11-8. Plan View of Palisade Located in Concentration B (23-SG-5)

excavated postmold was 52 centimeters deep (from the ground surface) and 31 centimeters in diameter.

Historical descriptions of early French colonial houses discuss palisades or fences surrounding house lots (Brackenridge 1868; Peterson 1949a). Although the excavations in Concentration B were limited, the evidence suggests that the linear feature may be the remains of a palisade trench. The circular postmolds located on either side of the linear stain appear to have contained supporting posts for the palisade.

Concentration C. Major work undertaken during 1986 was the excavation of a rectilinear *poteaux en terre* feature in the southern portion of Area V (fig. 11-3). The northern trench was 6.6 meters long, averaged 53 centimeters wide (fig. 11–9), and extended an average of 37 centimeters below the base of the plowzone. Two major artifact classes were recovered from the fill of the wall trench. Hand-forged nails were located along the midline of the north wall, approximately 10 centimeters below the plowzone-subsoil interface. Several small

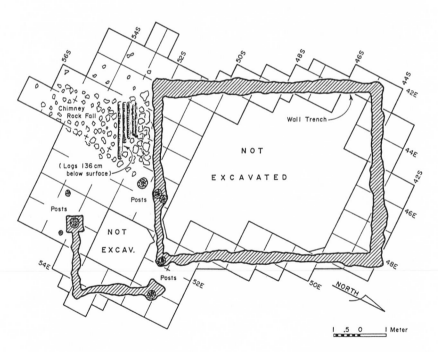

Figure 11-9. Plan View of *Poteaux en Terre* Structure Excavated in Concentration C (23-SG-5)

pieces of limestone (10–15 centimeters long) were found near the base of the trench. The circular arrangement of several pieces of limestone suggests they may have been placed along the base of posts to assure the uprights remained vertical. This configuration suggests the feature represents a builder's trench for a *poteaux en terre* structure.

A series of two-meter-square units was excavated to expose the east and west wall trenches. The west wall trench was 8.7 meters long, averaged 47 centimeters wide, and extended an average of 37 centimeters below the base of the plowzone. Several clusters of irregular-shaped pieces of limestone were found positioned along the base of the west wall trench, which terminated at the southern end of the structure under limestone chimney-fall rubble (fig. 11-9). The east wall trench of the structure was 8.6 meters long, averaged 36 centimeters wide, and extended an average of 29 centimeters below the plowzone base. A large slab of limestone found at the base of the wall trench at the juncture of the eastern and southern walls probably functioned as a brace for the corner of the structure.

An enigmatic feature associated with the structure was an L-shaped wall trench paralleling the southeast corner of the main structure (fig. 11-9). The apex of the lower arm of the "L" is one meter due east of the southeast corner of the main structure and extends 3.5 meters to the south, where it turns west for 3.2 meters, approximately one meter from the south wall. Two large postmolds were found at either end of the feature, and several creamware sherds were recovered from the bottom of the feature.

Defining the south wall of the main structure was difficult, as fireplace and chimney-fall rubble along and in the south end of the structure obscured the feature. The southeast corner of the structure was defined easily, as was 3.6 meters of the east portion of the south wall. Dark organic soils from the apparent fireplace and cellar area (discussed below) partially obscured the remaining portion of the wall trench. However, the majority of the south wall was visible and has been reproduced in figure 11-9. Test trenching of the cellar feature later revealed the size and configuration of the wall trench in profile. Based on the portion of the south wall trench excavated, the width of the trench averaged 39 centimeters, with an average depth of 37 centimeters. Estimated length of the wall is considered to be the same as the north wall trench, 6.6 meters. Limestone rubble and a large area of dark, organically stained soil were encountered, suggesting that the fireplace and chimney were located at the end of the feature. The chimney and fireplace appear to have collapsed to the west, parallel to the south wall of the structure.

Below the rubble, outside the southwest corner of the structure, a large cowbell, the base of a large cauldron, and several hundred fragments of animal and bird bone were recovered. The faunal assemblage includes the remains of cow, pig, horse, goat, deer, wild turkey, mallard duck, and rat. Domestic pig represents the largest part of the assemblage, and butchering marks are present on cow and pig elements. Almost all pig elements identified belonged to animals killed at about two years of age.

A dark brown, rectangular stain measuring 3.2 meters north-south by 3.3 meters east-west was defined below the chimney/fireplace rubble. The stain was located adjacent and parallel to the south wall trench, slightly offset to the west of center. Test excavations and soil probing indicated a depth of 1.4 meters for the feature and fill consisting of rubble and artifacts. Two one-meter-wide trenches were excavated to bisect the feature on the north-south and east-west axes. Feature fill consisted of limestone rubble, historic ceramics, brass buttons, bones, plaster, gun parts, a spoon, and metal.

A floor of parallel cedar poles positioned in a checkerboard fashion (fig. 11-10) was encountered at the base of the feature. Seven poles were oriented along a southeast-northwest axis, and three poles were positioned below the seven (as supports) and were oriented southwest to northeast. This rectangular pit feature appears to represent a small, floored cellar. It was constructed adjacent and parallel to the south wall of the structure and appeared to undercut slightly the southern wall trench. The cedar beams probably served as a rudimentary floor for keeping stored items off the dirt floor.

Martin's (1985:79) discussion of structure 1 at the Mill Creek site in Michigan is informative regarding cellar construction in *poteaux en terre* structures. He reports the presence of a shallow cellar that extended 5 ft beneath the floor of one room of the structure. The cellar measured 14 feet by 9 feet and contained a large volume of fill. This description generally conforms to the cellar partially excavated in Area V, although the cellar at 23–SG-5 was smaller in all dimensions.

Although wraparound porches, or galleries, are common elements of French architecture, test excavations placed outside of the rectangular builder's trench failed to locate any evidence of attached architectural features.

The ceramic assemblage recovered from surface collections and excavations in area V exhibits the greatest variation of any subarea assemblage from 23-SG-5. Included in the assemblage are examples of undecorated, handpainted, and bat-printed creamwares; underglaze blue transfer-printed, handpainted, and blue and green shell-

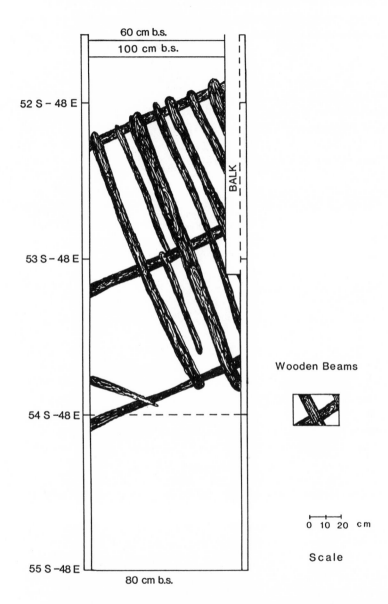

Figure 11-10. Plan View of Cedar Logs Positioned at Base of Probable Cellar at the Southern End of the *Poteaux en Terre* Structure (23-SG-5)

edge (rococo and scalloped) pearlwares; Chinese export porcelain; Jackfield; and undecorated faience (fig. 11-11). The presence of these ceramics indicates a date range for the *poteaux en terre* structure between ca. 1775 and 1810.

OTHER SITES IN THE LOWER SALINE VALLEY

Other sites examined in the lower Saline Valley include salt furnaces, residential areas, possible maple-sugar production sites, and combi-

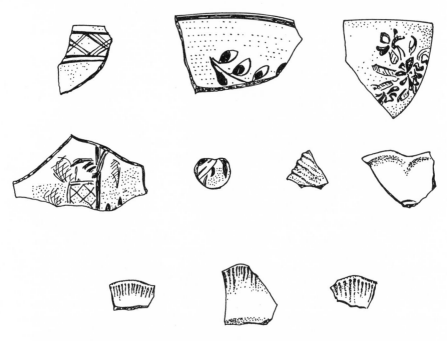

Figure 11-11. Ceramic Sherds from 1985-86 Excavations at 23-SG-5: *top,* cobalt-blue handpainted underglaze decoration in oriental style, bowl-rim interior, pearlware; cobalt blue handpainted underglaze decoration in oriental style, saucer-rim interior, pearlware; blue, red, green, yellow, and brown handpainted overglaze floral decoration, cup-rim exterior, creamware; *middle,* green and brown handpainted overglaze enamel decoration in oriental style, interior plate-base sherd, creamware; gaming piece made from plate sherd with reddish-brown handpainted overglaze enamel decoration on interior, creamware; press-molded teapot-spout fragment, creamware; plate with molded rim, "Royal" pattern interior, creamware; *bottom,* green "rococo"-style, shell-edge plate rim, interior pearlware; two blue "rococo"-style, shell-edge plate rims, interior, pearlware.

nations thereof. Site 23-SG-184 is a salt-production area lacking associated residential or other activity-oriented features and is characterized by a scatter of limestone and iron-kettle fragments. The site was cleared in this century for cultivation, and two field piles containing limestone slabs and kettle fragments are located on the edge of the field. The site may be associated with site 23-SG-185, a possible occupation located to the east and across a small drainage from 23-SG-184. Ceramics, predominantly of English manufacture (e.g., creamwares, blue transfer-printed and handpainted pearlwares), date 23-SG-185 to approximately 1790–1820. A metal drill bit dating from the mid-1700s was also recovered, suggesting a possible earlier date for an occupation. These two sites may represent isolated structures depicted on the de Finiels map (fig. 11-2).

A possible salt furnace or maple-sugar production site (23-SG-186) is located to the north of site 23-SG-185, across Saline Creek. The site dates to approximately 1795–1840. The site was identified on the basis of a small scatter of kettle fragments, shell-edge ceramics (scalloped rim), glass, brickbats, and small limestone fragments located on the surface of a large, dark organic stain. Unlike other salt-furnace sites in the valley, there are no large, semidressed limestone slabs on the site, nor are there any field piles along the margins of the cultivated field.

A small site (23-SG-188) containing depressions, stone foundations, and a single salt furnace appears to represent a short-term salt-production site. Although the ceramics (handpainted and blue shell-edge pearlwares, undecorated and handpainted creamwares, and Chinese export porcelain) predominantly date from ca. 1790–1810, a document in the Ste. Genevieve archives almost certainly refers to the site. The document records a sheriff's sale of "a certain tract of land containing 60 arpen[t]s . . . on Saline Creek in the same district adjoining the Upper Saline" (4 March 1811, Land Record Book, pp. 119–20, SGA). The following features are listed: a salt well, a "good" dwelling house, kitchen, counting house, and stone spring house. Archaeological features on the site include a salt furnace, two stone foundations, three depressions, and a rock alignment with associated depression.

Another site representing early exploitation and occupation of the valley is 23-SG-7, the Cole site. Originally reported by Keslin (1964) as the Cole site and the Fortnight site, the two sites represent a continuous scatter of historic materials and features relating to the production of salt and associated residential activities. Numerous surface features are present in four distinct areas. Keslin's Fortnight site

(23-SG-7, Area A) exhibits stone-chimney fall, a rock alignment, and a high-density surface scatter of historic materials. The area is on a plateau above an area containing nine furnaces, ash piles, and associated features (sixteen total features). Ceramics, metal fragments, kettle fragments, and limestone slabs occur in high frequencies across the site. A single fragment of British delftware (tin-glazed earthenware), dating from the last quarter of the eighteenth century, was collected from the plateau. Most of the other ceramics from the site are lead-glazed refined earthenwares of English origin that date from the 1790s to the 1820s. The assemblage includes undecorated and handpainted creamwares; handpainted, transfer-printed, and edge-decorated pearlwares; and Chinese export porcelain.

The Cole/Fortnight site represents one potential location of the Petite Saline community referred to in documentary sources. The de Finiels map depicts a configuration of three isolated households on the upper Saline with an identification of the "Petite Saline" nearby (fig. 11-2). Considering their location vis-à-vis one another, sites 23-SG-184, 23-SG-185, and 23-SG-186 may represent the three isolated structures labeled "Petite Saline" on the de Finiels map. However, documentary sources suggest that the Petite Saline designation represents a much larger community than that containing the three isolated sites. The Cole site may, in fact, represent this community, or a major part of it, as it is much larger and contains a much higher frequency and diversity of cultural materials. When the road system depicted on the de Finiels map is compared with the road system depicted on a 1922 USGS topographic map, the three isolated structures appear to best fit the location of the community. We believe the Petite Saline community referred to in documentary sources represents a dispersed, conglomerate community below the forks of the Saline rather than a single, closely knit community.

Summary

To date, our investigation has indicated that there is no single attribute that clearly differentiates a French colonial archaeological site from a structurally similar site of different ethnic origin. Simply put, we have been unable to discover an archaeological signature for French colonial sites in the Saline Creek Valley. Where a French architectural style can be identified, such as at site 23-SG-5, a predominance of English-made ceramics exists. Where a French household pattern is depicted on the de Finiels map at the location of one of the sites that may comprise the Petite Saline "community" (23-SG-185), English ceramics and a French gunflint were recovered together in the same excavation unit, at the same level. It is our contention that faience is not necessarily an indication of French ethnicity, nor does French architectural style make a site French. Shovel testing and surface collection to the north, west, south, and northwest of the metal-working area at 23-SG-5 (fig. 11-3) produced more faience than did any other area in the valley. That particular area of the site holds promise for investigating early French occupation of the Grande Saline community.

It is our opinion, based on the limited investigation to date, that settlement patterns in the Saline Valley differ from those in areas immediately surrounding the towns of Kaskaskia and Ste. Genevieve. In particular, we see land use and settlement of the valley as having been tied to the exploitation of specific, often seasonally exploited resources (e.g., salt and sugar maples) and not simply to agricultural pursuits.

It could be argued that settlement and land use were influenced by the issuance of two major land grants in the lower valley, which precluded the establishment of small freeholds. However, our assessment based on documentary evidence is that Peyroux's control over his land grant was minimal. A 1798 land-concession document (4 February 1798, Land Concession, 1759–1805, folder 86, SGA) is instructive regarding land acquisition for the express purpose of maximizing extraction of resources. The translated summary of the document reads:

> [Etienne Bolduc and Louis Bolduc, brothers] having wife, children, and slaves . . . desire to establish each his own habitation on a place safe from the floods, and suitable for the cultivation of various produce needed for the livelihood of their families all year-round and particularly feed for their animals during the winter. They located two tracts [on the south fork of the Saline], quite close to each other and *suitable for different purposes.* . . . [T]he said grants will enable them to establish themselves there and cultivate the land which will be suitable; as well as advantageous, for the grazing of their animals; the manufacturing of sugar from the syrup found in the maples here [emphasis added].

In summary, settlement and resource-extraction patterns in the lower Saline Valley appear to have been more functionally related than ethnically determined. Thus, even though the area was settled by a multiethnic population, material-culture differences may have become blurred at an early date due to the fact that settlers, whether French or English, were exploiting the same resources with probably very similar technologies. Another factor is that at least by the latter part of the eighteenth century, the British appear to have been the primary suppliers of ceramic and metal goods.

Acknowledgments

Work on the archaeology of and the documentary background pertinent to the lower Saline Creek Valley has been funded by research grants to the University of Missouri–Columbia from the Center for Field Research/Earthwatch in 1985, 1986, and 1988, the National Endowment for the Humanities (RO-21429–87) in 1987, the Weyerhaeuser Foundation, and the Wenner-Gren Foundation. The Missouri Historical Society, St. Louis, has been especially generous in their support of the project from its inception in 1987 to the present. From that institution, Dr. Robert Archibald, president, and Mr. Peter Michel, director of library and archives, must be singled out for special thanks. We also extend our gratitude to Gregory L. Fox for substantive and technical advice regarding the chapter. R. Lee Lyman of the Department of Anthropology, UMC, examined the faunal remains recovered from the *poteaux en terre* structure at 23-SG-5. James E. Price (American Archaeology Division, UMC) analyzed the metal from 23-SG-5 and from the sites inventoried in 1987. We were aided in the preparation of figures by the following individuals: Thomas D. Holland (figure 11-3), Terry Dye (figures 11-4, 11-7, and 11-8), Julie Remley (figures 11-5, 11-6, and 11-10), and Susan J. Vale (figures 11-9 and 11-11). We owe a great debt of appreciation to Joseph P. Kreilich, Henry Cole, Leonard Grither, and other landowners in the project area who extended their hospitality and utmost cooperation to us during our research. Ste. Genevieve residents Margaret and Royce Wilhauk and Jesse Francis also were invaluable sources of help and support.

An Archaeological Perspective on Animal Exploitation Patterns at French Colonial Sites in the Illinois Country

12

Terrance J. Martin

Within the last ten years considerable research has been carried out on archaeological sites in the midwestern United States that are associated with the period of the French colonial occupation. These investigations have included military forts, trading posts, domestic sites, and Native American habitation sites. Coupled with the diversity of activities represented at these various sites, archaeological faunal assemblages suggest that there was considerable variation in animal exploitation patterns. The goal of this chapter is to provide an overview of these patterns and to explore some reasons for these differences.

Vital to the operation of the French colonial fur trade network in North America during the eighteenth century was the maintenance of trading posts such as at Detroit, Fort Michilimackinac, and Fort de Chartres. Substantial civilian population centers were also present in close proximity to many of these posts (e.g., Kaskaskia, Ste. Anne, and Cahokia in the central Mississippi Valley). Also important to the network were numerous smaller and less well known posts that functioned in more remote locations (e.g., Forts La Baye at Green Bay, St. Joseph in southwestern Michigan, and Ouiatenon on the Wabash River in northern Indiana). Inspection of historical and documentary sources reveals that the more obscure posts were not simply smaller and more remote versions of posts like Fort Michilimackinac; more substantial differences did exist (Tordoff 1983). Some of these differences may be related, as Keene (chap. 3) suggests, to agricultural and extractive economic pursuits of the specific sites.

According to Tordoff's model of the French colonial fur trade network, the various North American settlements can be placed into five hierarchical levels. Each level represents a general decrease in internal functional complexity coupled with the "branching out . . . of French exploration, missionization, and, ultimately and consequently, the fur trade" into the wilderness frontier (Tordoff 1983:39). The various levels with settlement examples are the port of entry (e.g., Louisbourg), government/economic centers (e.g., Montreal and Quebec), regional distribution centers (e.g., Detroit, Fort Michilimackinac, and Fort de Chartres), local distribution centers (e.g., Forts La Baye, Miamis, and Ouiatenon), and aboriginal population centers (e.g., the Bell, Guebert, and Waterman sites).

In 1748 the governor-general of New France suggested to the French minister that Detroit should have authority over the southern trading posts whereas the outlying northern posts should be subordinate to the regional distribution center at Fort Michilimackinac (Tordoff 1983:47). Although the Illinois Country was removed from the jurisdiction of New France early in the eighteenth century, Fort de Chartres was established as a regional distribution center for the new colony of Louisiane and later evolved into a government/economic center in the 1750s. Despite their particular situations, these posts shared several characteristics. Because of their positions along major transportation routes, these posts were the key channeling points for commodities that passed between the government/economic centers and the local distribution and/or aboriginal population centers. As the regional bases for government and business representatives, these posts functioned as regional military headquarters as well as provision depots and supply bases for the more remote posts. In addition to serving the local distribution centers in the wilderness, the regional centers attended to the needs of nearby Native American populations.

The need to maintain Indian alliances and the fur trade in light of increasing British competition resulted in the French establishing small fortified trading posts far beyond the main colonies of New France and Louisiane. More often than not the local distribution center was placed near one or more Indian villages and was home to small numbers of voyageurs, traders, and their families. Troops, if present at all, were mainly for appearance. The most prominent residents at the local centers were the blacksmith and the Jesuit priest. Gift-giving sessions, the repair of Indians' weapons by the post blacksmith, and the fur trade were the principal activities. As a rule, social interaction between the French and the local Indians was more intimate at the local centers than at the regional distribution centers.

By proposing this model of the French fur trade system, the thesis of Tordoff's dissertation (1983) was that differences described between the levels should be reflected in the archaeological record of representative fur trade sites. A series of hypotheses relating to expected differences between local and regional distribution centers was formulated and tested by comparing Fort Ouiatenon to Fort Michilimackinac in terms of artifact classes grouped into functional categories. In general, this comparison demonstrated that Michilimackinac was inhabited by persons of higher rank and more affluence who placed more emphasis on military defense as well as on storage and building security.

This perspective can be extended to the analysis of archaeological faunal assemblages. Employment of a comparative approach has the potential for calling attention to significant variation among sites. This allows us to explore factors that may account for these differences, such as environmental setting, site function, military/civilian/ethnic composition, and intensity of culture contact. An interdisciplinary approach to the history, archaeology, and zooarchaeology of French colonial sites employing a regional perspective will contribute to a better understanding of this period.

Review of Particular Faunal Assemblages

Fort Ouiatenon is located in the central Wabash River Valley near Lafayette, Indiana. Along with trading posts at Fort Miamis (Fort Wayne, Indiana) and Vincennes, Fort Ouiatenon functioned as a local distribution center that was inhabited by a small garrison of French marines and fewer than twenty French families with a large Native American population (including the Wea, Piankashaw, Kickapoo, and Mascouten) residing at five nearby villages. Excavations were carried out at the site by the Michigan State University Museum from 1974 through 1979 (Noble 1983; Noble, chap. 5; Tordoff 1983). Faunal remains from a variety of different contexts (wall trenches, refuse pits, an abandoned well, and sheet midden) were analyzed, resulting in 11,625 identified specimens (Martin 1986). A wide variety of mammals, birds, turtles, and freshwater mussels are represented. White-tailed deer was found to be the most abundant single species. Waterfowl, wild turkey, and raccoon are also numerous. Domesticated animals (cattle, pig, horse, and chicken) together contributed less than seven percent of the number of identified specimens (NISP) and minimum number of individuals (MNI) and approximately thirty-five percent of the biomass. Fish are represented by large individual channel catfish, redhorse, buffalo, and freshwater drum, but in proportions well below the potential annual yields for the area.

A distinct pattern of animal exploitation is represented at Fort Michilimackinac in northern Michigan (Heldman, chap. 13; Scott 1985). The mixed conifer-deciduous forest of the Canadian biotic province was unfavorable to white-tailed deer and other game animals. This was offset, however, by fish from the Great Lakes that were exploited as part of the inland shore fishery (Cleland 1982; Rostlund 1952). Fish, consisting mainly of lake trout and whitefish, contributed from fifteen percent to eighty-six percent of the meat represented from several midden deposits (Scott 1985:154–55). The importance of other wild animal resources (e.g., beaver, various mustelids, passenger pigeon, and waterfowl) may also reflect the fort's original function as a local distribution center, a role that lasted until the 1730s (Scott 1985:26). Perhaps domesticated animals would occur in greater proportions if more faunal samples from the period of 1744–63 were available.

The largest analyzed assemblage of animal remains from the French Colonial District of Illinois is from the Laurens site, a site that is suspected to be the first of three structures named Fort de Chartres. From its inception, Fort de Chartres functioned as a regional distribution center. In 1718 sixty-eight soldiers and officers along with some *engages* were dispatched from New Orleans to "Upper Louisiane" in order to establish a military presence in the region, create a civil government, and provide a base of operations for the Company of the West (Jelks, Ekberg, and Martin 1989). Within the stockade resided sixty soldiers, and by 1724 the adjacent village of Ste. Anne had a substantial civilian population. Over 2,200 identified faunal specimens were associated with stockade trenches, refuse pits, and cellars. The fill in many of these features undoubtedly contains refuse that was deposited following the military abandonment of the fort. Domesticated animals (cattle, pigs, and chickens) contributed approximately thirty-one percent of the identified specimens and sixty-five percent of the biomass. Deer bones make up twenty-three percent, and black bear elements are also numerous. Bison is represented by two bones. Just over forty percent of the assemblage is from birds, but many of these were recovered from the fill of one cellar. Avian species of importance include various waterfowl, wild turkey, sandhill crane, and shorebirds. Overall, fish remains are not abundant, but the identified species—buffalo, paddlefish, and very large blue catfish—indicate that exploitation focused on the main channel of the Mississippi River.

Large samples of faunal remains have also been obtained from excavations at the site of the third Fort de Chartres (Keene, chap. 3;

Cardinal 1977; Martin and Masulis 1988). Approximately 1,400 specimens were identified from contexts that include Drains A through E and a British latrine located near the northern end of the East Barracks (Martin and Masulis 1988). Considerable diversity exists among the various features analyzed; however, cattle and pig bones dominate the overall assemblage with significant numbers of deer bones also present. Birds are dominated by waterfowl, but wild turkey, prairie chicken, and domestic chicken are also present along with sandhill crane and passenger pigeon. Fish are represented by very large blue catfish and buffalo. Large red-eared turtles (or sliders) were recovered from all features, but are especially abundant in the British sample. Unfortunately, artifact analyses have revealed that few areas of the site have escaped mixing of refuse by later military and civilian occupations. As a result, it is not possible to attribute subsistence practices with much precision with the exception of the British latrine.

The animal exploitation practices of Native Americans who lived near Fort de Chartres as late as the 1760s are known from animal remains that were associated with the Waterman site. Despite the importance of deer and other wild game (e.g., muskrat, raccoon, black bear, and waterfowl) to the Kaskaskia and Michigamea inhabitants, the Indians obtained considerable quantities of animal foods from backwater lakes and sloughs as indicated by the prevalence of bowfin and bullheads. Aquatic turtle remains are also abundant.

The Cahokia Wedge site provides the first opportunity to inspect archaeological remains from a civilian domestic site associated with a French colonial village in the American Bottom (Gums et al., chap. 7). The site was inhabited between 1758 and 1766 by Etienne Nicolle. Over four hundred animal remains were associated with wall trenches from a *poteaux en terre* structure, a refuse pit, a limestone concentration, and a discrete midden area (Martin 1988). Although cattle, pigs, and domestic chicken are represented, the sample indicates a preference for white-tailed deer. Bison, black bear, beaver, waterfowl, marsh birds, aquatic turtles, and large fish were also exploited. Similar to the Laurens site is the presence of trumpeter swan, sandhill crane, and exceptionally large blue catfish.

Factors Responsible for Intersite Differences among Faunal Assemblages

Differences in the environmental setting of various sites make comparison of some faunal assemblages difficult. For example, comparison of animal exploitation patterns between Fort Michilimackinac and

French sites in Illinois and Indiana are somewhat problematical due to dissimilarities in environmental settings. In contrast to the prairie-deciduous forest ecotone in the upper Wabash River Valley, for example, the mixed hardwood forest of coniferous and deciduous trees in northern Michigan was generally unfavorable to large game animals (Cleland 1982:764–65). This is reflected in the apparent emphasis that was placed on open water lake fish at the Straits of Mackinac where fish comprised approximately twenty percent (Scott 1985:200) in contrast to less than one percent at Fort Ouiatenon. Although recovery techniques differed, this does not fully account for the disparity. Differences in resource availability must be considered when discussing contrasts in basic animal exploitation patterns.

A major source of variation in archaeological faunal remains is undoubtedly differences in site function. For example, domesticated animals were probably more important to the subsistence economy of the regional distribution centers (Tordoff 1983:61). This is not to imply that wild animal foods were insignificant. Ekberg (1985:303) recounts that Frenchmen in the central Mississippi Valley were much impressed by catfish that were available in the rivers, and that bear oil was praised as a delicacy and was used as shortening as well as for seasoning. Early census information, also from the Illinois Country, points out the importance of domesticated animals to the French colonies, however. In 1752 the census listed over 2,000 head of cattle (comprised of oxen, cows, bull calves, and heifers), 346 horses, and more than 1,500 pigs (Belting 1948:56–57). Vouchers indicate that domesticated animals were present at both regional and local distribution centers and were given as gifts to local Indians. Difficulties in transportation coupled with the smaller resident French populations would have relegated livestock to a less prominent role at the local distribution centers. This functional difference should be reflected archaeologically by a proportionately greater representation of domesticated animals at regional distribution centers.

Contrary to this expectation, however, comparison of Forts Michilimackinac and Ouiatenon reveals that domesticated animals are proportionately better represented at Ouiatenon in terms of number of identified specimens (NISP), minimum number of individuals (MNI), and biomass calculated from bone weight allometry (Reitz et al. 1987). Although extensive disturbances to French occupational middens resulted from the British rebuilding activities, the faunal samples studied by Scott (1985) include a variety of activity areas (i.e., streets, yards, and gardens) that should be reasonably representative. Perhaps the low representation of domesticated species reflects Fort Michilimackinac's original function as a local distribution center, a role that lasted until the 1730s (Scott 1985:26). The earliest context from which domesticated animal remains have been identified dates to the second expansion of the fort between 1744 and 1761 (Scott 1985:160). Perhaps greater consumption of domesticated species will be revealed if more middens are discovered from this later period of French occupation.

The contrast between local and regional distribution centers is readily apparent when the focus is turned to Fort Ouaitenon and the Laurens site. Not only does the artifact assemblage from Laurens seem to contain more high status items, but the respective faunal assemblages also reflect this dichotomy, especially with regard to the greater representation of domesticated animal species at the site of the first fort in the Illinois Country. At Ouiatenon, domesticated animals were important only as supplements to wild animals, especially white-tailed deer. Although the proportions of identifiable bird and fish remains are quite similar for the two sites, domesticated animals as a group and domesticated mammals considered as individual species were more abundant at the Laurens site, regardless of the quantitative technique used to measure relative importance.

Another possible source of variation among French colonial sites is the amount of interaction between the French inhabitants of various posts and their respective Indian neighbors. Because of more frequent and less formal contact situations between French and Indians at local distribution centers, we would expect to find a greater reflection of Native American subsistence practices at the smaller posts. The smaller number of French civilians and military personnel at these posts would also facilitate acculturation by the French to some of the indigenous daily subsistence activities. Interracial marriages may have resulted in Indian wives taking up occupancy at the fort.

Fort Ouiatenon was established in 1717 close to five Wea Indian villages, and the post attracted additional trade from the Kickapoo, Mascouten, and Piankashaw. The impression for this post formed from scant documents and archaeological research is one of self-reliance on local resources. Fort de Chartres, on the other hand, was established within twenty miles of the French village of Kaskaskia where *habitants* were already raising crops and animals on traditional ribbon farms (Belting 1948). At least three Indian villages are known from the American Bottom region: one inhabited by the Kaskaskia (Guebert site), another occupied by the Michigamea between 1720 and 1752 (the Kohlmer site), and a village inhabited by both the Michigamea and Kaskaskia in the 1760s (Waterman site). Whereas Fort Ouiatenon housed a small detachment of about a dozen marines and fewer than twenty French families, Fort de Chartres was garrisoned by sixty soldiers. By 1724 the village of Ste. Anne (originally Chartres), adjacent to Fort de Chartres, consisted of thirty-nine *habitants*, forty-two white laborers, twenty-eight married women, seventeen children, and an unknown number of slaves (Jelks, Ekberg, and Martin 1989:10).

Interestingly enough, the Fort Ouiatenon faunal assemblage includes several interesting examples reflecting trade, the presence of local Indians, and possibly the acculturation of French inhabitants to local Indian customs.

Approximately 200 turtle carapace fragments from several species were recovered, and nearly half were modified by humans. Similar to the Bell site, a late seventeenth/early eighteenth-century Fox village site in Wisconsin (Parmalee 1963:63), the Indians of the central Wabash Valley selected Blanding's turtle for modification, although a modified eastern box turtle carapace was also recovered. In all of the Ouiatenon examples, carapaces were modified into containers by removing the vertebrae and costal ribs and cutting and polishing the peripheral elements. Indian utilization of turtles has been discussed elsewhere by Adler (1968, 1969) for the Northeast and Great Lakes region. In the western Great Lakes region, various Indian groups had used Blanding's turtle for food, utensils, and ornaments since the Middle Woodland period (Flanders 1965; Halsey 1966).

One of two mammal bone projectile points recovered at Fort Ouiatenon has a socketed base and is diamond-shaped in cross section. A similar point made from antler has been reported from the Rhoads site, a late eighteenth-century Kickapoo camp in central Illinois (Parmalee and Klippel 1983:274).

Two modified black bear elements were also recovered. A pointed fibula was found inside the western area of the fort, and a mandible tool was recovered in a midden scatter outside the east stockade line. The mandible, with its large perforation in the ascending ramus that shows wear polish, resembles numerous bear mandible tools discovered at early historic sites in the northern Great Lakes region (including the south end of Georgian Bay in Ontario [Garrad 1969], the Tionontate and Marquette Mission sites at the Straits of Mackinac [James Fitting, personal communication, 1978; Branstner 1984], and the Rock Island II site at the mouth of Green Bay, Wisconsin [Mason 1986:181–84]). Although the distinctive bear mandible tools have usually been attributed to Huron/Petun and Ottawa groups, their association with Fort Ouiatenon and the Potawatomi component at

Rock Island II may imply that the ethnic affiliations may not be as precise as previously believed.

Also thought to reflect interaction with local Indians is the presence of certain animals among the faunal assemblage. Although insignificant in terms of their overall dietary contribution, the presence of over two hundred freshwater mussel valves from seventeen species at Fort Ouiatenon suggests that bivalves were exploited as an occasional food item. Songbirds and small shorebirds were among the ten most plentiful bird groups encountered at Ouiatenon. Algonquian peoples commonly exploited songbirds in order to obtain their colorful feathers for decoration (e.g., Parmalee and Klippel 1983:272–73).

In contrast to Fort Ouiatenon, the only modified bones from the Laurens site and Fort de Chartres III are all typical of European manufacturing techniques. Examples include cutlery handles, buttons, combs, and a die. The proportion of turtle remains at the American Bottom French forts is similar to that at Fort Ouiatenon, yet none of these show signs of cutting or scraping. Freshwater mussels are rare, as are bones from songbirds.

This selective comparison between French colonial sites in the central Wabash Valley and the central Mississippi Valley serves to accentuate the different functions of the respective French settlements. In contrast to a reliance on domesticated animals in the Illinois Country that was facilitated by the proximity of well-established French agricultural villages, Fort Ouiatenon exemplifies a remote outpost with a small French civilian and military population that was dependent on the fur trade and on animal food resources that could be obtained from the local environment as well as from the large, local Indian populations.

One does not necessarily have to look outside the Illinois Country, however, to encounter interesting differences among faunal assemblages associated with this period. Albeit similar to the Fort de Chartres collections in terms of the presence of blue catfish of giant sizes, sandhill cranes, trumpeter swans, and large red-eared turtles, the Cahokia Wedge site exhibits an unexpected abundance of wild animal remains, especially white-tailed deer. In aggregate, cattle, pigs, and chickens contribute less than fourteen percent of the identified bones and less than forty-seven percent of the biomass. Other noteworthy species include bison, black bears, beavers, large birds, and aquatic turtles. The faunal assemblage at Cahokia Wedge is more similar to that from the post–French regime Michigamea occupation at the Waterman site (Parmalee and Bogan 1980) in that at both sites, domesticated mammals and birds are underrepresented, wild species are plentiful, and examples of modified trumpeter swan wing bones were recovered. In contrast to both Fort de Chartres assemblages and Cahokia Wedge, however, the remains from the Waterman site reveal that the local Indians in the American Bottom exploited the sloughs and backwater lakes for fish instead of the main river channel that the French preferred. In contrast to the French and Indians of the central Wabash Valley, neither the French nor the Indians of the Illinois Country took much effort to manufacture containers from turtle carapaces.

An interesting aspect of animal exploitation for this period in the Midwest involves the hunting of bison. Purdue and Styles (1986:7) have noted that despite documentary evidence of bison in southern Illinois (and in the central Wabash Valley of Indiana), occurrences of archaeological bison bones have been most common at sites in northern Illinois during the Early Historic period, the most noteworthy being the Zimmerman site (Cardinal 1975; Parmalee 1961; Rogers 1975a, 1975b). Recent analyses have disclosed the occurrence of bison at an early eighteenth-century Illini camp at the Naples-Abbott site in Scott County in the lower Illinois River Valley (Styles, Martin, and Masulis 1987), as well as at the Slim Lake site (also in Scott County) where an isolated scatter of poorly preserved bison bones were found associated with material that yielded a radiocarbon date of 330 ± 70 B.P. (ISGS #1717) (Stafford 1989:81–82). It seems plausible that bison killed on the prairie were processed away from the major habitation sites with only the meat and possibly the hides brought back, especially in light of Hennepin's description of bison hunting by the Miami from the 1670s (Thwaites 1903:147). At all of the French sites analyzed to date, most of the diagnostic large bovid bones that have been identified have been from domestic cattle. Sites that have yielded bison bones include Fort Ouiatenon (one bone), Laurens site (two bones), Cahokia Wedge (one bone), and Naples-Abbott (one bone).

Conclusions and Future Prospects

A review of several eighteenth-century French colonial sites in the midwestern United States indicates frontier adaptations were not uniform. Considerable diversity in local subsistence patterns seems to be related to social, cultural, and economic differences at various sites and not simply to local environmental settings. In the central Mississippi Valley, documents attest to the importance of agriculture to the various French settlements, and archaeological faunal remains from both the Laurens site and Fort de Chartres III indicate a primary reliance on domesticated livestock. Families that lived outside of the major French settlements, as exemplified by the Cahokia Wedge site, were more self-sufficient and exploited more of the wild animal populations. In contrast, the smaller resident French population at Fort Ouiatenon, which was more heavily involved in the Indian fur trade, followed an animal exploitation pattern more reminiscent of local Native American groups in the central Wabash Valley. More effort was directed at wild animal procurement, with most of the agricultural products being furnished by nearby Indian villages and, in times of crisis, from French settlements at Detroit or in the Illinois Country. The nature and quantity of modified faunal remains also suggest that the minority French civilian population may have been adopting local Indian subsistence patterns. The contrast between Fort Ouiatenon and the two Fort de Chartres sites seems to reflect social factors and differences between a small remote trading post and trapping settlement and a larger, more sedentary agricultural population that was closely involved with a government and economic center.

These generalizations are admittedly based on a small number of archaeological sites from which faunal assemblages of widely varied sample sizes have been analyzed. Much more work is needed to substantiate these observations and investigate in more detail other aspects of the French colonial subsistence system. An abundance of small duck bones (teals) in the fill of one cellar at the Laurens site implies that faunal remains may eventually be used to demonstrate differences in socioeconomic status among various inhabitants of French colonial sites. A focus on small, domestic sites, such as the Cahokia Wedge site, offers considerably more promise for archaeological investigations of behavioral patterns because it is more feasible to assign refuse deposits to specific households than has been possible at most of the sites of forts that have been investigated.

Historical documents disclose that trade at various French posts was carried out at different times under different regulations, and these regulations also changed when adminstration of many of these sites was transferred to the British after 1763. These differences in regulations and economic climate of the fur trade may be reflected by some variation among faunal assemblages at various sites. At Fort Ouiatenon, for example, deposits of animal remains that were associated with different periods of occupation can be used to suggest tentatively that wild animal resources may have been even more important following the collapse of the French regime (Martin 1986). In the Wabash River Valley, this may possibly be due to greater isolation of the old French settlements as a result of the breakup of the

French fur trade network and the administrative abandonment of many of the remote local distribution centers by the British following the years of Pontiac's Rebellion. Attempts should be made to test these trends using archaeological data from other French sites.

Another topic for investigation is the interaction between French settlements and neighboring Native American villages. Comparison of the Waterman site to Fort de Chartres shows some interesting differences in their respective faunal assemblages. Investigation of early historic Indian sites in the vicinity of Fort Ouiatenon in the central Wabash River Valley by Neal Trubowitz (1987) has the potential to compare and contrast animal exploitation patterns between the French and Indian settlements with special attention to species composition, butchering patterns, and modified animal remains. Research at these sites should contribute to a better understanding of acculturation processes and culture contact situations in the Wabash Valley.

These topics along with others not yet envisioned offer great potential for future investigations of French colonial sites. In this chapter I have demonstrated how a comparative approach to the study of faunal remains from several eighteenth-century sites has resulted in insights into the reasons for some of the variation in quantitative species composition that has been observed. It is hypothesized that most of these differences can be attributed to social factors and the functional role of various sites involved in the French colonial network.

The French in Michigan and Beyond: An Archaeological View from Fort Michilimackinac Toward the West

13

Donald P. Heldman

Throughout the seventeenth and eighteenth centuries, French set-tlements at the Straits of Mackinac played a major role in the European colonization of New France (fig. 13-1) (Heldman and Grange 1981:1–54). While French policy from Versailles at first stressed missionary activity and exploration of the inland waterways, it was the commercial raison d'être of New France that gradually came to predominate, namely trapping furs to enrich the French national treasury. French expansion from the Great Lakes region into the Mississippi Valley and the Gulf region at the beginning if the eighteenth century was a direct result of that increasing prosperity (Usner 1987).

At Fort Michilimackinac archaeologists have found three French settlement patterns, juxtaposed one upon another (fig. 13-2) (Heldman 1979). They are, of course, important not only in the evolution of the settlement itself but in its changing relationship to larger events throughout New France and, indeed, the rest of North America. These three earliest patterns outline Michilimackinac as it existed when established in 1715, in the 1730s when it was greatly expanded, and in 1744 when a few fortification defenses were added to the 1730s fort. A fourth pattern is British, a major expansion of the palisade walls to the north and south in 1764–65 (Heldman 1984; Heldman and Grange 1981:1–11; Gerin-Lajoie 1976; Maxwell and Binford 1961).

The late seventeenth-century Marquette mission at St. Ignace, on the north shore of the Straits of Mackinac (1671–1705), and the earliest eighteenth-century settlement of Fort Michilimackinac on the south shore (fig. 13-3) both resulted from the missionary/exploration/fur trade policies of Versailles (Beers 1964). In fact, this was a period when the fur trade, through a frontier exchange economy between

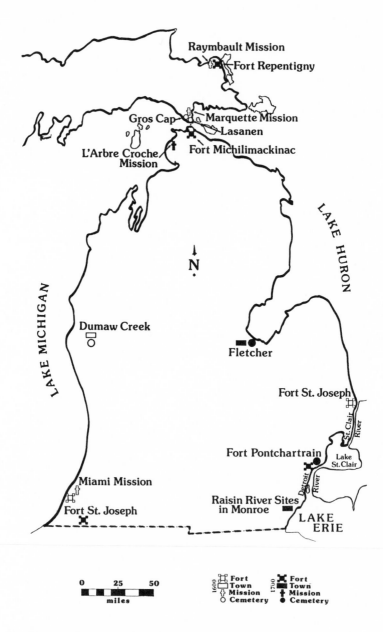

Figure 13-1. French and Indian Sites in Michigan

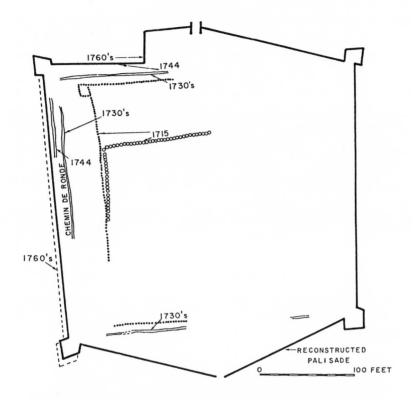

Figure 13-2. Expansion of the Palisaded Curtains at Fort
Michilimackinac

Europeans and Indians, began in earnest in isolated regions throughout North America (see, for example, Branstner 1985; Usner 1987).
At the time Michilimackinac was founded ca. 1715, policymakers in
France still counted somewhat upon missionaries to carry out French
policy, despite the fact that by 1717 only a dozen missions existed in
all of New France. The mission at Michilimackinac was built after
the close of the seventeenth century, the period of fervent mission-
izing, because it was a major part of the French and Indian alliance
against the Iroquois (Minutes of the Council of the Marine, 26 February 1717, Archives des Colonies C11A, 123 and Archives de la
Marine, bk. 19:163). Indeed, the earliest settlement pattern found by
archaeologists at Michilimackinac, and discussed in historic documents
as well, is a small and imperfectly known square or rectangular palisaded compound with a mission church outside the palisade walls

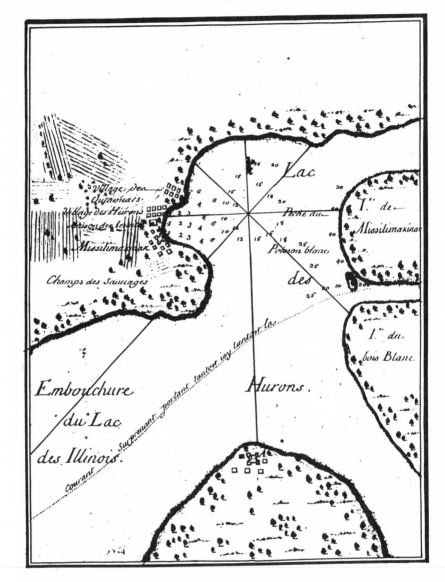

Figure 13-3. Straits of Mackinac

(fig. 13-4) (Heldman 1979; Heldman and Grange 1981:16–19; Maxwell and Binford 1961:26–30).

By the 1720s, however, either the palisades surrounding the tiny
compound were somewhat expanded, possibly because of population

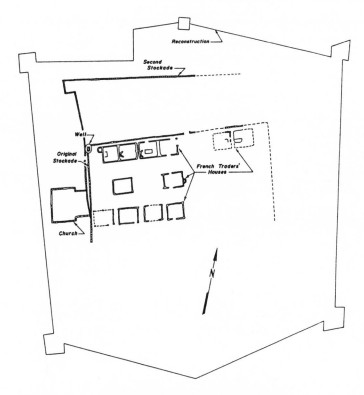

Figure 13-4. Archaeological Map of Mission/Fort

growth due to the growing importance of the fur trade in the eighteenth century or the entire settlement was moved slightly northward toward the shoreline. We do not know which. We do know that by 1732 Versailles responded positively to a plea to rebuild Michilimackinac completely as "a more solid fort" to accommodate the growing fur trade (Archives des Colonies, series B, Ministère des Colonies, vol. 57–1, Public Archives of Canada). Sometime in the 1730s, the old mission-fort was completely torn down and a greatly enlarged, well-planned trading town in the Vauban tradition was built in its place (fig. 13-5) (Heldman 1979, 1984; Heldman 1978:1–4; Heldman and Grange 1981:19–24; Binford 1978:267; Heldman and Minnerly 1976:1–2; Heldman and Minnerly 1977:4; Maxwell and Binford 1961:30–33).

By the 1730s and early 1740s, prosperity came to New France and the Louisiane colony (Usner 1987). In fact, during several of those

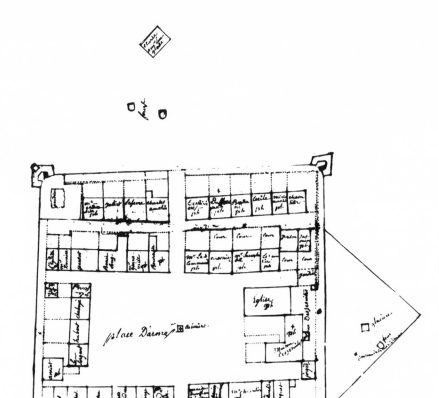

Figure 13-5. Map of Fort Michilimackinac in 1749

years New France actually experienced a favorable balance of trade with the mother country (Nish 1968:31 and table 3; also see Heldman 1980). The site of Michilimackinac reflects that prosperity (Heldman 1979). This new, greatly enlarged settlement, overwhelmingly of *poteaux en terre* architecture, consisted of seven lengthy row houses, a powder magazine, a new parish church erected on the foundations of the old mission, and a rectory, all enclosed within the palisades. Both the documents (Gerin-Lajoie 1976) and the archaeological record (Heldman and Grange 1981:19–24) are rich with data about this expanded and rebuilt palisaded fur-trading community.

More than three decades of peace and relative economic prosperity ended in 1744 when France and Britain once again went to war. At Michilimackinac the French added a second palisade in 1744, completely surrounding the 1730s fort "at a distance of 6 or 7 [French] feet," and the space thus created between the two formed yet another defense termed a *chemin de ronde* or sentry beat (Gerin-Lajoie 1976:6; Heldman and Grange 1981:24–29). These were, however, little more than minor additions to the 1730s fortified town (Heldman 1984; Heldman 1979:8–12, Heldman 1978:54–55; Maxwell and Binford 1961:12 and 34–35). Hostilities led to the final collapse of New France in 1761, with British occupation of many of the former French settlements east of the Mississippi River.

British arrival in 1761 did not mean an end to French activities at Michilimackinac. French, *metis,* and American Indians lived uneasily with the British military inside the fort (Heldman and Grange 1981:35–39; Stone 1974:352–55). After the successful Indian uprising and occupation of Michilimackinac in 1763–64, British authorities rebuilt much of the settlement (fig. 13-6). In so doing, they expanded the palisade into a hexagonal outline and had the French rebuild most if not all seven of the long row houses inside it (Heldman and Grange 1981:29–35). In 1765 the British forced some of the growing fur-trading community to build houses outside the fort (Gen. Thomas Gage to Maj. Robert Roberts, 2 September 1767, Gage Papers, Clements Library, Univ. of Michigan, Ann Arbor). Most French buildings, both inside and outside the palisade, were rebuilt in the old *poteaux en terre* style, architectural construction which evidently continued at Michilimackinac until the community departed the fort for Mackinac Island in 1781 (Williams and Shapiro 1982).

This sequence of settlement patterns results from a tedious piecing together of thirty consecutive years of archaeology; we now know it is more correct than earlier proposed sequences for the site (for example, Maxwell and Binford 1961:27–86). And we possess much data for comparison with other eighteenth-century French sites in the upper Great Lakes and beyond simply because no other French colonial frontier site has undergone such extensive excavation and analysis.

The purpose of this chapter is to compare some of the data from Michilimackinac to contemporary sites to the west and south and to suggest other possibilities for comparative studies. For starters, take the settlement patterns themselves. The two major plans (see figs. 13-4 and 13-5), those of 1715 and the 1730s, are square to rectangular in outline and have towers or bastions at each of the four corners. When one looks at engineering drawings and the precious few fortified

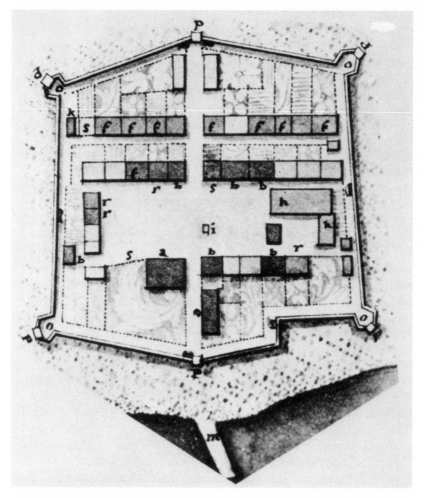

Figure 13-6. Map of Fort Michilimackinac in 1766

settlements revealed by archaeology, the same pattern of frontier fortification (fig. 13-7) appears over and over again, from the entire Great Lakes region into the Mississippi Valley and southward into the Louisiane colony (Peterson 1949a: fig. 1; Saucier and Seineke 1969:208, 211–12, and 215; and, for example, drawings in the Map Room and the Burton Historical Collections, Detroit Public Library). This simple fortification plan was designed by the marquis de Vauban in the late seventeenth century (Vauban 1795). As a confidant of

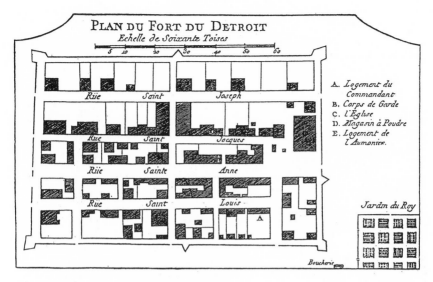

Figure 13-7. Map of Fort Pontchartrain

Louis XIV, Vauban established a corps of military engineers in France, some of whom came to North America. This *corps du genie,* which survived Vauban's early dismissal as commissary-general of fortifications, brought to the colonies engineering manuals that contained, among other more complicated fortifications for major centers, plans for the simple four-bastioned frontier fortification, and variations thereof (Vauban 1742). And they built great numbers of them in the vast area between the Appalachians and the Mississippi River.

Most of these frontier settlements were built of wood and usually contained buildings of simple *poteaux en terre* construction (fig. 13-8). Frequently the buildings were long row houses, like the seven inside the 1730s fort at Michilimackinac. In fact, only the ecclesiastical buildings at Michilimackinac were of *piece sur piece* style. Thanks to the historian Dennis Au (personal communication, 1987) and to others (for example, Bald 1961:58), we know that in Michigan in the seventeenth and eighteenth centuries, French dwellings were almost exclusively of post-in-the-ground architectural style. At Green Bay, documents suggest that the *metis* settlement of La Baye (1763–1812), while unknown archaeologically, evidently contained the same kind of buildings (Trask 1987:4–5). According to Collot, Napoleon's "spy" in the Great Lakes and the Mississippi Valley, post-in-the-ground architecture was the "Typical Habitation of the Illinois Country" (Pe-

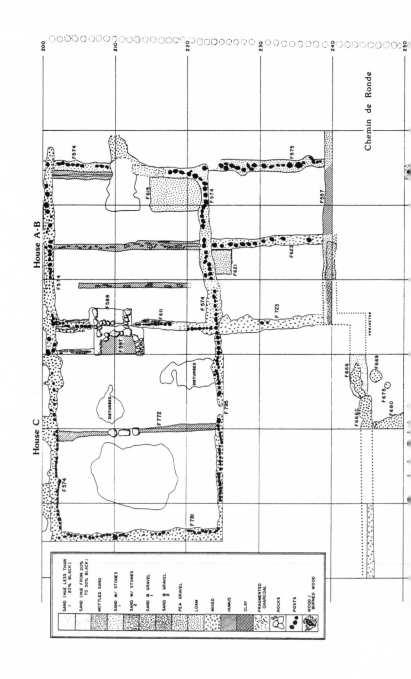

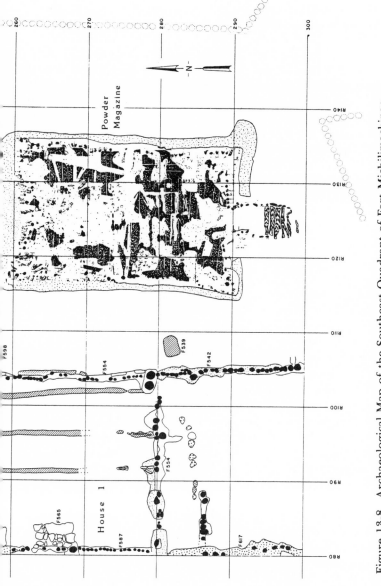

Figure 13-8. Archaeological Map of the Southeast Quadrant of Fort Michilimackinac

terson 1949a:34–35). It is known archaeologically from early to mid-eighteenth-century sites such as Fort de Chartres I (Edward B. Jelks, personal communication, 1988). Although the French mission on top of Monks Mound (ca. 1735–52) evidently is a combination of both *poteaux en terre* and *poteaux sur sole* (posts on sill) styles (Walthall and Benchley 1987:27), it is an exception. In the Louisiane colony post-in-the-ground buildings were probably the most common as well. Typical examples have been found at Fort Toulouse (1717–62) in Alabama (Ray 1976), and were common elsewhere in the Louisiane colony (see Dumont de Montigny 1753).

At Michilimackinac archaeological and historical research have proceeded to the extent that archaeologists can discuss social status and class structure in terms of neighborhoods (fig. 13-9) (Heldman 1986:28–32). Documents state that the northwest row house, protected from the prevailing northwesterly winds by a high fortification palisade, was occupied in the 1730s fort by "junior officers" and wealthy traders (Gerin-Lajoie 1976:5). Binford (1978:267) dubbed the structure "status row" for the later British period, but it is clear from excavations of the 1970s and 1980s elsewhere on the site that it housed the privileged even earlier, beginning with the 1730s rebuilding (Scott 1985; Halchin 1985; Heldman 1980, 1983, 1986). While *poteaux en terre* buildings were lived in by privileged and commoner alike at Michilimackinac, the larger structures generally are associated with high-staus artifacts, the kinds of goods only people of means would have owned in the eighteenth century (Heldman 1977:78–86; see also Heldman 1983).

Studies of ethnicity and gender to reveal class structure are only beginning at Fort Michilimackinac, but we hope to develop methods by which both may be identified in the archaeological data (Scott 1987). Historical documents do tell of differences in status, differences which tend to correlate with dietary studies at the site (Scott 1985, 1986). But actual cultural assemblages resulting from specific ethnic practices other than those of the expected French or British have thus far gone virtually undetected. A lone exception is that of two Jewish entrepreneurs who conducted the Indian trade in the summers between 1765 and 1780 from their home at Michilimackinac. The royal notary recorded the sale to these two traders of the house found archaeologically (Halchin 1985; Heldman 1986). However, only the location of their trading house in a low-status neighborhood and the complete lack of any British military artifacts from sheet deposits within the building point to archaeological evidence of the occupation of the house by Jewish fur traders (Halchin 1985: Heldman 1986:26–

28). In no other dwelling excavated thus far, whether that of a trader or soldier, has a complete absence of British military artifacts been recorded, suggesting eighteenth-century northern European anti-Semitism toward the occupants of the house. An analysis of the dietary remains of the sheet deposits in and around this structure is presently underway and may demonstrate a "Jewish" diet for the occupants of the house.

In French colonial deposits at Fort Michilimackinac, the fur-trade pattern is present not only in and around buildings where the Indian trade was conducted (see, for example, Halchin 1985:120–83) but in many other areas and features as well (see Heldman and Grange 1981:206–8). This is true regardless of the activities defined for any given area. Which is to say, it occurs in areas where one would not expect it. For example, a powder magazine on French colonial sites is usually thought to have contained armaments (Heldman and Minnerly 1977). However, behavorial analyses of the area immediately outside the only door leading to the magazine, which was located inside the fort, shows "that the magazine enclosure and probably the magazine itself were used for the movement and storage of armaments *and trade goods*" during the 1760s (Heldman and Grange 1981:225–27, emphasis added). Thus while the British army used it for military purposes, evidently traders used it to store quantities of trade goods as well. In other words, fur trading permeated almost all other activities at Michilimackinac. This may hold true at other French fur-trade sites and even at British and American sites that postdate French hegemony and whose function(s) seemingly have little to do with the fur trade.

One area for possible comparison of Michilimackinac to other French colonial sites is the occupation deposits. For the French period (1715–61), they are always of a gray, sandy loam; after 1761 French deposits, like those of the British, are always of a brown sandy loam (Heldman 1984). This is true for primary or sheet deposits as well as for the secondary deposits comprising most of the features on the site. We do not know why these color differences exist, despite several attempts to find out. Even though the color of soil deposits varies considerably on French colonial sites, there may be a difference in the minimal quantity of organic matter French deposits contain compared to later British deposits at Michilimackinac. This difference may result from variations in behavior and population size between the French and British inhabitants of Michilimackinac and, more importantly, may be present in French and British colonial deposits elsewhere in North America.

Figure 13-9. Archaeological Master Map of Fort Michilimackinac

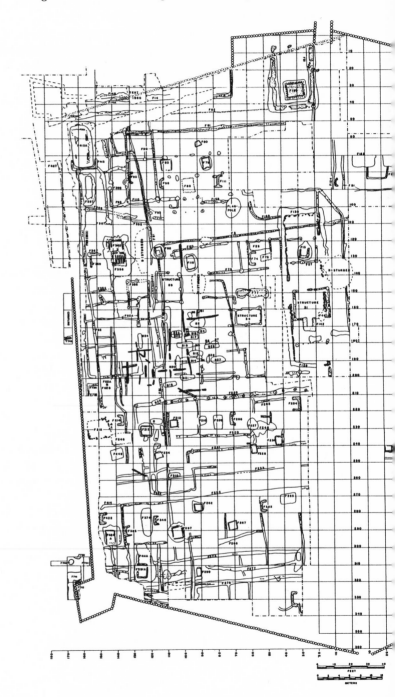

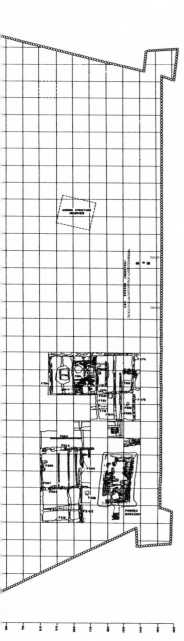

SHIMMIN

Dietary studies and refuse disposal patterns during the French period may also be a lucrative area for comparison. While dietary differences exist for different social classes of people at Michilimackinac (Scott 1986), the French in general depended less on imported foods and more on local flora and fauna than did the later British. This is in contrast to eighteenth-century French settlements in the east of New France and to frontier British settlements, including Fort Michilimackinac (Scott 1985; Shapiro 1978). It seems clear that the farther inland and west in New France one moves from Louisbourg and Quebec, which is to say away from ports on dependable sea routes, the greater the dependence on wild animals in the French diet (Heldman 1984; Scott 1985; see also Wallerstein 1974). In Illinois and Louisiane a similar dependency upon established trade routes at New Orleans and Mobile may be possible to demonstrate (see Usner 1987:169 and 180–88). Test excavations at the Laurens site (Martin, chap. 12), for example, thought possibly to be Fort de Chartres I, suggest that as a major military post Fort de Chartres I imported a surprisingly high quantity of its meat. It was situated along a major trade route. However, a study of the faunal remains from Fort Ouiatenon (Martin, chap. 12) shows that, like Michilimackinac, the occupants depended largely on wild animals for meat. Ouiatenon was not located along a major trade route. Nor were many of the isolated settlements in the Louisiane colony, and like settlements in the western Great Lakes, they depended heavily upon Indians to trade and sell indigenous foods (Usner 1987). One major problem in comparing the Fort de Chartres I and Ouiatenon samples to that from Michilimackinac results from the absence of water-screened samples at the Indiana and Illinois sites (Martin, chap. 12). We need such water-screened samples, not only from these two sites but also from Fort Toulouse and Dauphin Island in Alabama, from Fort St. Pierre on the Yazoo in Mississippi, and from a large number of sites throughout the Louisiane colony, before anyone may speak with any certainty of French adaptation generally.

Another possible area for comparative studies is refuse disposal. Among the French at Michilimackinac, refuse disposal patterns differ from those of the later British. French period deposits evidently contain few, if any, refuse pits, in stark contrast to the later British period (Scott 1985; Shapiro 1978:163). Rather, the French simply tossed refuse into the yards or gardens behind the row houses. Little refuse made it to the streets outside garden fences. But in the British period, along with great numbers of refuse pits, refuse disposal took place in areas beyond the yards of the row houses: the streets and lanes and even in the enclosed powder magazine area (Heldman and Grange 1981:233). Edward B. Jelks (personal communication, 1988) thinks the pits at Fort de Chartres I are either French refuse pits or filled-in root cellars that existed beneath floors of buildings inside the stockade. In order to make valid comparisons, we need large-scale block excavations of these features, and the resulting secondary deposits should be water-screened. Indeed, we need similar excavation techniques at sites throughout Illinois and the Louisiane colony.

This brings me to a plea for both slow, careful field techniques in excavation and for water-screening the excavated deposits. Few sites in the country undergo water-screening but with it the difference in specimen recovery is astonishing. In one study conducted by the Mackinac Island State Park Commission at the Old Mill Creek site, a late British colonial and early American farm and grist mill complex, deposits were first screened with standard quarter-inch mesh. Specimens recovered from the quarter-inch screen were bagged and recorded separately. Then the deposit from the quarter-inch screen was water-screened, with the result that the number of total specimens recovered nearly doubled (an increase of forty-five percent). If we throw away almost half the data we should be recovering, as that study suggests, the conclusions we reach very well may be skewed. We may, in fact, be doing more harm than good. At sites protected as parks, such as Michilimackinac, de Chartres, Toulouse, and the others, we really have no excuse; their protection is in perpetuity.

This paper is dedicated to the memory of Dr. Gary Shapiro.

Variability in Trade at Eighteenth-Century French Outposts

14

Dean L. Anderson

In a brief review of the ways in which historical archaeology has been defined, Deagan (1982:152–53) states that there seems to be general agreement among historical archaeologists that the existence of a documentary record of the peoples and cultures they study is the distinguishing feature of their discipline. Access to the documentary record as a source of data independent of the archaeological record adds another dimension to the archaeological study of historical period peoples. As Deetz (1977:8) points out, the archaeological record and the documentary record complement one another in historical archaeological research. The foundation of the research potential of historical archaeology lies in incorporating the documentary record into the process of archaeological inquiry.

The documentary record presents a diverse array of data that can be exploited by historical archaeologists. The focus of attention here is upon those documents that contain an explicitly material record of the past, specifically, in this case, account books. Documents like account books include detailed lists of material things, and in this way they bear similarity to the archaeological record. Account books and other documents present a form of the material record to historical archaeologists which is independent of the archaeological record. This documentary record is also different from the archaeological record in an important way. Account books represent a record of material things while they were actively functioning in a cultural system, in other words, while they were in systemic context (Schiffer 1972, 1976). Excavated data, on the other hand, represent the material record in archaeological context. As a result, documentary material data have different properties than archaeological data and offer different analytical opportunities in historical archaeological research.

This study makes use of documentary data to address a problem in fur trade archaeology. Specifically, the purpose of the study is to examine trade at French period outposts in the western Great Lakes region. The data used are taken from eighteenth-century accounting records kept by merchants in Montreal. These data provide a detailed material record of trade goods shipped to the western country and, in this way, lend themselves to the investigation of French trade in that region.

Variability in the French-Indian Trade System

One of the important trends in historical archaeology today is the effort to interpret sites and archaeological data in the context of broad spatial and temporal frameworks (Cleland 1988). Such an approach is exemplified in the body of research that has been generated regarding the spatial and functional dynamics of frontier development and the archaeological manifestations of that process (Hardesty 1985; Lewis 1984). In addition, recent work in urban archaeology has endeavored to place sites in the systemic context of city growth and integration (Cressey and Stephens 1982; Rubertone 1982). These studies, and others like them, strive to understand archaeological sites in the context of the larger community, city, political structure, or system of which they were a part.

A good example of such an approach to the archaeology of the French period is Judy Tordoff's (1983) analysis of French colonial outposts in the western Great Lakes region. As part of her study, Tordoff sought to develop a broad spatial framework that would help elucidate the relationships between individual French period trading post sites. To do this, Tordoff proposed that French outposts be viewed as components of the trade and logistical system developed in New France during the eighteenth century. She constructed a model of that system, which organized French settlements into a four-level hierarchy: port of entry, government and economic centers, regional distribution centers, and local distribution centers. In this hierarchy, French outposts in the Great Lakes area were represented by the last two settlement types: regional distribution centers and local distribution centers.

The key to the differentiation between the two types of posts was relative functional complexity. Regional distribution centers, such as Michilimackinac and Detroit, were larger posts, had more diverse populations, and were more militarily and administratively oriented. As a result, a greater range of activities took place at these posts. In contrast, local distribution centers such as Green Bay, Ouiatenon, St. Joseph, and Nipigon were smaller, less diverse settlements at which a narrower range of activities took place. In this model then, variation between French outposts could be related to the functional disparity between regional distribution centers and local distribution centers.

In this systemic approach to understanding French period outpost sites, Tordoff proceeded to consider a number of functional attributes that might be expected to vary among these posts. Her treatment of one of these attributes—trade—is the focus of the analysis in this chapter. One of the issues Tordoff raised was the question of how trade, as a primary function of French posts, varied between different posts. Toward this end, she conducted an archaeological evaluation of differences and similarities in trade at Michilimackinac, a regional distribution center located at the northern tip of the lower peninsula of Michigan, and at Ouiatenon, a local distribution center located on the Wabash River in northwestern Indiana (see fig. 1-1).

Tordoff proposed to investigate trade at Michilimackinac and at Ouiatenon by examining the traffic in trade goods that occurred at each post. This was done archaeologically on the basis of the trade materials recovered from each of the sites. To facilitate the comparison of trade at the two posts, Tordoff identified a commercial/trade artifact category and placed those items commonly recognized as trade goods in that group. In this way, the archaeological occurrence of trade goods at Michilimackinac and at Ouiatenon was interpreted as a reflection of trade activity at those posts.

Tordoff hypothesized ways in which differences in trade between regional distribution centers and local distribution centers would be manifested archaeologically. For example, regional distribution centers were expected to exhibit more evidence of commercial activity and a greater incidence of high-status gift items than local distribution centers were. She also suggested that there would be similarity in trade at regional and local distribution centers in that a comparable variety of trade goods would be present at both. Tordoff's archaeological analysis provided support for the latter hypothesis, as it was demonstrated that the variety of trade goods recovered from Michilimackinac was similar to that recovered from Ouiatenon. Beyond this, however, Tordoff's analysis met with limited success. The archaeological evidence did not offer a strong basis on which to accept or reject hypotheses concerning contrasts in trade at the two posts.

Although Tordoff's analysis of trade met with difficulties, she raised an important question concerning variability in commercial activity at posts in the French trade system. A better understanding of trade at French outposts contributes to a better understanding of the French colonial settlement system as a whole. As a problem in the historical archaeology of the French period, the issue bears further consideration. The purpose of this chapter is to build on Tordoff's effort to understand variation in trade in the system of French outposts on the western frontier during the eighteenth century.

In this effort, however, a different approach to the problem is taken. Like Tordoff's, this study proceeds with the supposition that the investigation of the traffic in trade goods holds potential for understanding variability in trade at different French posts. However, in pursuing this investigation, this study takes advantage of one of the major strengths of historical archaeology: the opportunity to consult the documentary record as an independent body of data. In this case, a material record of the traffic in trade goods contained in eighteenth-century account books is used as a source of data for examining differences in trade.

The Data

The documentary data used in this study are contained in a series of account books and ledgers known collectively as the Montreal Merchants' Records (Michigan State University Library, microfilm no. 19014, East Lansing). The documents in this collection represent portions of the business records of several merchants who were active in the city of Montreal during the eighteenth century. As part of their business, these merchants supplied trade goods to individuals engaged in the fur trade in the western country. The merchants' account books contain invoices for the sale of trading outfits to traders bound for various French outposts. An outfit is an assemblage of trade goods and supplies purchased for a trading expedition into the interior. Not uncommonly, the compilation of a single outfit would be recorded in two or more separate invoices in the account books. An individual outfit is considered as all of the materials purchased by a trader or a partnership of traders in a single year for trade at a specific post.

The invoices for these outfits are scattered throughout the account books but they are usually very similar in form and include several kinds of information. At the head of the invoice, the date of the sale is recorded. Next, a brief statement appears that identifies the purchaser and usually gives the destination of the outfit. The main body of the invoice follows, consisting of an itemized listing of the goods and services sold to the trader. The entries sometimes include descriptive detail about the trade goods such as size, color, or type. The quantity of each item and the unit of measure in which it was sold is recorded, such as 10 axes, five pounds of beads, or 50 *ells* of cloth. In addition, each invoice entry includes the unit price for the item and the total cost for the quantity purchased. In some invoices, profit margin is added to the itemized charges. All of the price information in the account books is recorded in the French-Canadian monetary system of the period consisting of *livres, sols,* and *deniers* (20 *sols* equal one *livre,* 12 *deniers* equal one *sol*).

As mentioned previously, the account books record trade goods in systemic context whereas excavated trade goods appear in archaeological context. This attribute of the documentary data is important to the discussion of trade. Most trade goods shipped to the interior passed into Indian hands and thus were not incorporated into the archaeological record at European posts. Those materials that did enter the archaeological record did so as a result of two processes. First, some of the goods intended for trade entered archaeological context through loss. Second, many types of trade goods were used by Europeans as well as by Indians. These materials entered archaeological context through use and discard by the European occupants of the posts. Consequently, trade goods in archaeological context at a European post site may be a residue of trade activity at the site or a product of European use of trade goods. This creates potential difficulty in interpreting whether trade goods recovered archaeologically are a reflection of European use or whether they are a reflection of trade.

On the other hand, the Montreal Merchants' Records account books record trade goods in systemic context prior to archaeological deposition. The invoice lists represent a body of goods intended for trade to Indians. Ultimately, most of the materials recorded probably were traded to Indians and were transported away from the post. Thus it may be reasonably argued that these goods primarily reflect trade at French posts rather than the European use of trade goods.

This study focuses on a comparison of trade at the French posts of Michilimackinac, Detroit, Green Bay, and Ouiatenon (see fig. 1-1) between the years 1715 and 1758. A total of fifty-eight outfits is used in this study, fifteen for Green Bay, fifteen for Detroit, fourteen for Michilimackinac, and fourteen for Ouiatenon. These outfits are distributed over a number of years for each post (see table 14-1).

The number and distribution of outfits shown in table 14-1 illustrates the unevenness of the data for these four posts in the Montreal Merchants' Records. The merchants dealt with different traders from year to year, so that outfits for specific posts appear at different in-

Table 14-1. Outfits by Year for Each Post

	Green Bay		Detroit		Michilimackinac		Ouiatenon	
	yrs.	outfits	yrs.	outfits	yrs.	outfits	yrs.	outfits
	1724	(1)	1715	(1)	1725	(1)	1721	(1)
	1725	(2)	1721	(4)	1732	(1)	1731	(10)
	1739	(1)	1724	(1)	1734	(1)	1736	(2)
	1740	(2)	1731	(1)	1736	(2)	1738	(1)
	1741	(1)	1732	(2)	1739	(2)		
	1742	(3)	1734	(1)	1740	(1)		
	1743	(1)	1736	(2)	1744	(1)		
	1744	(1)	1737	(2)	1745	(1)		
	1745	(1)	1758	(1)	1746	(3)		
	1747	(1)			1747	(1)		
	1748	(1)						
Total	11	(15)	9	(15)	10	(14)	4	(14)

tervals and with varying frequency throughout the account books. This unevenness is especially evident in the case of Ouiatenon, where most of the outfits recorded for that post were shipped in a single year. Because of this variance in the number and frequency of outfits recorded for the different posts, all outfits for a single year at each post were combined. In this way, comparisons could be made on a per-year basis.

Analysis

As a first step in organizing the invoice data for the purpose of examining traffic in trade goods, items that were probably not intended for trade were removed from each outfit. Such articles included canoe gear, supplies, and personal possessions. The remaining trade goods data were organized to look at three aspects of trade at the four posts: the variety of goods traded, the volume of trade, and the composition of the inventories of goods traded.

The materials that appear in the Montreal Merchants' Records do not, of course, account for all of the trade goods that went to the posts recorded in those documents. They are a sample of the traffic in trade goods that flowed through different French posts during the eighteenth century. Are the Montreal Merchants' Records data representative of the trade carried out at the western posts?

The Montreal Merchants' Records are comprised mainly of the accounting records of the Moniere family. Most of the trade outfit data are contained in the Moniere books. This raises the possibility that the traffic in trade goods as depicted in the Moniere records was shaped by the Monieres' inventory of goods rather than by variability in trade at different posts. But portions of the accounting records of several other merchants are also included in the Montreal Merchants' Records. Comparison of the Moniere records with those of the other merchants indicates that they all carried a comparable inventory of trade goods and supplies. As a result, it is assumed that the Montreal Merchants' Records invoices offer a generally reliable representation of the content of trade outfits and the variety of goods shipped to interior posts.

The question of whether the Montreal Merchants' Records data provide an accurate representation of the relative volume of trade conducted at various posts must be approached more cautiously. Each merchant did business with several traders destined for different trading posts. The relative volume of trade for a particular post depended upon the number of traders outfitted for that post and the size of their outfits. While a comparative view of the relative volume of trade at posts in the western Great Lakes region can be obtained from the account book data, it is unclear whether the Montreal Merchants' Records present an equally representative sample of the traffic in trade goods for each of the different posts mentioned.

Variety of Goods Traded

The procedure for assessing the relative variety of goods traded at the posts was fairly straightforward. Based on the inspection of individual invoice entries, a list of the range of goods destined for each post was compiled. For this purpose, varieties of goods were collapsed into a single, basic category. In other words, different types of knives were all included in the category "knives," and different types of cloth were all included in the category "cloth."

Table 14-2 summarizes the comparison of the variety of goods traded at Michilimackinac, Detroit, Green Bay, and Ouiatenon. To

Table 14-2. Variety of Goods

Green Bay	Ouiatenon	Detroit	Michilimackinac
Mean Number of Different Types of Goods Per Year			
40.7	26.3	23.7	22
Total Variety of Goods Over All Years			
70	61	57	60

make this comparison, the number of different kinds of goods shipped to each post per year and the total number of kinds of goods sent to each post for all years were computed. Ouiatenon, Detroit, and Michilimackinac exhibit roughly similar mean values for the range of goods shipped per year. Green Bay, however, shows a substantially higher mean number of different types of goods traded per year.

A similar relationship occurs in the comparison of the total range of goods represented in all outfits for each post. Ouiatenon, Detroit, and Michilimackinac again display very similar values but a somewhat larger overall variety of goods was traded at Green Bay.

Volume of Trade

In order to compare the relative volume of trade at the four posts, price information recorded in the account book invoices was used. This approach was taken to avoid problems in using quantity as a basis for comparison. The units of quantity in which different goods were sold varied considerably. Some items, such as pins and needles, were sold by count; others, such as glass beads, were sold by the pound or by the "mass," still other items were sold by the bundle, and so on.

Because of this situation, certain items could make a significant difference in the size of an outfit on the basis of quantity. If pins or needles were included in an outfit, they could increase the total quantity of goods by hundreds or thousands. This creates the potential for the presence or absence of items like pins or needles to have a considerable impact on the relative quantity of goods sent to the different posts.

Expressing volume of trade in terms of trader expenditure circumvents this problem. Unlike quantity, the monetary units of price are consistent variables among all types of trade goods. Thus trader investment in trade goods provides a common basis for comparison.

Table 14-3 presents the expenditure figures representing the relative volume of trade. The amount of money spent per year for trade goods and the total expenditure for all years combined are indicated for each post. The mean yearly value for each post is also given. All of these figures are expressed in terms of the monetary system in the account books. Three-part decimal numbers are used to indicate *livres, sols,* and *deniers.*

These data suggest contrasts in the level of trade at the four posts. The mean yearly figures suggest that the largest volume of trade was consistently conducted at Green Bay, followed by Ouiatenon, Detroit, and Michilimackinac.

Table 14-3. Expenditure for Trade Goods by Year

Green Bay		Detroit		Michilimackinac		Ouiatenon	
1724	8929.02.09	1715	1808.10.00	1725	4109.06.06	1721	552.05.00
1725	8357.01.06	1721	902.01.00	1732	47.03.00	1731	10074.16.03
1739	3711.19.09	1724	4057.16.00	1734	3368.15.03	1736	1400.02.06
1740	8537.05.04	1731	297.00.00	1736	361.09.06	1738	455.05.00
1741	10004.16.05	1732	4025.17.05	1739	1128.02.04		
1742	9671.12.06	1734	969.04.06	1740	1731.10.09		
1743	6497.01.11	1736	940.00.09	1744	814.10.07		
1744	7782.00.11	1737	447.14.04	1745	1367.14.05		
1745	5069.13.02	1758	12496.08.04	1746	3767.19.02		
1747	20626.02.02			1747	1659.05.10		
1748	10344.14.04						
	99531.10.09		25944.12.04		18355.17.04		12482.08.09
Mean	9048.06.06		2882.14.08		1835.11.09		3120.12.02

The position of Ouiatenon in this sequence is difficult to assess due to the single large value for the year 1731. That figure, combined with the fact that there are only four years' worth of outfits for Ouiatenon, results in a yearly mean greater than that for both Detroit and Michilimackinac. Because of the small number of years recorded for Ouiatenon and the discrepancy between the 1731 total and the totals for the other three years, it is unclear how valid a representation this is of the relative volume of trade at Ouiatenon.

The main contrast in relative volume of trade is in the disparity between Green Bay and the other three posts. The Green Bay yearly totals are generally considerably higher than those for the other posts, reaching a peak in 1747 at 20,626.02.02. The yearly mean value at Green Bay—9,048.06.06—is more than three times higher than the mean yearly expenditure for Detroit and more than four times higher than the mean yearly expenditure for Michilimackinac.

Composition of the Trade Good Inventories

Trader expenditure was also used as a basis for comparing composition of trade good inventories. In this analysis, the outfits shipped to Green Bay for all years were combined and the total expenditure for all trade goods was calculated. Then the percentage of total expenditure represented by each type of trade good was computed. This allowed the total inventory of types of goods sent to Green Bay to be rank ordered according to the proportion of expenditure each type of good comprised. This was done for each of the other posts as well, allowing comparison between the ranked order of goods for each post. Table 14-4 presents the ranked ordering of those goods that comprise at least one percent of the total expenditure at each post.

This analysis revealed some interesting consistencies between the four posts. First, at each post, cloth comprises the largest proportion of expenditure by a substantial margin. Second, a very small number of goods accounts for a very high percentage of the total expenditure for each post. The top five items at Green Bay represent 61.6 percent of the total, at Michilimackinac 68.5 percent, at Detroit 75.2 percent, and at Ouiatenon 60.6 percent. Further, while their ranked order varies somewhat, the top five items are virtually identical at all four posts. Cloth, blankets, gunpowder, and shirts represent four of the top five items at all four posts. Capotes is the fifth item at three of the posts, whereas brandy is the fifth item at Detroit.

As another aspect of the composition of trade good inventories, the frequency at which different types of goods were shipped to the posts was examined. This was accomplished by determining how often each trade item was taken to a post out of the total possible number of years for that post. Table 14-5 summarizes the frequency distributions for each post.

Again, the primary result of this analysis is the contrast indicated between Green Bay and the other three posts. At Detroit, Michilimackinac, and Ouiatenon the pattern is one of a relatively limited number of goods consistently shipped to each post and an increasingly larger range of goods that were taken infrequently. At Green Bay there was a relatively large number of goods commonly taken to the post, a small number of items that were taken about half the time, and then a larger range of goods that went to the post infrequently.

A simple breakdown of the data helps illustrate this point. At Detroit, fourteen of fifty-seven items appeared in the outfits in over half of the nine years represented at that post. At Michilimackinac, fifteen of sixty items appeared in over half of the ten years represented. At Ouiatenon, thirteen of sixty-one items occurred in over half the years represented. But at Green Bay, thirty-nine of seventy items appeared in over half of the eleven years represented. It may be noted that an important component of the larger range of goods shipped to Green Bay is the consistent appearance of clothing articles in the outfits: capotes, shirts, leggings, sleeves, and mantelets.

Conclusions

This analysis of data in the Montreal Merchants' Records account books offers a number of insights into contrasts in French period

Table 14-4. Ranked Order of Trade Goods Which Account for at Least One Percent of the Total Expenditure for All Trade Goods

Item	Percent of Total Expenditure
A. Detroit	
1. cloth	54.7513
2. blankets	7.9581
3. gunpowder	6.6141
4. shirts	3.2367
5. brandy	2.6133
6. kettles	2.4994
7. wine	2.2095
8. trim	2.0663
9. musketballs	2.0081
10. guns	1.9033
11. stockings	1.6974
12. knives	1.5971
13. thread	1.1141
14. shot	1.0783
15. capotes	1.0079
B. Green Bay	
1. cloth	22.1779
2. blankets	13.8905
3. gunpowder	10.3656
4. capotes	8.6634
5. shirts	6.5178
6. shot	3.7748
7. leggings	3.7539
8. brandy	3.6982
9. mantelets	3.6924
10. sleeves	3.0210
11. knives	2.3120
12. kettles	2.1803
13. guns	2.1679
14. vermilion	1.9865
15. axes	1.7120
16. tobacco	1.5330
17. musketballs	1.0151

Table 14-4 Continued

Item	Percent of Total Expenditure
C. Michilimackinac	
1. cloth	35.4459
2. gunpowder	9.8034
3. blankets	8.9797
4. shirts	8.9688
5. capotes	5.2980
6. vermilion	2.6940
7. brandy	2.1328
8. knives	2.1281
9. mantelets	2.0668
10. leggings	2.0305
11. tobacco	1.9834
12. gartering	1.8200
13. thread	1.2608
14. trim	1.1963
15. kettles	1.1016
16. sleeves	1.0106
D. Ouiatenon	
1. cloth	26.2732
2. gunpowder	12.0169
3. shirts	9.0487
4. capotes	7.2622
5. blankets	6.0245
6. brandy	5.2794
7. vermilion	4.1418
8. guns	3.7813
9. kettles	3.5610
10. knives	3.2886
11. wine	1.6693
12. musketballs	1.6023
13. shot	1.4020
14. axes	1.3459
15. tobacco	1.1182
16. stockings	1.0054

trade activity at Green Bay, Michilimackinac, Detroit, and Ouiatenon. The documentary data used in this study are especially important to the results produced by the analysis. The Montreal Merchants' Records provide a record of trade goods in systemic context, which primarily represents Indian trade at the posts. This body of data is well suited to examining the traffic in trade goods at different French period posts.

First, with regard to variability in trade, a very comparable variety of goods was traded at Michilimackinac, Detroit, and Ouiatenon. At Green Bay, however, a larger variety of goods was marketed. This greater variety was apparent in both the range of goods shipped to Green Bay on a yearly basis and in the overall range of goods that went to the post over the course of the entire period.

Second, the Montreal Merchants' Records data suggest discrepancies between all four posts in the volume of trade conducted. The mean yearly expenditure for trade goods computed for each post suggests the highest volume of trade was carried out at Green Bay, followed by Ouiatenon, Detroit, and Michilimackinac. The results of this comparison of the relative volume of trade are considered tentative because the representativeness of the data is uncertain. It would appear that, except for the year 1731, these particular merchants did very little business with traders destined for Ouiatenon. With data for only four years available and the pronounced discrepancy between 1731 and the other three years, the mean yearly value produced for Ouiatenon is difficult to evaluate. While the data for the other posts are more comparable, the degree to which they reflect the volume of trade at each post is not completely secure. If the merchants that appear in the Montreal Merchants' Records sold goods to several traders destined for some posts but sold to very few traders destined for others, the volume of trade at certain posts could be underrepresented. While keeping this caveat in mind, it should also be noted that this analysis suggests, at least, that there may have been a substantially greater volume of trade at Green Bay as compared to the other three posts.

Third, there are both similarities and differences in the composition of the trade inventories at the four posts. An element of consistency among the posts is exhibited in the fact that a nearly identical group of five trade items commanded a large percentage of trader expenditure. However, the trade good inventories varied with respect to the frequency at which different types of trade goods were shipped to the posts. This discrepancy was most apparent between Green Bay and the other three locations. For Michilimackinac, Detroit, and Ouia-

Table 14-5. Number of Years Each Item Was Taken to Forts

A. Green Bay

11	10	9	8	7	6	5	3	2	1
cloth	mantelets	leggings	guns	ice chisel	pipes	wire	breeches	pistols	dress st.
blankets	vermilion	mskktball	wine	hawk bells	scissors	darts	daggers	gun cocks	dresses
gunpwdr.	tobacco	yarn	caps	hats	buckles	hoes	gowns	handrchief	beads
capotes	tomahawks	trim	shoes	gunsheaths			hair puller	fish line	adze
shirts	gartering	awls	stockings				verdigris	garters	cod line
shot	combs		firesteel					jew's harp	gun screw
brandy	fngr ring		gunworms						lioncloth
sleeves									pins
knives									shawls
kettles									gun locks
axes									fishhooks
gl. bead									pwdr horn
thread									blck lead
mirrors									tacks
gunflint									
needles									

Table 14-5 Continued

B. Detroit

9	8	7	6	5	4	3	2	1
cloth	gl. bead	blanket	brandy	pins	shirts	guns	capotes	ornament?
gunpowder	combs	wine	musketball	tobacco	kettles	stocking	gloves	hawk bells
knives		trim	shot	mirrors	caps	yarn	hoes	mantelets
		thread	vermilion	hndrchief	scissors	buckles	tomahawk	cod line
		gunflint			needles	axes	necklace	tuques
					firesteels	shoes	awls	thimbles
					pipes	buttons	spoons	gartering
					finger ring	girters	tacks	jew's harp
						gunworms		fans
						wire		brushes
								forks
								ladles
								brooches

Table 14-5 Continued

C. Michilimackinac

10	9	8	7	6	5	4	3	2	1
cloth	yarn	tobacco	gunpowder	brandy	mirrors	mantelets	wine	capotes	guns
knives		gl. bead	blankets	gartering	firesteel	leggings	shot	kettles	necklaces
			shirts	shoes	gunflints	axes	stocking	sleeves	musketballs
			vermilion	combs		fngr ring	caps	hndkrchief	gunsheaths
			thread			wire	tomahawk	hawk bells	hair puller
			trim			needles	darts	verdigris	breeches
						awls	hoes	azure	mittens
						scissors	pipes	pins	gloves
						gunworms			hats
									scarves
									ice chisels
									bayonets
									cod line
									garters
									jew's harp
									buckles
									tacks

Table 14-5 Continued

D. Ouiatenon

4	3	2	1	1 (cont.)
brandy	cloth	shirts	capotes	daggers
knives	gunpowder	vermilion	guns	hawk bells
wine	blanket	kettles	musketballs	brooches
	axes	shot	tomahawks	garters
	tobacco	stockings	wire	azure
	combs	hndrchiefs	gunworms	buttons
	glass beads	needles	hats gun-	scissors
	caps	shoes	sheaths	tacks
	thread	trim	shawls	fishhooks
	firesteels	mirrors	cod line	
		finger rings	mittens	
		gunflints	scarves	
		awls	yarn	
		necklaces	breeches	
		pipes	hoes	
			laces	
			gloves	
			forks	
			hoods	
			jews harps	
			pins	
			loincloths	
			buckles	
			fans	

tenon, a very small number of items was consistently included in the trade outfits over the years. For Green Bay, on the other hand, a relatively large group of goods appeared regularly in the outfits taken to the post.

The main result of this comparison of trade is the suggestion that there was a marked contrast in commercial activity at Green Bay in relation to the other three posts. Based on this analysis of the traffic in trade goods that moved through these four French period posts, it appears that a more ambitious trade with Indians was conducted through Green Bay than at Detroit, Michilimackinac, or Ouiatenon. The evidence in the Montreal Merchants' Records indicates that a wider variety of goods was consistently traded at Green Bay. Further, the data suggest that a relatively high volume of trade was conducted through that post.

To a certain extent, these results lend support to Tordoff's argument that trade at different posts varied on the basis of dfferences in functional complexity between regional distribution centers and local distribution centers. In her hierarchical model, Green Bay represents a local distribution center and Michilimackinac and Detroit are regional distribution centers. It appears that Green Bay may have been a much more *intensive* trade location whereas Michilimackinac and Detroit, as more *extensive* settlements, were not as focused on trade activities.

For the most part, however, the comparisons made in this study suggest that with respect to the function of trade, variation among French outposts did not follow the regional distribution center–local distribution center model. According to that model, trade at Green Bay and Ouiateneon, two local distribution centers, was similar, and it contrasted with trade at Michilimackinac and Detroit, which were regional distribution centers. This study suggests an alternate perspective. Although the Montreal Merchants' Records data are not conclusive, they suggest that trade at Ouiatenon was more similar to trade at Michilimackinac and Detroit than it was to trade at Green Bay. Further, Tordoff's suggestion that the variety of goods traded was consistent at both regional distribution centers and at local distribution centers was not supported by this analysis. The documentary data indicate that while the variety of goods traded was similar at Detroit, Michilimackinac, and Ouiatenon, it differed at Green Bay.

The results of this analysis suggest that additional factors need to be considered in the comparison of trade at different posts. For example, Eccles (1974:146–47) points out that various trade policies were instituted by the government of New France at different French posts in the West. He notes that at Michilimackinac, trade was open

236 / French Colonial Archaeology

to licensed traders. Detroit, in contrast, was maintained as a king's post or crown monopoly in order to keep prices competitive with those set by English traders. Johnson (1971:43, 48), however, indicates that the commandant at Detroit often granted permits to trade to the residents of the settlement.

During at least the 1740s and 1750s, it appears that a monopoly on the Green Bay trade was held by the person or partners who acquired the lease for the post (Eccles 1974:146; Kay 1978:144; Harris 1987: pl. 40). Further, Eccles (1974:147) states that the Green Bay trading territory included an extensive region stretching from Green Bay to the Mississippi River and from Lake Superior to the southern Wisconsin area. He goes on to say that the trade at Green Bay was especially lucrative and, as a result, that it was one of the most desirable and profitable trading locations in the West.

It appears that factors such as these had an important bearing upon the substantial trade developed at Green Bay as suggested by the Montreal Merchants' Records data and echoed in Eccles's comments. Green Bay was the base of operations for an extensive trading territory, and a leaseholder maintained monopoly trading rights over the region. These conditions figured prominently, no doubt, in fostering the large-scale, high-volume trade that developed at Green Bay.

This investigation suggests that a complex set of conditions contributed to variability in trade at French period outposts. While Tordoff's hierarchical differentiation between regional distribution centers and local distribution centers is useful in understanding other functional variation, such as population size and military presence, it is not as effective in representing contrasts in trade between posts. This study suggests that the French system of trade in the western country varied over space in several respects. It is part of the ongoing challenge of French period research to gain a better understanding of this variability and of the underlying factors that contributed to it.

Acknowledgments

I would like to thank Charles Cleland for his insightful comments on earlier drafts of this chapter and Peggy Anderson for her help in organizing the data and for proofreading the final draft.

French Presence in Minnesota: The View from Site Mo20 near Little Falls

15

Douglas A. Birk

Since 1982 the Institute for Minnesota Archaeology (IMA) has sponsored field and archival research to give sharper regional definition to the era of French presence (ca. 1640–1760) south and west of Lake Superior. Among the IMA's most notable work is the continuing investigation of site 21-Mo-20 (or "Mo20"), the archaeological remains of a mid-eighteenth-century French colonial outpost in central Minnesota. With private funds and the support of other groups, the IMA has now acquired the site for preservation and public interpretation. This chapter considers the importance of perspective in studying early French sites, discusses the material record of French presence in the Minnesota area, and reviews some preliminary results of the Mo20 project.

The Fur Trade: A Confining Vision?

Early Great Lakes history is often treated topically and chronologically as an era of European-Indian transactions known as the *fur trade*. In Minnesota a long line of scholars with widely different backgrounds and expertise have written papers, dug sites, exhibited materials, and attended conferences — all in the name of the fur trade. To categorize their work and subject matter under this single unified theme may be working to oversimplify the past, mislead the public, stifle creative research, and inhibit the preservation of important archaeological sites.

There is no doubt that *fur trade* is a loaded term steeped in romantic imagery. A large segment of the public, content with an uncomplicated vision of the past, sees it as a time when carefree voyageurs sang and paddled their way across the continent in search of furs and adventure.

Others, less afflicted by the Hollywood drill, view the fur trade as a procession of explorers and company mergers, a series of conflicts and treaties, a web of cultural ecological shifts, or an arena where the Old and New Worlds met to exchange merchandise, ideas, and genes.

Most scholars are aware of this "identity crisis" and accept fur trade studies as a field of research covering a broad range of human and natural topics. They recognize that the nature of their inquiries is changing and welcome the trend toward new interests and approaches (e.g., Judd and Ray 1980:3). Rather than redefine their subject matter they are content to say there were many "fur trades," involving different people, times, and places and requiring diverse explanations.

Others in the historical and anthropological professions embrace a more parochial view. They see *the* fur trade as a trite and requisite part of Great Lakes history that uniformly conditioned intercultural encounters and led to inevitable Euro-Canadian or Euro-American domination in the nineteenth century. Some privately argue that fur trade studies have been overdone and seriously question the utility of researching a subject or time that is so completely known!

Fur trade archaeology in Minnesota began in the 1850s when antiquarians dug into sites as a form of recreation or as a means to verify "facts" gleaned from paper records. Later, public works programs used field excavation as a means to create jobs and reconstruct early historic buildings. Excavators paid little attention to artifact provenience and even less to artifact groups and patterns. Despite changes in the profession during the 1960s and 1970s, the reconstructionist approach has had a lingering impact on public perception. Archaeology, to many, remains a discipline with lots of sex appeal but with only minor application, best suited to generating historical footnotes or items for museum display.

Combining the idea that the fur trade was a romantic era now being studied to death with the notion that archaeology is a trivial pursuit has done little to excite public support for fur trade archaeology in Minnesota. The general lack of enthusiasm has also inspired few efforts to preserve historic sites identified with *the* fur trade. The generic, one-explanation-fits-all fur trade concept may even lead to prophetic scholarship in the sense that it can seriously affect how early historic records and materials are gathered and used. To consider the rich and diverse legacy of Great Lakes area Indian-European interactions as just so many facets of a single, uniform economic experience may be limiting our capacity to know and explain many broader issues.

For these reasons, when studying French fort sites in the Minnesota area I prefer not to think of them simply as fur trading posts, but rather as places associated with European global expansion and cultural exchanges that went far beyond the mere act of swapping furs and kettles. Minnesota's French forts are material expressions of past human thought and enterprise—frozen time capsules that reflect the ability and resolve of French colonials in dealing with austere and often uncertain conditions on the western edge of their known world. Those fort sites that survive contain unique information about their occupants and the natural and cultural environments in which they lived. In archaeological soil can be found evidence relating to their social organization, technological capability, life-styles, world view, and even their decision-making processes. The plant and animal remains are equally vital in reconstructing diets, butchering practices, human-land relationships, game population dynamics, and local vegetation. The range of potential research topics often seems more limited by the methods and goals of excavation than by any inherent limits in the data themselves.

The role of archaeologists digging such sites is not to sweep up the stray and aberrant crumbs of history, but to illuminate French presence and all that presence involved, *including* the trafficking of furs. Although hardly revolutionary, this approach inspires freer discussion of the commercial, political, religious, settlement, and biological aspects of western French penetration. It also leaves room to explore the same historic era from the other side of the frontier, emphasizing the North American Indian experience.

The French Regime in Minnesota

The French regime in the Minnesota area began with the earliest French explorations in the 1600s and ended with the British conquest of Canada in 1763. During this dynamic period, small numbers of colonial French entered the West where their presence influenced the movement, alienation, or alliance of numerous Indian groups. The French introduced new language, religions, technologies, diseases, modes of warfare, and a paternalistic Indian policy (Eccles 1969; Elliott 1975:xi). In turn, they borrowed extensively from native cultures and adapted to a broad range of natural and human conditions encountered in the West.

The French regime accounts for about one-third of recorded "historic" time in the Minnesota area, yet remains poorly known. To promote a better understanding of this formative period, a system has been proposed for dividing it into lesser temporal units or phases

(Birk 1982:118). These phases broadly reflect shifting colonial interests and the concomitant rhythms of French presence in the Northwest. For archaeologists, this scheme offers an alternative to the Quimby
historic dating system, which is only marginally useful in regions west
of the Great Lakes (Quimby 1966:7).

The Initial or *French Contact phase* (ca. 1640–1702) was marked by
western geographical discovery and the opening of cross-cultural relations with contacted native groups. During this formative period
the French entered the upper Mississippi Valley, met the powerful
Siouan-speaking Dakota nations, and encountered the vast treeless
plains of the West. Regional historians have independently characterized the French Contact phase as an "era of pristine discovery"
or an "era of hope and achievement" (Kellogg 1908:150; compare
with Turner 1977:29–38; Blegen 1963:53–62).

From 1702 to 1713 France was embroiled in Queen Anne's War
and the French largely withdrew from the Great Lakes to promote
their political advantage elsewhere. This disruptive period is a wa-
tershed between seventeenth- and eighteenth-century French activities
in the Minnesota area.

The Late or *French Expansion phase* (ca. 1713–63) saw a renewed
demand for western furs, a reopening of French interests through
the Great Lakes, and the reestablishment of direct trade with the
Dakota. An increased French presence led to the construction of a
number of licensed posts in the Northwest, including the transship-
ment center of Fort Michilimackinac. The French Expansion phase
has been depicted as an "age of exploitation" (Kellogg 1908:150).

French period forts in the Minnesota area were situated with regard
to resources, transportation lanes, exchange opportunities, and defense. Actual site selection might be made through the invitation or
direction of Indian groups (Turner 1977:38). Remote, contested, or
poorly populated areas were usually bypassed. The vast, Dakota-dom-
inated grasslands of western Minnesota formed a sort of physical and
psychological barrier to French movement and were probably avoided
for siting forts. Although early recognized as a Dakota settlement,
the Mille Lacs Lake region was apparently too confined, underpopu-
lated, and unstable to attract a permanent French post.

The most prominent French forts in the Minnesota area were tribal
or multiband level exchange centers built on major waterways in game-
rich locales near the prairie-forest edge (fig. 15-1). Some of the largest
facilities were at lucrative and accessible points on the Minnesota, St.
Croix, and Mississippi rivers in southeastern and east-central Minnesota. Others, such as Fort St. Charles and Fort St. Pierre, were on

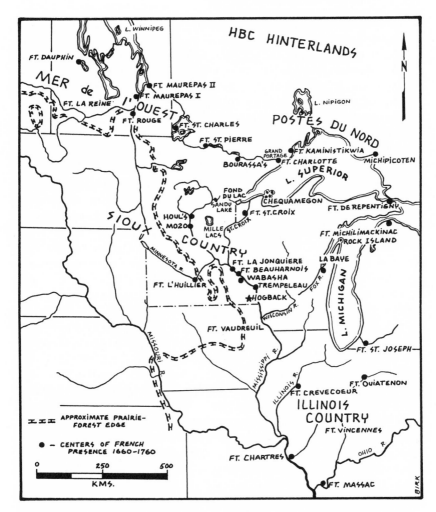

Figure 15-1. Selected French Sites in the Western Great Lakes Region

northern waterways along the present international border with Canada. The forts were pockets of French influence and points of distribution for European goods. In theory, each was part of a broad security and logistical network that promoted French interests in the western Great Lakes. In reality, Minnesota area forts were temporally and spatially dispersed and, because of Indian loyalties and the jealousies or cross motives of their builders, were often in conflict.

The establishment and use of the Minnesota area posts was largely reliant on external forces like political and economic affairs in Europe and the Americas, or the whim of the French colonial governors. Equally important were conditions along the western frontier itself. Use of French posts in the Lake Pepin region, for example, hinged on the real or perceived disposition of such groups as the Dakota, Fox, Sauk, and Illini. French interests at Chequamegon, in the greater Mississippi Headwaters, and in the northern border lakes region were more closely linked to Assiniboine-Cree-Ojibway-Dakota relations and, at times, dealings with "fugitive" eastern tribes like the Ottawa.

Because the French interacted with different native groups in so many different locations, Minnesota's French regime also lends itself to spatial division. The challenge is in trying to find names that acceptably portray these divisions during the century of sparse and discontinuous French occupation. Much of the problem stems from the evolution of French geographical knowledge, shifting political boundaries, and the inconsistent early use of names to define western territories or locales (e.g., Innis 1956:100, 413–14).

French forts along the present international border, between Lake Superior and Lake-of-the-Woods, were part of what became known as the *Mer de l'Ouest* (or the Posts of the Western Sea). This French interaction sphere, with roots in late seventeenth-century exploration, eventually extended beyond Lake Winnipeg to the foothills of the Rocky Mountains (Eccles 1969:145). The *Mer de l'Ouest* involved cultural exchanges with northern Indian groups (including the Cree and Assiniboine), use of the "Voyageur's Highway," competition with the Hudson's Bay Company, and an unrequited effort to find a passage to the Pacific Ocean (Wisconsin Historical Collections 1906, 18:187–88). The French entered this area by water routes through Kaministikwia and Grand Portage, or the St. Louis (Fond du Lac) River that empties into Lake Superior at present-day Duluth (Morse 1969:80; Thompson 1969:5–11). The boundaries of the *Mer de l'Ouest* were elastic and changed in response to waxing and waning French interests (Burpee 1968:7; Birk 1982:117–18).

In the region northeast of Grand Portage, on the north side of Lake Superior, were the French *Postes du Nord* that included facilities at Michipicoten and Nipigon (Morton 1973:168; Wisconsin Historical Collections 1906, 18:191). In broader terms, all French forts within the area of Lake Superior and its dependencies were sometimes considered as northern posts (Guillet 1966:9).

The Sioux Country comprised the western hinterlands of the Green Bay and Chequamegon trade districts and extended from near Prairie du Chien northward in an arc through the Minnesota, Mississippi, and St. Croix river basins to the head of Lake Superior. This inter-action sphere was separated from the *Mer de l'Ouest* by the boglands and closed forests of northern Minnesota. In the southeast it cornered on the Illinois Country. French posts in the Sioux Country were accessed from Lake Superior through the St. Louis and Brule rivers, from Green Bay via the Fox-Wisconsin route, or from the south by way of the Mississippi (Wisconsin Historical Collections 1906, 17:57). Modern use of "Sioux Country" as a geopolitical or logistical concept is not completely satisfying. Several forts in this area attracted Indian groups other than Dakota and some posts in the Mississippi-St Croix headwaters regions after 1745 may have catered exclusively to non-Dakota groups such as the Cree and Ojibway.

The natural environment in Minnesota during the French regime broadly approximated that observed by land surveyors in the mid-to-late 1800s. In general, the state was dominated by two great biomes, prairie and forest, that merged to form a vegetal transition running diagonally across the state from northwest to southeast (fig. 15-2). West of this transition were tall and mixed grass prairies and to the east were broadleaf, conifer-hardwood, and boreal forests (Shay 1985:31). The land surface comprised an uneven mix of lakes and swamps, lakeless plains, hilly moraines, and rocky escarpments. The "unglaciated" Mississippi Valley area of southeastern Minnesota was a contradiction of floodplains and uplands that inspired many a French pen to dwell on its beauty and fertility.

Pollen evidence suggests climatic conditions in the western Great Lakes were quite stable from about 2000–300 B.P. Beginning about three hundred years ago, with the commencement of historic time in Minnesota, world climate became generally cooler. It was during this period, sometimes called the Little Ice Age, that the state's transitional woodlands developed into the particular patterns recorded at the time of white settlement. The transformations may have been most dra-matic in those parts of southern Minnesota that promoted growth of the "Big Woods" (Grimm 1985:14–16; Shay 1985:36). Early records, like Andre Penicaut's observation in 1700 that the "great cold" and severity of Minnesota winters began in September (McWilliams 1953:47–48), give a human dimension to the scientific data.

Because climatic change can affect the distribution of plants and animals, people reliant on those resources for survival might respond by altering their settlement and ranging habits. The ecological shifts of the Little Ice Age, in tandem with other disruptions such as growing native participation in a fur trade economy and human population

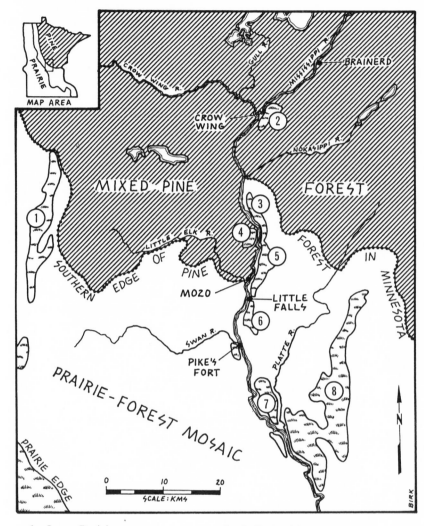

1   Long Prairie   5   Belle Prairie
2   Crow Wing Prairie   6   Little Falls Prairie
3   Olmstead Prairie   7   Bellevue Prairie
4   Green Prairie   8   Rich Prairie

Figure 15-2. Major Vegetation Features in the Little Falls Area of Central Minnesota

loss through intensified warfare and disease, may have influenced conditions and events in Minnesota in ways we do not yet understand.

For example, a suspected precipitation increase during the Little Ice Age could have inhibited the start and spread of fires, resulting in decreased annual burnings and an expansion of the forest into the prairie (Wright 1974:14). Grassland loss combined with increased hunting pressures would likely favor a reduction in the size and range of bison and elk herds, particularly in east-central and southeastern Minnesota. Both Ojibway oral accounts and French records hint at a growing depletion of big game in these areas in the eighteenth century (e.g., Warren 1957:97; Shea 1861:173). As their ability to exploit and manipulate the prairie-edge diminished, forest-fringe dwellers like the Mdewakanton Dakota may have had to travel greater distances during their seasonal western hunting forays to capture large game (Johnson 1985:156–57, 161). If real, such shifts could have hastened the Dakota abandonment of the Mille Lacs region in the eighteenth century and influenced the location and use of French forts in central and southern Minnesota.

There is, in fact, an oral tradition that the westward emigration of the Dakota was partly inspired by their need for greater food resources and their desire to escape the increasingly harsh climate about the head of Lake Superior (Grant 1960:346). Another Dakota claim is that they surrendered no lands that were not already destitute of game and therefore not worth spilling blood over (Parker 1966: 197). Such ecological explanations have been overlooked by those promoting a strict military cause for the Dakota exodus from Mille Lacs Lake. More likely the Dakota were both propelled and drawn from their former homelands in a lengthy process involving a number of complex and interrelated political, ecological, economical, and historical factors. The final catalyst for Dakota withdrawal may have been the condition of French presence, which often served to enhance tribal differences, stimulate territorial movements, and deplete animal resources.

The Archaeology of French Presence

Data gleaned from written and material records suggest Minnesota's French-related sites can be grouped according to function, and the duration and intensity of use, as follows: (1) fortified *entrepots* designed for extended use and often occupied by traders, troops, craftsmen, or missionaries (such places, like Isle Pelee and Forts l'Huillier, Beauharnois, La Jonquiere, and St. Charles, were typically named after geographical entities, statesmen, sponsors, or religious figures); (2) temporary, although likely fortified, outposts built for trading, political, or religious purposes (these commonly bore the names of agents like Bourassa, Deruisseaux, and Houl, or select geographical locations like St. Croix, Trempeleau, and Sunrise); (3) accommodations used by visiting, captive, or resident Frenchmen or French *coureurs de bois* at Indian villages; (4) special activity areas like transient camps, seasonal fishing or hunting camps, kill sites, battle grounds, portages, mines, burials, and the like; and (5) canoe accident sites or other places where items might be lost or discarded.

Unlike Fort de Chartres (Keene, chap. 3) and Fort Massac (Walthall, chap. 4) in the Illinois Country, no elaborate stone or earth-banked fortresses were built by the French in the Minnesota area. Forts there might consist of one or more log houses chinked with clay and surrounded by an enclosure of closely spaced vertical posts or "pickets." Stone fireplaces with wattle-and-daub (*bousillage*) chimneys were the principal sources of interior heat and light. Temperature extremes, frost heave, and heavy snows played havoc with buildings made of wood and bark. The same structures were also susceptible to shrinkage, warping, fire, and rot. Extended use of such facilities demanded heavy maintenance and was probably attended by a layering, overlapping, exaggeration, or intrusion of archaeological features. Because French forts were often built on older prehistoric sites, the superimposition or intermixing of site components can add to the complexity of the archaeological record. Forts were abandoned due to political shifts, changing economic interests, hostilities, competition, fear, flooding, and fires, or the exhaustion of local fur, food, or fuel resources.

To date, few French period sites or site components have been found and studied in Minnesota. Some that have are the Hogback site (Wilford and Brink 1974), the Mille Lacs sites (Johnson 1985), the "Sturgeon Lake Post" (21-GD-88) at Prairie Island (Birk 1985), 21-Mo-20 (Birk 1987), Fort Charlotte (Birk 1975; Birk and Wheeler 1975), and Fort St. Charles (Birk 1982). The latter two sites are along Minnesota's northern border. The others are situated in central and southern parts of the state.

Before the involvement of the Institute for Minnesota Archaeology, there was no sustained and systematic effort to locate, study, or preserve French colonial sites in Minnesota. An early antiquarian interest in places associated with French presence climaxed in 1908 with the discovery of Fort St. Charles on Lake-of-the-Woods. More recent attempts to find French fort sites at Mankato, Wabasha, Frontenac,

Sturgeon Lake (Prairie Island), and in the St. Croix Valley have gone largely unrewarded. As yet no one has satisfactorily identified the remains of a fort or structure in Minnesota dating to the French Contact phase. Fort St. Charles, one of only two sites identified from the French Expansion phase, was largely damaged by landscaping activities in the 1950s. The preservation clock is ticking, and because most forts were built in areas now widely developed or altered, hope is diminishing for future discoveries.

Site 21-Mo-20: A New Contender

The only French fort site identified in Minnesota in the past eighty years is 21-Mo-20. "Mo20," as the site is generally known, is the remains of a French outpost built in the mid-eighteenth century. It is the oldest European habitation site yet found in the Mississippi Headwaters region of central Minnesota and is one of a few short-term French wintering posts known archaeologically in North America. The site was listed to the National Register of Historic Places in 1984.

Mo20 lies in Morrison County 3.5 kilometers north of the city of Little Falls and 200 kilometers southeast of Lake Superior (fig. 15-1). The site is on the west bank of the Mississippi on a level terrace about two meters above the river. The French component of Mo20 is thinly buried beneath a few centimeters of soil and, except for some pothunting scars and its former use as a sheep pasture, is remarkably preserved. The remains of three French houses and other habitation features are visible on the ground surface (fig. 15-3). All appear to be contained in an area measuring about thirty by forty-five meters. For security reasons, the IMA has enclosed the site with a chainlink fence topped with barbed wire.

Mo20 sits in a small clearing bordered on its north and west sides by a thick deciduous forest. Several hundred meters to the west, on higher ground, is a dense stand of red and white pine. An open field begins near the south edge of the visible site remains and extends along the river. This grassy opening supports an interesting variety of prairie plants. It was cultivated with horses prior to 1945 and later pastured with sheep. The field is bounded on the south by the Little Elk River, a tributary stream that enters the Mississippi about 500 meters below Mo20. Although now diminished, the Little Elk once served as a link in an overland canoe route to the Minnesota River.

During its occupation, Mo20 was on the southern edge of Minnesota's extensive pine woods and about fifty kilometers from the western tall grass prairies (fig. 15-2). The fort occupied a mosaic,

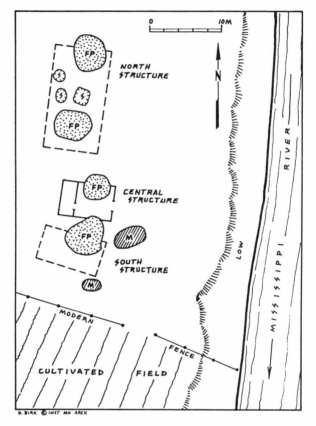

Figure 15-3. Site Mo20 Surface Feature Map

transitional forest zone dotted with oak openings and small tracts of prairie. Forest edge was plentiful. Opposite the fort was the Belle Prairie, a narrow grassland that paralleled the east bank of the Mississippi. Other nearby openings included Long, Olmstead, Green, Little Falls, Bellevue, and Rich prairies. These grasslands attracted elk and white-tailed deer and provided suitable forage for wintering herds of bison. The presence of large ungulates and meat and fur-producers such as beaver and bear were likely incentives for the French to build at the Little Elk. Other attractions probably included accessible building materials and firewood, convenient water transportation, and receptive Indian groups that might allow exploration of more remote areas.

Before arrested by the Little Falls dam, the Mississippi River below

Mo20 had an average gradient of seven feet per mile and accommodated several stretches of whitewater called the Little Elk Rapids (Upham 1969:353). Other rapids extending up the Little Elk River are less affected by the dam and remain active. Historical records hint that Indian portages may have bypassed turbulent sections of both rivers near their confluence. If so, Mo20 may also have been sited to control or benefit from the use of these trails.

It is traditionally believed that "Elk," as applied to the Little Elk River, comes from a Frenchman named (or nicknamed) La Biche who was supposedly killed at that location by the Dakota. The Ojibway called this stream the Omoshkos Sibi (variably spelled) meaning the "Elk River" (Bray 1970:52). The change to Little Elk, was apparently made to differentiate the Morrison County stream from another Elk River that enters the Mississippi in Sherburne County farther south. The name change has led to some confusion about the location of the historic Elk River battles fought between the Dakota and Ojibway, most probably at the mouth of the Sherburne County stream (Warren 1957:236–41). No further record of the hapless La Biche has been found, and it is not presently known if he was related to the French presence at Mo20.

Rocky exposures of schist and near-black slate at the mouth of the Little Elk extend northward along the Mississippi to beyond Mo20. In part these exposures coincide with the Little Elk Rapids. Because the slate is jointed and easily broken into portable slabs, it has seen nominal use as a local building material. Some of the slate is marbled with occasional veins of white pheno-crystalline quartz (Upham 1884:95). The Ojibway saw a visual resemblance between the quartz intrusions and layers of animal fat and named them the "Winin wabik" or "fat rock" (Brower 1902:122).

Jacob Brower, a pioneer Minnesota archaeologist, was drawn to the Little Elk around 1900 while pondering the notion that ancient "paleolithic" peoples once inhabited central Minnesota. White quartz chips found in local floodplain deposits fueled speculation that "Glacial Man" populations had used Little Falls area quartzes in the manufacture of tools. The subject was one of great controversy and attracted the attention of such scholars as W. H. Holmes of the Bureau of American Ethnology, F. W. Putnam of the Peabody Museum, and Theodore Lewis, Newton Winchell, and Warren Upham of Minnesota. From the melee also emerged Minnesota's first woman archaeologist, Frances Eliza Babbitt (Brower 1902:33–47).

Brower examined the "Winin wabik" formations and noted the quartz was angularly fractured (brecciated) and of poor quality for making tools. The few prehistoric artifacts he did find at the mouth of the Little Elk were in sparse deposits disturbed by modern quarries and the construction of mills and dams (Brower 1902:63).

The IMA has since determined the limits of these and other prehistoric sites in this locale using interval shovel testing. Materials found at Mo20, such as prehistoric hearths, ceramics, and stone tools and debitage, suggest the site area was used intermittently from at least 400 B.C. through A.D. 1760. The French occupation represents the last major phase of site use.

IMA surveys also identified the remains of a suspected historic dwelling about 150 meters downstream from Mo20 on the west bank of the Mississippi. Preliminary observation suggests this partly cultivated property may date to about 1840 and may be the site of a cabin used by the Ojibway war chief Hole-in-the-Day the Elder while trying to solidify his territorial claims in central Minnesota. An imposing grass-covered mound of earth and slate marks the location of the cabin's collapsed fireplace. Similar mounds with protruding slate blocks and granitic cobbles appear with the French component at Mo20 and likely discouraged cultivation of the fort area.

Persons who once hunted arrowheads in the plowed field between the cabin and fort sites came to view these rock piles as "Indian mounds." In fact, a tradition persists that the cabin's fireplace heap is actually the grave of an Indian chief and his horse. Although the origin of this story is uncertain, it is interesting that the site has continued to be identified with a Native American male of high status.

The "Indian mound" idea was another factor that worked to save the fort and cabin sites. Early landowners believed the mounds marked human burials that should not be disturbed. Their convictions were so strong that even today some persons will not consent to be interviewed on this subject. This preservation ethic was not broken until circa 1965, when stories of possible Indian battles, graves, and artifacts inspired some youths to explore the sites with shovels and screens. These adventurers, two boys and two girls all under the age of fifteen, were related to the landowner. One of the group, Bruce Mellor, about thirteen years of age, later emerged as a poet and writer of local history.

Digging in the mounds turned up several artifacts, none of which appeared to the youthful excavators to be very old or very Indian. Though disappointed, they shared their finds with a prehistorian (not trained in historical archaeology) who thought the materials might date to "early pioneer" times. The digging ceased, and by 1968, at the landowner's insistence, some backfilling was done.

In 1972, while doing National Register surveys for the Minnesota Historical Society, I was part of a group that talked to the landowner about the old Indian mission, flour mills, and other sites at the mouth of the Little Elk. In the course of our conversation he mentioned the "stone Indian mounds" and implied that human remains had been found in these features. Although skeptical, I made sketch maps of the "mounds" at both Mo20 and the nearby cabin site. Because the survey was designed to be only a rapid inventory of potential National Register sites, it allowed no time to test any of the three hundred or so archaeological properties visited that summer in the Mississippi Headwaters region. The dense vegetation precluded surface collection at Mo20 and plans to return to the Little Elk the following year were later scrapped.

There matters stood until my chance meeting with Mellor in February 1978. At the time he was gathering information to write an epic poem about Hole-in-the-Day the Elder. During our conversation Mellor mentioned that he was one of the Little Elk diggers and still had the materials excavated in 1965. In fact they were in a shoebox under his bed. His mother had long viewed this dusty packet with suspicion and had even tried to throw it out with the garbage (Birk 1983).

As we talked, I learned for the first time that the "mounds" had yielded more than just bones and that the bones themselves were small and heavily burned. Among materials not previously mentioned were "square nails" and ceramic sherds from "dishes like you might have in your kitchen cupboard." According to Mellor, most of these finds were made near the base of the mounds in what appeared to be thick deposits of ash. With this new information, it was immediately clear that the Little Elk mounds—at least those at the site of Mo20 — were the collapsed remains of historic fireplaces.

Mo20: A Working Hypothesis

Having jumped that initial hurdle, the query shifted to determining the age and identity of the fireplaces. Who built Mo20 and when? How long did the occupants stay? What were they doing at the Little Elk? Could their presence be linked to written records?

The problem of dating was tentatively answered a week later when Mellor returned to my office with his shoebox of treasures. In his collection were a handful of calcined animal bone, a heavily burned prismatic gunflint, and several hand-forged square nails (fig. 15-4). Also present were sherds from a tin-glazed earthenware ("faience")

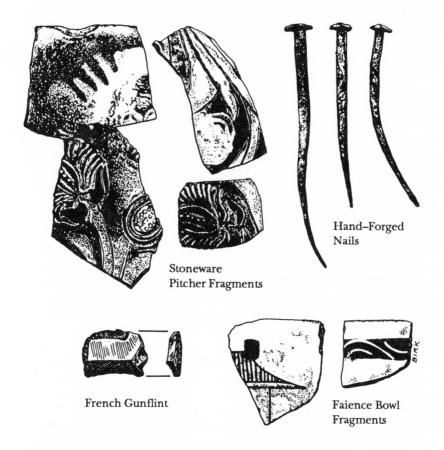

Stoneware
Pitcher Fragments

Hand–Forged
Nails

French Gunflint

Faience Bowl
Fragments

Figure 15-4. Selected Artifacts Found at Mo20

bowl with a handpainted, blue-on-white Chinese exterior motif. Finally, there were several pieces of what appeared to be a gray, salt-
glazed, Rhenish-style stoneware pitcher or mug. Exterior decoration
on this vessel consisted of a busy array of floral appliques, incised
lines, and zoned blue glazing. The presence of such distinctive ceramics so far west hinted that their owners possessed a measure of
social and economic importance. In the absence of later refined earthenwares, they also suggested the historic component at Mo20 must
represent a pre-1760 occupation (Birk 1983:26). Given this evidence,
the site's geographical location became another important dating
mechanism.

Mo20 is in a region that served as a contested intertribal buffer between the Dakota and Ojibway Indians from the mid-1700s until after 1800 (Hickerson 1970). Theoretically, one should not expect to find a Euro-Canadian or American site in this war zone dating to the last half of the eighteenth century. The history of recent events in this region is fairly well known from written accounts, yet no post-1800 trading posts or forts are recorded at the Little Elk. The oldest historic structures documented there are linked with the activities of Methodist-Episcopal missionaries and Hole-in-the-Day the Elder, in the late 1830s. The location of Mo20, in concert with its artifacts, suggested the site must predate the escalation of Dakota-Ojibway conflicts and therefore must be identified with the early French presence. It must, in fact, be the remains of a little-known or "lost" French fort.

My revitalized interest in Mo20 led to closer ties with landowners, Spencer and Rusty Nelson. The Nelsons had purchased the Little Elk property in 1950 for recreational use and, beyond building a cabin and barn, had chosen to leave most of the land undeveloped. Once informed that a probable "French fort" was lying in their old sheep pasture, they offered me free and unlimited access to the site. Like others now privy to its identification, they were sworn to silence. One of my greatest concerns was keeping the site a secret until its preservation was certain. Later, I learned that Bruce's mother, Jo Ann Mellor, was so moved by this intrigue that she placed the "shoebox" artifacts in her safety deposit box!

My initial work focused on nondestructive means to study Mo20 and its potential for controlled excavation. Specialists were enlisted to conduct floral, magnetometer, and color infrared aerial photo-graphic surveys of the site. Working behind the scenes, Jan Warner, the director of the Morrison County Historical Society, provided in-formation and leads relating to local history and legends. Soil scientists and other archaeologists were also consulted. While useful, none of these avenues promised to unlock the secret of the fort's identity. In attempting to answer that basic question from documentary sources, I also encountered some limitations in dealing with old French records.

A search of published and archival materials turned up few references to a French fort that might be identified with Mo20. The best leads were found in the papers of Joseph de la Marque (la Malgue), sieur de Marin, a noted explorer and officer in the French colonial regular troops. That Marin built a fort in central Minnesota was learned from his 1753–54 manuscript *journal* and letters housed in the collections of the Henry E. Huntington Library in San Marino,

California. These papers remained unknown to Minnesotans until 1951, when they were used by historian Grace Lee Nute in describing the closing years of the French regime in the upper Northwest (Nute 1951). Nute's pioneering work presented much new information on French presence in the Minnesota area and illuminated the Marin family's remarkable role in shaping events in the upper Mississippi Valley in the mid-1700s.

Joseph Marin was the son of Pierre-Paul de la Marque, sieur de Marin, a man of undoubted energy and broad experience in military, political, and commercial matters in the western Great Lakes (Eccles 1974:431). Joseph was baptized at Montreal in 1719. In 1732, at the tender age of thirteen, he was sent west by his father to explore the country around Michilimackinac and Green Bay. He soon mastered the art of Indian diplomacy and became a fluent speaker of Siouan and several Algonkian dialects (Chaput 1979:512).

In 1739 Joseph served in the French campaign against the Chickasaw in the lower Mississippi Valley. About the same time, Paul conferred with the Dakota "at the River of the Swan on the Mississippi" (Wisconsin Historical Collections 1906, 17:316–17), a location which, some speculate, could be the Swan River that enters the Mississippi ten kilometers south of Mo20 (fig. 15-2). There is no known evidence to suggest this meeting included the construction of a fort.

The following year Joseph negotiated peace and trade agreements with the Dakota and in 1745 was recalled with his father to fight the British in Acadia and along the New York frontier. Soon after, he became the son-in-law of Francois-Pierre de Rigaud de Vaudreuil, the future governor of New France (Chaput 1979:512).

In 1749, with the restoration of the trade licensing system, Joseph returned to the west as head of the Chequamegon post. At the time his father was commander at Green Bay. Their combined influence and political connections gave the Marins control of French relations in the vast country west of Lakes Michigan and Superior (Eccles 1974:431). Among their supporters was the governor, the marquis de la Jonquiere, who assigned the elder Marin a small garrison of troops and a liberal allowance for Indian presents (Wisconsin Historical Collections 1906, 18:63). Paul responded by building an outpost called "Fort La Jonquiere" somewhere in the Lake Pepin area. This fort, maintained by the Marins for six years, helped funnel Dakota furs through the entrepot at Green Bay (Kellogg 1925:379–80; Nute 1951:227–29).

Under the Marins, the *voyageur* labor force in the Green Bay district grew from six in 1738 to at least 190 by the year 1750 (Eccles

1974:431). The alleged financial rewards of deploying such a large work force caused some to charge the Marins with making excessive profits and paying political kickbacks in exchange for their monopoly trade positions (Kellogg 1925:381). Others accept that their dealings benefited a broader strategy designed to cement the allegiance of the western tribes to the French cause (Eccles 1974:431). Whatever their gain, their smug political position was soon altered by the death of la Jonquiere. The new governor, the marquis de Duquesne, pressed the need for colonial regulars to protect the frontiers of New France from British incursion. In 1752 Paul Marin was recalled to fight in the Ohio Valley. He died in broken health in 1753 while attempting to reach Fort Duquesne (Pittsburgh) at the forks of the Ohio. Meanwhile, Joseph was promoted full ensign in the colonial regulars in 1750 and spent the following year in garrison at Quebec (Chaput 1979:512). In 1752, at the direction of la Jonquiere, he was back in the upper Mississippi in control of the Sioux posts (Nute 1951:227).

Building on his father's authority, Joseph hoped to use his monopoly trade position to extend French influence in the Mississippi Headwaters. His agenda included searching for mines and minerals and discovering a route to the Western Sea. He also sought to pacify the western Indians and rally them against the growing threat of Anglo-American influence in the east. To accomplish his mission, Joseph Marin continued the use of Fort La Jonquiere and built another Mississippi River post below Prairie du Chien he called Fort Vaudreuil (Nute 1951:227). The latter facility Marin described as a walled fort enclosing "four houses and a storehouse" (Bailey 1975:71). This crucial reference helps archaeologists to visualize the size and appearance of the western forts.

In two years Joseph claims to have traveled over two thousand leagues in pursuit of his mission, much of it under wintry conditions and wearied by fatigue. His journeys purportedly brought twenty Indian nations into the French sphere and established peace among the Fox, Sauk, Winnebago, Sioux of the Lakes, Sioux of the Prairies, and the Menominee and Illini (Nute 1951:227). By his own assessment, "this peace was of the greatest consequence, for if these nations had not been reconciled, the French of the colony established at the Cahau [Cahokia] at the forts of Chartres and the cas [Kaskaskia] would have been obliged to abandon their settlements" (Bailey 1975:xi).

When Joseph Marin went to Green Bay, his former position among the Ojibway at Chequamegon was assigned to a rival named Joseph La Verendrye. The latter was a member of the adventurous La Verendrye family that had earlier opened and solidified French trade in the *Mer de l'Ouest*. Marin and La Verendrye soon entered a dispute over who had lawful control of affairs in the headwaters of the Mississippi and St. Croix rivers. It was during this period, on the eve of the expanding Dakota-Ojibway wars, that Joseph Marin built a third fort, a temporary outpost he named Fort Duquesne, somewhere on the Mississippi above St. Anthony Falls. Marin's writings suggest that his Fort Duquesne was occupied during the winter of 1752 and for part of the following year.

Minnesota historians have long used Marin's *journal* and letters to place his Fort Duquesne in the area of Crow Wing or Brainerd, Minnesota, about thirty to forty kilometers north of Mo20 (fig. 15-2) (e.g., Nute 1951:228, 234; Nute 1960:99; Blegen 1963:60; Breining and Watson 1977:63). Although based on scant, inconclusive, and somewhat contradictory information, this opinion is now widely embraced and is regarded as sacrosanct by many professional and lay historians. I am less convinced. In 1980, after considering the evidence for French presence in central Minnesota, I suggested Mo20 could be associated with the Marins and might well be the remains of the obscure Fort Duquesne.

The archaeological record of the Little Elk fort, including the artifacts and features, the architectural style, and the size and configuration of the site, all support the notion that Mo20 marks the remains of a 1750s French outpost. There are few such facilities documented for central Minnesota. The best known are Fort Duquesne and "Houl's" post that Marin commissioned at Crow Wing in 1753 (fig. 15-1). Houl (also spelled Houle and Hout) was assigned by Marin to proceed to Crow Wing and there to meet the Yankton Dakota and defuse hostilities between the Cree and Dakota in central Minnesota. If Fort Duquesne was already at Crow Wing, where Houl was ordered to set up, it seems likely that Marin would have simply ordered him to reoccupy that post.

Arriving at Crow Wing from the south, Houl was soon confronted by La Verendrye who entered the Mississippi Headwaters from the east through Sandy Lake. La Verendrye claimed exclusive rights to affairs in this region and seized Houl's outfit. He immediately sent Houl and his associates down the Mississippi with the admonition that they return to Fort La Jonquiere and not winter at Fort Duquesne (Nute 1951:232–33). La Verendrye then apparently occupied Houl's intended Crow Wing post and from this position continued to thwart Marin's commercial and political ambitions in the Mississippi Headwaters. Evidence suggests that Houl and fellow agents later reascended the Mississippi to confront La Verendrye a second time. Thus deployed, they may have taken temporary shelter at Fort Duquesne before being expelled again by their northern rival (Bailey 1975:78).

Although it is impossible to tell from Marin's writings just where Fort Duquesne was established, it seems likely that its location was somewhere other than at Crow Wing. Crow Wing was a strategic point for controlling southern entry into the Mississippi Headwaters and the logical place for La Verendrye to stop the northward penetration of Marin's men. The admonition that Houl and his associates not winter at Fort Duquesne after being forced from Crow Wing suggests that the 1752 fort was somewhere to the south, but close enough to make La Verendrye nervous. The nature and location of Mo20 makes it a prime candidate for such an elusive fort. As a working hypothesis of Mo20 research, at least, that notion is now being tested by every new turn of a trowel or archival page.

Field Discoveries

In 1982 I began the intensive study of Mo20 through the newly formed Institute for Minnesota Archaeology (IMA). One of my first tasks at IMA was to substantiate the mid-eighteenth-century date of Mo20 and to gather evidence that might further reveal the site's purpose and identity.

Using visible surface features as a guide, a two-meter-by-two-meter test unit was opened on the west edge of what later proved to be the "north structure" (fig. 15-3). Excavation was halted at a depth of 15 centimeters when a section of charred, palisaded (*poteaux en terre*) wall line was uncovered. This evidence suggested the structure was destroyed by fire. Habitation debris found on the east or interior side of the wall line included animal bone (food refuse), glass beads, part of an iron axehead, and faience and probable window glass sherds. Coincidentally, one of our faience sherds fit one of those found by the youths in 1965 (fig. 15-5A). This single discovery not only served to "verify" their artifact collection but, perhaps more than anything else, helped promote IMA's quest to save Mo20.

The IMA decided to buy the site in 1982 when the Nelsons announced their intention to sell part of their Little Elk property. At the time IMA was a new organization striving to initiate statewide programs in archaeological research, education, and preservation (Birk 1983:28–31). We were also a nonprofit group in need of financial support. After several false starts, IMA approached the Minnesota Parks Foundation (MPF), a group dedicated to making advance land purchases for the state park system. Responding to our request, MPF

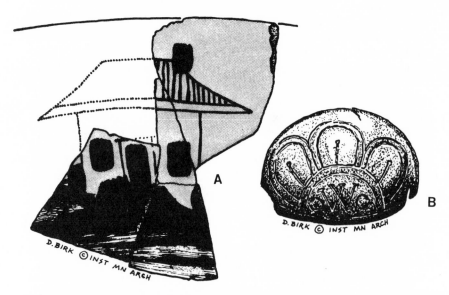

Figure 15-5. Additional Mo20 Artifacts

acquired title to Mo20 and some adjoining acreage in 1983. There-after the IMA-MPF partnership led to the acquisition of other his-torical properties on both sides of the Little Elk River. Ownership of this ninety-three-acre archaeological park—now known as the Little Elk Heritage Preserve—was transferred to IMA in 1988.

The 1983 field season at Mo20 was one of great toil and surprise. IMA research associate Dean Anderson (a doctoral candidate at Mich-igan State University) and I spent two months establishing a permanent metric grid and gathering ground elevation and soil data. We also dug several test pits and defined and implemented methodological procedures since used in additional fieldwork. The desire to maximize recovery of small artifacts, like glass and shell beads, lead shot, pins, needles, and microflakes, led to water-screening all soils associated with the French component.

Despite efforts to go "high-tech," the most useful tool in our arsenal in 1983 proved to be a power lawnmower. Our task of recording over 3,000 surface elevations across the site necessitated the prior removal of brush, small trees, and dead wood. As we proceeded we also mowed and raked the underlying grass. The job was perfectly awful, due largely to the intense summer heat, and had us wondering some days whatever happened to the "romance" of archaeology. We soon found out!

During our ordeal, Dean and I witnessed a spectacular transformation in the site's appearance. Features once veiled by vegetation now emerged in full contour. As we studied the features from various angles and heights under different lighting conditions, they began to take on new form and meaning. Finally, the verdict was clear. The remains of at least three houses, four fireplaces, and several middens and depressions were visible on the ground surface. Other disturbances suggested the location of perimeter fortifications, bastions, borrow or "puddling" (clay-mixing) pits, and other possible buildings. We could also distinguish scars left by the digging in 1965.

With these discoveries we came to appreciate just how tenuous site preservation had been. Definite French period features were visible within three meters of the dead furrow at the north edge of the old cultivated field. Had earlier landowners farmed another half acre of land along the river, all of Mo20 would likely have been plowed under!

We called the three visible house sites the "north, central, and south structures." These fallen remains were rectangular in outline, yet exhibited differences in size, character, and orientation that seemed related to functional and socioeconomic aspects of site use (fig. 15-3).

The largest and most imposing building site is that of the north structure. It sits on the highest ground and occupies a "leveled" space of 7.5 by 14 meters (about 105 square meters). Its long axis is oriented north-south. Collapsed fireplace mounds appear at opposite ends of the structure. One, set in the north wall, was considerably disturbed in 1965. The other, centered within the south end of the structure, appears largely intact. Towards the middle of the building site are two circular depressions and a gaping squarish hole that has the outward appearance of having been a cribbed cellar. Outside and parallel to the north, west, and south wall embankments are several apparent borrow pits. A contour break in the east wall embankment suggests a doorway. Developing evidence now shows that only the north end of this house was destroyed by fire. Because of the north structure's ambitious size, elevated location, dual fireplaces, subfloor pits, and associated artifacts (including "status items" like ceramics, a key, and a shoe buckle frame), it has been tentatively identified as the commandant's quarters or "Bourgeois House" (Birk 1987:4).

More recent work done in and around the north structure tends to support this interpretation. Excavation in 1986 showed that one of the two circular depressions was a steep-sided, bark-lined, subfloor pit containing charred corn and nut shells. This fact, and the nearby presence of a second depression of similar size and appearance, hints that both served the common purpose of food storage pits. To find such pits so close together implies that an east-west partition wall ran between them and divided the north structure into two compartments, each with its own fireplace.

If so, we might infer from this evidence that the building was shared by persons of some elevated social status who lived and messed separately. On the other hand, excavations done in 1988 along the southeast exterior of the building hint that at least part of the structure may have been used for the storage and exchange of trade goods. Either way, our limited excavations in and around the north structure have produced the richest variety of French period artifacts yet found at Mo20.

A one-meter-by-three-meter trench placed in the south structure in 1983 suggests its use by those at the opposite end of the social scale. This well-defined building site occupies a somewhat elevated space of 4.75 by 9 meters (about 43 square meters). Unlike the north structure, its long axis is east-west. A lone fireplace in the north wall was largely, if not completely potted in 1965. The hole dug in this feature was big enough for the landowner to ask that it be backfilled "before one of his sheep fell into it and broke a leg" (Dacken 1983:2).

Our excavations in the south structure reveal the exterior walls were built of *poteaux en terre* construction. The daub or *bousillage* used to chink the walls was a blend of fine river sediments intermixed with leaves and other plant materials. The collapsed south wall was plastered on only the exterior surface, apparently to keep dried and aging *bousillage* from falling into the house where it might create dust and contaminate provisions and furs. The roof of this structure may have been covered in part with birch bark. The floor treatment is unknown. The quantity of charred timbers and burned daub indicates the south structure was destroyed by a massive conflagration. The most notable artifact found in our exploratory trench is part of a cast brass "circarch" bell with the letter "W" on its face (fig. 15-5B). It is not unlike examples reported from other eighteenth-century sites by Ian Brown (1979:199–200).

In 1984 IMA fielded its first large crew at Mo20 and began inviting greater public visitation and news coverage. We were fortunate to get a regional utility company, Minnesota Power, to donate and install an electric cable to the site. Other "Friends of the IMA" helped acquire or assemble the security fence, water screens, electric water pump system, excavation canopies, and a small office trailer complete with telephone. It was also the year that IMA curator-archaeologist Kim

Breakey joined the project as my assistant, a position she has held every year since.

IMA excavations during the 1984–86 and 1988 field seasons focused on opening a 240 square meter block of units from an area in and around the central structure (fig. 15-3). This prepared but unelevated building site had the poorest surface definition of the three. Its size, orientation, and visible features approximate those of the adjacent south structure. Complete excavation shows that the central structure measured 5 by 7.5 meters and had two rooms enclosing a total space of about 37.5 square meters (fig. 15-6). The east room, roughly 5 meters square, had an exterior doorway facing the river and a single fireplace built into the north wall. It served as a living area and work space. The smaller, unheated west room, only accessible through an interior doorway, was likely a storage area. The north-south walls of the central structure were of *poteaux en terre* construction, whereas the flanking east-west walls were made of horizontal timbers. A deep postmold at the midpoint of each of the north-south walls marks the location of three large vertical timbers that likely supported a central ridge pole for a gable roof.

Because only part of the central structure was damaged by fire, many details of the building's construction and appearance were lost.

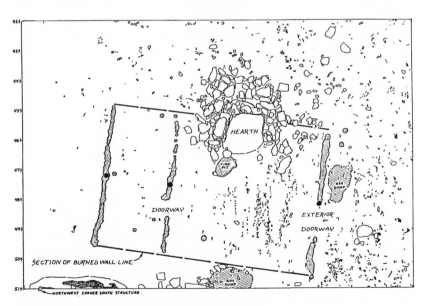

Figure 15-6. The Central Structure at Mo20

Heavy charring, confined to the southwest corner of the house, suggests ignition from the intense heat of the burning south structure. Why the flames did not spread to envelope the entire central structure is unknown. However, the evidence for separate fires in the north and south structures—at opposite ends of the fort complex—implies the blazes were deliberately set. The validity of this observation will be tested in future excavations.

Artifacts found in and around the central structure suggest its occupants lived a spartan life-style with few material luxuries. Window glass and ceramic vessels are missing from the artifact assemblage and only one small, white clay smoking pipe fragment was recovered. Gun-related objects such as lead shot and balls, gunflints, and gunworms are plentiful, as are items of adornment such as glass beads, tinkling cones, and brooches. Among the unique artifacts is a small octagonal mirror box (or compact), and a signet ring bearing the intaglio bust of a male flanked by the initials "C-F." Lead runnels and other evidence found on the hearth show that circular lead brooches, similar to examples from the River L'Abbe Mission at Cahokia (Walthall and Benchley 1987:61, fig. 23), were manufactured in front of the fire-place. Bone and lead gaming pieces found nearby hint that some idle time was devoted to gambling.

As a general practice, soils relating to the French occupation at Mo20 are excavated with trowels, brushes, or smaller tools. The materials exposed by this process are piece plotted in situ before being removed for shipment to the laboratory. This effort is supported by the routine recovery of small artifacts through water-screening and flotation. The meticulous mapping and retrieval of materials has given strong indications of activity areas and disposal and traffic patterns important in determining how the French organized and used space and budgeted time (fig. 15-7). The great quantities and good preservation of food waste, fireplace sweepings, and artifacts on the site lend themselves to this approach. Much, in fact, would be lost if the digging was done with less stringent methods.

Piece plotting has benefited the field research in other ways as well. The great volumes of wood ash and animal bone scattered about the "front yard" east of the central structure were found to end abruptly in a line paralleling the river bank. Although yet uncertain, this line may mark the location of an east curtain wall, a feature that has otherwise escaped archaeological detection in the deep "prairie soil."

Piece plotting also led to an unexpected discovery in the east room of the central structure. Careful mapping of the animal bone in that area revealed their distribution trended in very subtle yet obviously

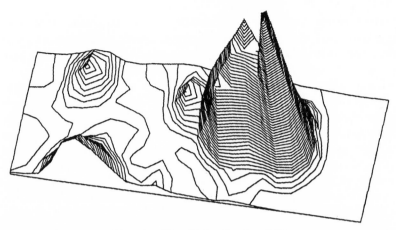

Figure 15-7. Drawn Glass Seed Bead Distribution. This computer-generated view, looking southeast, shows how the distribution of seed beads coincides with cultural features in the area of the central structure. Visible on the right is the house with its two rooms, and on the left are several trash middens found in the front yard.

paralleling north-south rows. In some parts of the room these rows were associated with rich organic soils and small artifacts like lead shot or gunflints. The rows are now believed to indicate the spaces between wooden, puncheon "floor boards" that had long since rotted away (fig. 15-6).

Another important discovery was made during the excavation of the central structure fireplace. Probably like all the fireplaces at Mo20, this feature consisted of a rock fire chamber topped by a wood frame and clay chimney. When weakened and decayed by time, it eventually collapsed into a circular mound. Excavation of the mound uncovered the C-shaped base of the fire chamber with its walls intact to the level of four or five courses of rock. On the hearth and spilling out the front of the fireplace was a thick stratum of wood ash separated into two layers by a seam of clay rubble. The ash appeared to have been deposited in two episodes, with the rubble having fallen from the chimney sometime before the second ash layer was formed. Preliminary observation indicates that the top layer of ash contained a considerable quantity of migratory waterfowl bones, an expected by-product of fall hunts in this northern latitude.

A scenario built on the idea that Mo20 is Fort Duquesne can be constructed to explain this circumstance. The bottom layer of ash could be the residue of fires built during the first winter's occupation of the fort. Evidence from around the central structure shows that large quantities of wood ash were also discarded outdoors during that initial use. When the occupants left for their traditional summer rendezvous, some accumulated ash was left in the fireplace. During their absence rain washed down the chimney, "caking" the ash and dislodging pieces of clay from the flue lining. When the fort was reoccupied the following autumn, the inhabitants did not choose to remove the accumulated ash and rubble. They simply resumed building fires and during their stay tossed the scraps from their meals of ducks and geese into the blaze. The second occupation of the fort was terminated before the ash was considered of sufficient depth to necessitate removal. Sometime later the fireplace collapsed, encapsulating its ashy contents.

If this scenario and my understanding of Joseph Marin's affairs are correct, then the bottom layer of ash and most of the ash piles scattered outside the central structure could relate to the first occupation of Fort Duquesne. In other words, they would date to the winter of 1752–53. If so, then the clay rubble must have fallen during the spring and summer of 1753. It follows that the top layer of ash accumulated during a short autumn reoccupation of the fort by Houl or his associates sometime before they were run off by La Verendrye. Further excavations in the north and south structures should help test this explanatory model (Birk 1987:5–6).

Another important test will be the formal analysis of bone material from the fireplace, a task now being done by Dr. Terrance J. Martin of the Illinois State Museum in Springfield. Martin, the author of many faunal studies in the western Great Lakes, will eventually be able to compare food waste from the various houses at Mo20 to see who was eating what and where. He will also be able to compare the faunal assemblage from Mo20 with assemblages from other French sites, such as Forts de Chartres I, Ouiatenon, and Michilimackinac.

Equally interesting will be faunal comparisons with the nearby ca. 1840 Little Elk cabin and mission sites. Unlike Mo20, where fish remains appear to be scarce, the cabin site produced a sizable collection of fish bones in the first one-meter-by-one-meter test pit. Other useful comparisons might be made with faunal evidence from Mille Lacs Lake (Johnson 1985) and nearby British and American period wintering sites (Birk 1984). One of these, a post occupied by Zebulon Pike's American expeditionary force at the Swan River in 1805–6 (fig. 15-2), is now being studied by IMA. Pike's journals reveal the kinds, numbers, and habits of large game animals probably available in this resource regime during the French occupation of Mo20. They also shed light on how Minnesota's changing seasons shaped human diets before the period of white settlement.

Other inquiries should be no less informative. I, for one, am anxious to see if evidence exists to show a measurable effect of Catholic religious beliefs on western French diets. One source suggests that devout French Canadians came to observe 143 days of abstinence from eating meat or milk by-products. Many of these devotees apparently considered fish a disagreeable alternative. To compensate, it is said that they ate beaver, muskrat, and otter, which were allowed because they are amphibious animals (Denys 1908:361–63; Jacoby 1983:14). Beaver tail was among the culinary delicacies not dispensed with even in Lent (McKenney 1959:201).

Conclusions

Mo20 is more than just a "fur trade" site, historic place, or curiosity. It is a material archives of unique and vital information about the past. It is a *source* that yields to thoughtful investigation with the potential to inform about a broad range of topics and events. From it we can learn simple facts such as the nature of French architecture and the caliber of French guns, or more complex things such as the process and extent of mid-eighteenth-century French contacts and exchanges in the Mississippi Headwaters.

Much of the information recovered from Mo20 is specific to a particular time and place and cannot be duplicated from other sources. What better defines the nature and setting of a French fort than the remains of the fort itself? Where else can we gain fresh insights about the *voyageurs*, that illiterate class of French Canadian laborers so often ignored in contemporary written records? How did they live? What material items did they possess and use in daily lives? How did they relate to their natural surroundings? What did they eat? How did their diet differ from that of their bourgeois or other associates? Is the privilege of rank reflected in which animal parts were eaten or how they were prepared by different social classes? Did the French introduce trade silver ornaments into the western Great Lakes before 1760? Did the French "melt into the wilderness" on their western voyages or did they build conventional style houses and live in a manner reminiscent of their parent culture? How do population dynamics of mid-1700s white-tailed deer herds in central Minnesota (as gleaned from the archaeological record) compare with those of today? What does the presence of intact, eighteenth-century trash deposits tell us about the need for greater restraint in our continued promiscuous use of the environment?

The full scope and value of Mo20 will only be realized when excavation and analysis are completed. The site's ultimate impact might best be measured by how its many "lessons" are absorbed into mainstream historical thought, where they might more sharply focus our visions of the past and help us better understand how we got where we are today. To meet this challenge, IMA is developing plans to extend public interpretation of Mo20 and the many other historical and natural properties at its Little Elk Heritage Preserve. At the same time IMA is supporting broader research to uncover and explain more fully French presence throughout the region south and west of Lake Superior. I think Marin, Le Sueur, Duluth, and the La Verendryes would be pleased.

Acknowledgments

This paper was prepared at the Institute for Minnesota Archaeology, 3300 University Avenue Southeast, Minneapolis, MN 55414 as IMA Report of Investigations, no. 38.

The Mo20 Project has benefited from assistance provided by the Elmer L. and Eleanor J. Andersen Foundation, Blandin Foundation, Bush Foundation, First National Bank of Little Falls, La Compagnie, Minnesota Historical Society, Minnesota Parks Foundation, Minnesota Power, Morrison County Highway Department, Morrison County Historical Society, Pap's Sport Shop of Little Falls, Mr. Carl A. Weyerhaeuser, and the many volunteers and contributors who comprise the Friends of the IMA. Special recognition is due Mr. and Mrs. Robert J. Sivertsen for their steadfast interest, encouragement, and support.

The author also wishes to acknowledge the help of Sam Morgan, Bob Binger, the late Tom Savage, and other members of the Minnesota Parks Foundation; Clark Dobbs and Elden Johnson, IMA; Paulette Pappenfus, Chair, Little Elk Task Force; Jan Warner, Director, Morrison County Historical Society; the late Robert C. Wheeler of St. Paul; Douglas Forsythe, Ted Lofstrom, and Diana Mitchell-Keefe of Minneapolis; and James Engholm, Larry and Kathy Engholm, Earl and Esther Knutson, Jo Ann and Bruce Mellor, the late Spencer Nelson and Rusty Nelson, and Al Stoltman of Little Falls. A special thanks to Kim Breakey, Dean Anderson, and the many other archaeologists and volunteers who have served on Mo20 field crews.

Bibliography

Adler, Kraig
  1968 Turtles from Archaeological Sites in the Great Lakes Region. *Michigan Archaeologist* 14(3–4):147–63.
  1969 The Influence of Prehistoric Man on the Distribution of the Box Turtle. *Annals of the Carnegie Museum* 41(9):263–80.

Alvord, Clarence W.
  1906 The Finding of the Kaskaskia Records. *Transactions of the Illinois State Historic Association for the Year 1905.*
  1907 *Cahokia Records 1778–1790.* Collections of the Illinois State Historical Library, vol. 2, Springfield.
  1922 *The Illinois Country 1673–1818.* A. C. McClurg, Chicago.

American State Papers
  1860 *Documents of the Congress of the United States in Relation to Public Land.* 38 vols. Washington, D.C.

Avery, Kevin W.
  1988 Early French Sites in Peoria. In *Intensive Archaeological Explorations for Peoria's 18th Century Village,* by Keith L. Barr, Jerry J. Moore, and Charles L. Rohrbaugh, pp. 87–113. Illinois State University, Midwestern Archaeological Research Center Research Report no. 7. Normal.

Bailey, Kenneth P. (editor)
  1975 *Journal of Joseph Marin.* Irvine, Calif.

Bailey, Lynn R.
  1966 Preliminary Archaeological and Feasibility Study, Fort Massac. Ms. on file, Center for Archaeological Investigations, Southern Illinois University, Carbondale.

Bald, F. Clever
  1961 *Michigan in Four Centuries.* Harper and Brothers, New York.

Baldwin, Elmer
  1877 *History of LaSalle County, Illinois.* Rand McNally, Chicago.

Ballance, Charles
  1870 *The History of Peoria, Illinois.* N. C. Nason, Peoria.

Bareis, Charles J.
1975a Report of 1971 University of Illinois-Urbana Excavations at the Cahokia Site. *Papers in Anthropology* 3:9–11. Illinois State Museum, Springfield.
1975b Report of 1972 University of Illinois-Urbana Excavations at the Cahokia Site. *Papers in Anthropology* 3:12–15. Illinois State Museum, Springfield.

Barr, Keith L., Jerry J. Moore, and Charles L. Rohrbaugh
1988 *Intensive Archaeological Explorations for Peoria's 18th Century French Village.* Illinois State University, Midwestern Archaeological Research Center Research Report no. 7. Normal.

Barton, Kenneth J.
1977 The Western European Coarse Earthenwares from the Wreck of the Machault. *Occasional Papers in Archaeology and History* 16:45–71. Canadian Historic Sites, Ottawa.
1981 *Coarse Earthenwares from the Fortress of Louisbourg.* History and Archaeology no. 55. National Historic Parks and Sites Branch, Parks Canada, Ottawa.

Beck, Lewis C.
1823 *A Gazetteer of the States of Illinois and Missouri.* Albany, New York.

Beers, Henry P.
1964 *The French and British in the Old Northwest: A Bibliographical Guide to Archive and Manuscript Sources.* Wayne State University Press, Detroit.

Belting, Natalia M.
1943 The French Villages of the Illinois Country. *Canadian Historical Review* 24:14–23.
1948 *Kaskaskia under the French Regime.* Illinois Studies in the Social Sciences 29(3). University of Illinois, Urbana.

Benchley, Elizabeth D.
1974 *Mississippian Secondary Mound Loci: A Comparative Functional Analysis in a Time-Space Perspective.* Ph.D. dissertation, University of Wisconsin-Milwaukee. University Microfilms, Ann Arbor.

Binford, Lewis R.
1978 A Discussion of the Contrasts in the Development of the Settlement at Fort Michilimackinac Under British and French Rule. In *Historical Archaeology: A Guide to Substantive and Theoretical Contributions,* ed. Robert L. Schuyler, pp. 267–68. Baywood Publishing, Farmingdale, N.Y.

Birk, Douglas A.
1975 Fort Charlotte. In *Voices from the Rapids,* ed. Robert C. Wheeler, pp. 85–93. Minnesota Historical Archaeology Series no. 3. Minnesota Historical Society, St. Paul.
1982 The La Verendryes. Reflections on the 250th Anniversary of the

French Posts of La Mer de l'Ouest. In *Where Two Worlds Meet: The Great Lakes Fur Trade*, ed. Carolyn Gilman, pp. 116–19. Minnesota Historical Society, St. Paul.

1983 Our Search for Minnesota's Unwritten History. *The Minnesota Volunteer* 46(267):25–31. Minnesota Department of Natural Resources, St. Paul.

1984 John Sayer and the Fond du Lac Trade: The North West Company in Minnesota and Wisconsin. In *Rendezvous: Selected Papers of the Fourth North American Fur Trade Conference, 1981*, ed. Thomas C. Buckley, pp. 51–61. North American Fur Trade Conference, St. Paul.

1985 *The Continuing Search for 21–GD-88, a Suspected French-Period Fort Site on Prairie Island, Goodhue County, Minnesota.* Report of Investigations no. 5. The Institute for Minnesota Archaeology, Minneapolis.

1987 Tracking the Voyageur: Archaeologists in Search of Our French Connection. *HSP Journal* 2(1):3–6. La Compagnie des Hivernants de la Riviere Saint Pierre Historical Society, Burnsville, Minn.

Birk, Douglas A., and Robert C. Wheeler
1975 Fort Charlotte Underwater Archeology Project. *National Geographic Research Reports 1975*, pp. 791–99. National Geographic Society, Washington, D.C.

Blegen, Theodore C.
1963 *Minnesota: A History of the State.* University of Minnesota Press, Minneapolis.

Bossu, Jean Bernard
1771 *Travels Through That Part of North America Formerly Called Louisiana.* T. Davies, London.

Boylan, Rose J.
1939 Report of the Cahokia Memorial Survey from August 1, 1938 to February 1, 1939. Ms. on file, Illinois State Historical Library, Springfield.

1949 Life as Illustrated by Legal Documents, 1772–1821. In *Old Cahokia*, ed. John F. McDermott, pp. 93–189. The St. Louis Historical Documents Foundation, St. Louis.

Brackenridge, Henry M.
1868 *Recollections and Places in the West.* Philadelphia.

Brain, Jeffrey P.
1979 *Tunica Treasure.* Papers of the Peabody Museum of Archaeology and Ethnology, vol. 71. Harvard University, Cambridge, Mass.

Branstner, Susan
1984 Huron-Petun Occupation of the Marquette Mission Site, 1671–1700. Paper presented at the Midwest Archaeological Conference, Evanston, Illinois.

1985   Excavating a Seventeenth-Century Huron Village. *Archaeology* 38(4): 58–59.

Bray, Martha C. (editor)
1970   *The Journals of Joseph N. Nicollet.* Minnesota Historical Society, St. Paul.

Breining, Greg, and Linda Watson
1977   *A Gathering of Waters: A Guide to Minnesota's Rivers.* Minnesota Department of Natural Resources, St. Paul.

Briggs, Winstanley
1985   *The Forgotten Colony: Le Pays Des Illinois.* Ph.D. dissertation, University of Chicago.

Brink, McDonough, and Co.
1881   *History of St. Clair County, Illinois.* Brink, McDonough, and Co., Philadelphia.

Brooms, Bascom M., and James W. Parker
1980   Fort Toulouse Phase IV Progress Report. Ms. on file, Alabama Historical Commission, Montgomery.

Brower, Jacob V.
1902   *Kakabikansing.* Memoirs of Explorations in the Basin of the Mississippi, vol. 5. Minnesota Historical Society, St. Paul.

Brown, Ian W.
1974   Excavations at Fort St. Pierre. *The Conference on Historic Sites Archaeology Papers* 9:60–85.
1979   Bells. In *Tunica Treasure,* by Jeffrey P. Brain, pp. 197–205. Papers of the Peabody Museum of Archaeology and Ethnology, vol. 71. Harvard University, Cambridge, Mass.

Brown, Margaret Kimball
1970   An Analysis of the Archaeological Data from Fort Massac. Ms. on file, Center for Archaeological Investigations, Southern Illinois University, Carbondale.
1973   The Waterman Site, Archaeology and Systemic Change. Ms. on file, Colonial Studies Program, Illinois State Museum, Springfield.
1975   Preliminary Investigations at Fort de Chartres. *The Conference on Historic Sites Archaeology Papers* 8:94–107.
1976   *The 1974 Fort de Chartres Excavation Project.* Archaeological Service Report no. 49. Southern Illinois University Museum, Carbondale.

Brown, Margaret K., and Laurie C. Dean
1977   *The Village of Chartres in Colonial Illinois, 1720–1765.* Polyanthos Press, New Orleans.

Burnham, J. Howard
1914   *Destruction of Kaskaskia by the Mississippi River.* Transactions of the Illinois State Historical Society, vol. 20. Springfield.

Burpee, Lawrence J.
1968   *Journals of La Verendrye.* Greenwood Press, New York.

Bushnell, David I.
  1914 Archaeological Investigation in Ste. Genevieve County, Missouri. *Proceedings of the United States National Museum* 46:641–68. Washington, D.C.

Cardinal, Elizabeth A.
  1975 Faunal Remains from the Zimmerman Site–1970. In *The Zimmerman Site,* by Margaret K. Brown, pp. 73–79. Illinois State Museum Reports of Investigations no. 32. Springfield.
  1977 Faunal Remains from Fort de Chartres. In *The 1975 Season of Archaeological Investigations at Fort de Chartres, Randolph County, Illinois* by Charles E. Orser, pp. 164–67. Southern Illinois Studies, Research Records no. 16. Southern Illinois University, Carbondale.

Carter, Clarence E. (editor)
  1934 *The Territorial Papers of the United States 2.* United States Printing Office, Washington, D.C.

Casagrande, Joseph B., S. I. Thompson, and Peter D. Young
  1964 Colonization as a Research Frontier: The Ecuadorian Case. In *Process and Pattern in Culture,* ed. Robert A. Manners, pp. 281–325. Aldine, Chicago.

Chaput, Donald
  1979 Marin de la Malgue, Joseph. *Dictionary of Canadian Biography* 4:512–14. University of Toronto Press, Toronto.

Charlevoix, Pierre F. X. de
  1761 *Journal of a Voyage to North America.* 2 vols. March of America Facsimile Series no. 36. University Microfilms, Ann Arbor, 1966.

Clark, A. H.
  1968 *Acadia: The Geography of Early Nova Scotia to 1760.* University of Wisconsin Press, Madison.

Cleland, Charles E.
  1972 From Sacred to Profane: Style Drift in the Decoration of Jesuit Finger Rings. *American Antiquity* 37:202–10.
  1982 The Inland Shore Fishery of the Northern Great Lakes: Its Development and Importance in Prehistory. *American Antiquity* 47:761–84.
  1988 Questions of Substance, Questions That Count. *Historical Archaeology* 22:13–17.

Coles, Edward
  1834 Claims to Lots in the Village of Peoria, Illinois. *American State Papers, Public Lands* 3:476–86. Gales and Seaton, Washington, D.C.

Collet, George
  1942 Maps of the Illinois Country 1796. In *Indian Villages of the Illinois Country, Part I, Atlas,* comp. Sarah J. Tucker, plates 27 and 30. Illinois State Museum, Scientific Papers vol. 2, Springfield.

Cotter, John L.
1958 *Archaeological Excavations at Jamestown.* National Park Service, Washington, D.C.

Cox, Sandford C.
1970 *Recollections of the Early Settlement of the Wabash Valley.* Reprint, Books for Libraries Press, Freeport, New York. Originally published Chicago, 1860.

Craig, Oscar
1893 Ouiatenon. *Indiana Historical Society Publications* 2(8):317–48.

Cressey, Pamela J., and John F. Stephens
1982 The City-Site Approach to Urban Archaeology. In *Archaeology of Urban America: The Search for Pattern and Process,* ed. Roy S. Dickens, pp. 41–61. Academic Press, New York.

Dacken, Elaine
1983 Fort Duquesne: A French Fort near Little Falls. *Minnesota Power Contact,* October, pp. 2–3.

Deagan, Kathleen
1982 Avenues of Inquiry in Historical Archaeology. In *Advances in Archaeological Method and Theory,* vol. 5, ed. Michael B. Schiffer, pp. 151–77. Academic Press, New York.
1987 *Artifacts of the Spanish Colonies of Florida and the Caribbean.* Smithsonian Institution Press, Washington, D.C.

Deetz, James
1977 *In Small Things Forgotten.* Anchor Books, Garden City, N.Y.

Denman, D. D.
1979 History of La Saline: Salt Manufacturing Site, 1675–1825. *Missouri Historical Review* 73:307–20.

Denys, Nicolas
1908 *The Description and Natural History of the Coasts of North America.* The Champlain Society, Toronto.

Donnelly, Joseph P.
1949a Burial Records of the Holy Family Church. In *Old Cahokia,* ed. John F. McDermott, pp. 255–85. The St. Louis Historical Documents Foundation, St. Louis.
1949b The Founding of the Holy Family Mission and Its History in Eighteenth Century Documents. In *Old Cahokia,* ed. John F. McDermott, pp. 55–92. The St. Louis Historical Documents Foundation, St. Louis.
1949c *The Parish of the Holy Family, Cahokia, Illinois.* St. Louis University, St. Louis.

Drown, S. DeWitt
1844 *The Peoria Directory for 1844.* Peoria.

Dumont de Montigny, Jean F. B.
1753 *Memories Historiques sur la Louisiane,* part 2. Paris.

Eccles, William J.
  1969 *The Canadian Frontier, 1534–1760.* Holt, Rhinehart, and Winston, New York.
  1972 *France in America.* Harper and Row, New York.
  1974 Marin de la Malgue, Paul. *Dictionary of Canadian Biography* 3:431–32. University of Toronto Press, Toronto.

Ekberg, Carl J.
  1985 *Colonial Ste. Genevieve.* The Patrice Press, Gerald, Mo.
  1987 A Map of Ste. Genevieve. *Mapline* 45:1–3.

Ekberg, Carl J., and W. E. Foley (editors)
  1989 *An Account of Upper Louisiana by N. de Finiels.* University of Missouri Press, Columbia.

Elliot, John B. (editor)
  1975 *Contest for Empire, 1500–1775.* Indiana Historical Society, Indianapolis.

Emerson, Thomas E., and R. Barry Lewis (editors)
  1991 *Cahokia and the Hinterlands: Middle Mississippian Cultures of the Midwest.* University of Illinois Press, Urbana.

Esarey, Mark, and David Dycus
  1986 Phase I Investigations for the Franklin Street Bridge Cultural Resource Survey Project. Ms. on file, Illinois Department of Transportation, Springfield.

Faribault-Beauregard, Marthe
  1984 *La Population des Fortes Francais d'Amerique,* vol. 2. Bergeron Publishing, Montreal.

Farnsworth, Kenneth B., and Thomas E. Emerson
  1986 *Early Woodland Archaeology.* Center for American Archeology Press, Kampsville, Illinois.

Feister, Lois M.
  1984 Material Culture of the British Soldier at "His Majesty's Fort of Crown Point" on Lake Champlain, New York, 1759–1773. *Journal of Field Archaeology* 11(2):123–32.

Ferguson, Leland G.
  1977 An Archaeological-Historical Analysis of Fort Watson: December 1780–April 1781. In *Research Strategies in Historical Archaeology,* ed. Stanley South, pp. 41–72. Academic Press, New York.

Flanders, Richard E.
  1965 Engraved Turtle Shells from the Norton Mounds. *Papers of the Michigan Academy of Science, Arts, and Letters* 50:54–60.

Fortier, Edward J.
  1909 The Establishment of the Tamarois Mission. *Transactions of the Illinois State Historical Society* 13:233–39.

Fortier, John B.
1969 New Light on Fort Massac. In *Frenchmen and French Ways in the Mississippi Valley*, ed. John F. McDermott, pp. 57–72. University of Illinois Press, Urbana.

Franzwa, Gregory M.
1967 *The Story of Old Ste. Genevieve.* The Patrice Press, Gerald, Mo.

Garrad, Charles
1969 Bear Jaw Tools from Petun Sites. *Ontario Archaeology* 13:54–60.

Genêt, Nicole
1977 *La Faience à la Place Royale.* Activites Archeologiques 1976, dossier 31, Ministere des Affaires Culturelles, Quebec.

Gerin-Lajoie, Marie
1976 Fort Michilimackinac in 1749, Lotbiniere's Plan and Description. *Mackinac History*, vol. 2, Leaflet no. 5. Mackinac State Park Commission, Mackinac Island, Mich.

Giraud, Marcel
1953 *Histoire de la Louisiane Française le regne de Louis XIV*, vol. 1. Presses Universitaires de France, Paris.

Goggin, John M.
1968 *Spanish Majolica in the New World.* Yale University Publications in Anthropology no. 72. New Haven.

Good, Mary E.
1972 *Guebert Site: An 18th Century Kaskaskia Indian Village in Randolph County, Illinois.* Central States Archaeological Society Memoir no. 2. St. Louis.

Grant, Peter
1960 The Sauteux Indians About 1804. In *Les Bourgeois De La Compagnie Du Nord-Ouest*, ed. L. R. Mason, pp. 303–66. Antiquarian Press, New York.

Green, Mary S.
1983 *The Material Culture of a Pre-Enclosure Village in Upper Louisiana: Open Fields, Houses, and Cabinetry in Colonial Ste. Genevieve, 1750–1804.* Master's thesis, Department of Anthropology, University of Missouri, Columbia.

Grimm, Eric C.
1985 Vegetation History Along the Prairie-Forest Border in Minnesota. *Reprints in Anthropology* 31:9–30. J and L Reprint Co., Lincoln, Neb.

Guillet, Edwin C.
1966 *Pioneer Travel in Upper Canada.* University of Toronto Press, Toronto.

Gums, Bonnie L.
1988 *Archaeology at French Colonial Cahokia.* Studies in Illinois Archaeology, vol. 3. Illinois Historic Preservation Agency, Springfield.

Halchin, Jill Y.
1985   *Excavations at Fort Michilimackinac, 1983–1985: House C of the South-east Row House, the Soloman Levy-Parant House.* Archaeological Completion Report Series no. 11. Mackinac Island State Park Commission, Mackinac Island, Mich.

Hall, Robert L.
1986   Starved Rock as the Site of La Salle's Fort St. Louis. Paper presented at the Annual Meeting of the Central States Anthropological Society, Chicago.

Halsey, John R.
1966   Additional Hopewell Engraved Turtle Shells from Michigan. *Papers of the Michigan Academy of Science, Arts, and Letters* 51:389–98.

Hamilton, T. M.
1980   *Colonial Frontier Guns.* The Fur Press, Chardron, Neb.

Hardesty, Donald L.
1985   Evolution on the Industrial Frontier. In *The Archaeology of Frontiers and Boundaries,* ed. Stanton W. Green and Stephen M. Perlman, pp. 213–29. Academic Press, New York.

Harris, Donald A.
1971   A French Colonial Well: Its Construction, Excavation, and Contents. *The Conference on Historic Sites Archaeology* 5:51–80.

Harris, R. Cole
1987   *Historical Atlas of Canada,* Vol. 1: *From the Beginning to 1800.* University of Toronto Press, Toronto.

Heldman, Donald P.
1977   *Excavations at Fort Michilimackinac, 1976: The Southeast and South Southeast Row House.* Archaeological Completion Report Series no. 1. Mackinac Island State Park Commission, Mackinac Island, Mich.
1978   *Excavations at Fort Michilimackinac, 1977: House One of the South Southeast Row House.* Archaeological Completion Report Series no. 2. Mackinac Island State Park Commission, Mackinac Island, Mich.
1979   Archaeological Preservation at Michilimackinac: The First Twenty Years. Paper presented at the Twelfth Annual Meeting of the Society for Historical Archaeology, Nashville, Tenn.
1980   Coins at Michilimackinac. *Historical Archaeology* 14:82–107.
1983   *Archaeological Investigations at French Farm Lake in Northern Michigan, 1981–1982: A British Colonial Farm Site.* Archaeological Completion Report Series no. 6. Mackinac Island State Park Commission, Mackinac Island, Mich.
1984   East Side, West Side, All Around the Town: Stratigraphic Alignment and Resulting Settlement Patterns at Fort Michilimackinac, 1715–1781. Paper presented at the Seventeenth Annual Meeting of the Society for Historical Archaeology, Williamsburg, Va.
1986   Michigan's First Jewish Settlers: A View from the Soloman-Levy

House at Fort Michilimackinac, 1765–1781. *Journal of New World Archaeology* 6(4):21–33.

Heldman, Donald P., and Roger T. Grange
1981 *Excavations at Fort Michilimackinac, 1978–1979: The Rue de la Babillarde.* Archaeological Completion Report Series no. 3. Mackinac State Park Commission, Mackinac Island, Mich.

Heldman, Donald P., and William L. Minnerly
1976 *Fort Michilimackinac Archaeological Investigations, 1974 and 1975.* Archaeological Completion Report Series no. 7. Office of Archaeology and Historic Preservation, National Park Service, Washington, D.C.
1977 *The Powder Magazine at Fort Michilimackinac: Excavation Report.* Reports in Mackinac History and Archaeology no. 6. Mackinac Island State Park Commission, Mackinac Island, Mich.

Hickerson, Harold
1970 *The Chippewa and Their Neighbors: A Study in Ethnohistory.* Holt, Rhinehart and Winston, New York.

Houck, Louis
1908 *History of Missouri.* Chicago.

Hulse, Charles A.
1977 *An Archaeological Evaluation of Fort St. Joseph: An Eighteenth Century Military Post and Settlement in Berrien County, Michigan.* Masters thesis, Department of Anthroplogy, Michigan State University, East Lansing.

Innis, Harold A.
1956 *The Fur Trade in Canada: An Introduction to Canadian Economic History.* University of Toronto Press, Toronto.

Jacoby, Patrick E.
1983 *The Family of Theodore Bellefeuille.* Minneapolis.

James, J. A. (editor)
1912 *The George Rogers Clark Papers, 1771–84.* Illinois State Historical Society, Springfield.

Jelks, Edward B., and Joan Church
1978 Report of Archaeological Reconnaissance and Testing at Fort Creve Coeur State Park. Ms. on file, Illinois Historic Preservation Agency, Springfield.

Jelks, Edward B., Carl J. Ekberg, and Terrance J. Martin
1989 *The Laurens Site: A Probable Location of Fort de Charles I.* Studies in Illinois Archaeology no. 5. Illinois Historic Preservation Agency, Springfield.

Jelks, Edward B., and Joan Unsicker
1981 Archaeological Assessment of Seven Sites Purported to be the Location of La Salle's Fort Creve Coeur. Ms. on File, Illinois Historic Preservation Agency, Springfield.

Johnson, Elden
1985   The 17th Century Mdewakanton Dakota Subsistence Mode. *Reprints in Anthropology* 31:154–66. J and L Reprint Company, Lincoln, Neb.

Johnson, Ida A.
1971   *The Michigan Fur Trade.* Black Letter Press, Grand Rapids, Mich.

Johnson and Co.
1880   *The History of Peoria County.* Chicago.

Joutel, Henri
1962   *A Journal of La Salle's Last Voyage.* Corinth Books, New York.

Judd, Carol M., and Arthur J. Ray (editors)
1980   *Old Trails and New Directions: Papers of the Third North American Fur Trade Conference.* University of Toronto Press, Toronto.

Kay, Jeanne
1978   *The Land of La Baye: The Ecological Impact of the Green Bay Fur Trade.* University Microfilms International, Ann Arbor.

Keene, David
1988   Archaeological Excavations at Fort de Chartres 1985–1987. Ms. on file, Illinois Historic Preservation Agency, Springfield.

Kellar, James H.
1970   The Search for Ouiatenon. *Indiana Historical Bulletin* 47:123–33.

Kellogg, Louise Phelps
1908   The Fox Indians During the French Regime. *Proceedings of the State Historical Society of Wisconsin,* pp. 142–88. Madison.
1925   *The French Regime in Wisconsin and the Northwest.* State Historical Society of Wisconsin, Madison.
1935   La Chapelle's Remarkable Retreat Through the Mississippi Valley. *The Mississippi Valley Historical Review* 22:63–81.

Keslin, Richard O.
1964   *Archaeological Implications on the Role of Salt as an Element of Cultural Diffusion.* Missouri Archaeologist, vol. 26.

Krauskopf, Frances (editor)
1955   Ouiatenon Documents. *Indiana Historical Society Publications* 18(2):132–234.

Lagron, Arthur
1913   Fort Crevecoeur. *Journal of the Illinois State Historical Society* 5(4):451–57.

Lewis, Kenneth E.
1984   *The American Frontier: An Archaeological Study of Settlement Pattern and Process.* Academic Press, New York.

Linder, Jean R.
1975   Survey of the Archaeological Resources Along the Existing and Proposed Levees on Kaskaskia Island in Randolph County, Illinois. Ms. on file, Corps of Engineers, St. Louis.

Long, George A.
  1973 *Progress Report on Faience Research.* Research Bulletin no. 3, Canadian National Historic Sites Service, Ottawa.

Lowrie, Walter, and Walter S. Franklin (editors)
  1834 *American State Papers, Documents, Legislative and Executive of the Congress.* Public Land Series, vol. 2. Gales and Seaton, Washington, D.C.

McClurkan, Burney
  1971 Fort Desha: The Location of Arkansas Post. *The Conference on Historic Site Archaeology Papers* 6:32–39.

McDermott, John F. (editor)
  1949 *Old Cahokia.* The St. Louis Historical Documents Foundation, St. Louis.
  1965 *The French in the Mississippi Valley.* University of Illinois Press, Urbana.
  1969 *Frenchmen and French Ways in the Mississippi Valley.* University of Illinois Press, Urbana.
  1974 *The Spanish in the Mississippi Valley, 1762–1804.* University of Illinois Press, Urbana.

MacLaughlin, Ada G.
  1902 The Site of Fort Crevecoeur. *Journal of the Illinois State Historic Society* 5:179–89.

McKenney, Thomas L.
  1959 *Sketches of a Tour of the Lakes.* Ross and Haines, Minneapolis.

McWilliams, Richebourg G. (editor)
  1953 *Fleur de Lys and Calument, Being the Penicaut Narrative of French Adventure in Louisiana.* Louisiana State University Press, Baton Rouge.

Maduell, Charles R.
  1972 *The Census Tables for the French Colony of Louisiana from 1699 Through 1732.* Baltimore.

Mansberger, Floyd
  1989 An Architectural and Archaeological Assessment of the Proposed Bielfeldt-Homart Development Site. Ms. on file, Illinois Historic Preservation Agency, Springfield.

Martin, Patrick E.
  1985 *The Mill Creek Site and Pattern Recognition in Historical Archaeology.* Archaeological Completion Report no. 10. Mackinac Island State Park Commission, Mackinac Island, Mich.

Martin, Terrance J.
  1986 *A Faunal Analysis of Fort Ouiatenon, An Eighteenth Century Trading Post in the Wabash Valley.* Ph.D. dissertation, Michigan State University. University Microfilms, Ann Arbor.
  1988 Animal Remains from the Cahokia Wedge Site. In *Archaeology at*

French Colonial Cahokia, by Bonnie L. Gums, pp. 221–34. Studies in Illinois Archaeology, vol. 3. Illinois Historic Preservation Agency, Springfield.

Martin, Terrance J., and Mary Carol Masulis
1988   Preliminary Report on Animal Remains from Fort de Chartres (11-R-127). Ms. on file, Illinois Historic Preservation Agency, Springfield.

Mason, Ronald J.
1986   *Rock Island: Historical Indian Archaeology in the Northern Lake Michigan Basin.* Kent State University Press, Kent, Ohio.

Matson, Nehemiah
1874   *French and Indians of the Illinois River.* Princeton, Ill.
1882   *Pioneers of Illinois.* Knight and Leonard, Chicago.

Maxwell, Moreau S., and Lewis H. Binford
1961   *Excavations at Fort Michilimackinac, Mackinac City, Michigan, 1959 Season.* Museum Cultural Series, vol. 1. Michigan State University, East Lansing.

Maynard, Paul
1939   Archaeological Excavations at Cahokia Courthouse Site: June 26, 1939 to August 31, 1939. Ms. on file, Illinois Historic Preservation Agency, Springfield.
1942   Summary Report of the Archaeological Research and Preliminary Restoration: Fort Massac State Park, Metropolis, Illinois. Ms. on file, Illinois Historic Preservation Agency, Springfield.

Mereness, Newton D.
1916   *Travels in the American Colonies.* Macmillan, New York.

Mohlenbrook, Robert
1972   Fort Crevecoeur State Park. *Outdoor Illinois* 14:18–26.

Morse, Eric W.
1969   *Fur Trade Canoe Routes of Canada: Then and Now.* Queen's Printer, Ottawa, Canada.

Morton, Arthur S.
1973   *A History of the Canadian West to 1870–71.* University of Toronto Press, Toronto.

Mousnier, R.
1970   *The Institution of France Under the Absolute Monarchy, Society and the State.* Presses Universitaires de France, Paris.

Nish, Cameron
1968   *Les Bourgois-gentilshommes de la Nouvelle France, 1729–1748.* Fides, Montreal.

Noble, Vergil E.
1982   Excavating Fort Ouiatenon, A French Fur Trading Post. *Archaeology* 35(2):71–73.
1983   *Functional Classification and Inter-Site Analysis in Historical Archaeol-*

ogy: A Case Study from Fort Ouiatenon. Ph.D. dissertation, Michigan State University. University Microfilms, Ann Arbor.

Noël Hume, Ivor
1970 *A Guide to the Artifacts of Colonial America.* Alfred A. Knopf, New York.

Norris, F. Terry
1979 Old Town Ste. Genevieve—A Preliminary Assessment. Ms. on file, U.S. Army Corps of Engineers, St. Louis.
1984 Old Cahokia, An Eighteenth Century Archaeological Model. *Le Journal* 2(1):1–21.

Nute, Grace L.
1951 Marin Versus La Verendrye. *Minnesota History* 32:226–38.
1960 By Minnesota Waters. In *Minnesota Heritage,* ed. Lawrence M. Brings, pp. 89–119. T. S. Denison Co., Minneapolis.

Orser, Charles E.
1975 *The Kolmer Site: An Eighteenth Century Michigamea Village.* Master's thesis, Department of Anthropology, Wayne State University, Detroit.
1977 *The 1975 Season of Archaeological Investigation at Fort de Chartres.* Southern Illinois Studies no. 16. Southern Illinois University, Carbondale.

Paape, Charles W.
1938 Starved Rock in the History of Illinois. Ms. on file, National Park Service, Washington, D.C.

Palm, Sister Mary Borgias
1931 *The Jesuit Missions of the Illinois Country, 1673–1763.* Cleveland.

Parker, Donald D. (editor)
1966 *The Recollections of Philander Prescott, Frontiersman of the Old Northwest, 1819–1862.* University of Nebraska Press, Lincoln.

Parker, James W.
1982 *Archaeological Test Excavations at 1Su7, the Fort Tombecbe Site.* Journal of Alabama Archaeology 18(1).

Parkman, Francis
1869 *La Salle and the Discovery of the Great West.* Ungar Publishing, New York.

Parmalee, Paul W.
1961 Faunal Materials from the Zimmerman Site (Ls 13), LaSalle County, Illinois. In *The Zimmerman Site,* ed. James A. Brown, pp. 79–81. Reports of Investigations no. 9. Illinois State Museum, Springfield.
1963 Vertebrate Remains from the Bell Site, Winnebago County, Wisconsin. *The Wisconsin Archaeologist* 44(1):58–69.

Parmalee, Paul W., and Walter L. Klippel
1983 The Role of Native Animals in the Food Economy of the Historic Kickapoo in Central Illinois. In *Lulu Linear Punctate: Essays in Honor*

of George Irving Quimby, ed. Robert C. Dunnell and Donald K. Grayson, pp. 253–321. Anthropological Papers no. 72. University of Michigan Museum of Anthropology, Ann Arbor.

Pease, Theodore C. (editor)
1925 *Laws of the Northwest Territory.* Illinois State Historical Library, Springfield.

Pease, Theodore C., and Edward Jenison
1940 *Illinois on the Eve of the Seven Years' War 1747–1755.* Collections of the Illinois State Historical Library, vol. 29. Springfield.

Pease, Theodore C., and Marguerite Pease
1965 *The Story of Illinois.* University of Chicago Press, Chicago.

Penny, James S.
1981 *Archaeological Survey of Fort Massac State Park, Massac County, Illinois.* Research Paper no. 29. Center for Archaeological Investigations, Southern Illinois University, Carbondale.

Perino, Gregory
1967 The Kaskaskia Indian Village Site 1700–1832. *The Conference on Historic Site Archaeology Papers* 1:127–30.

Peterson, Charles E.
1949a *Colonial St. Louis, Building a Creole Capital.* Missouri Historical Society, St. Louis.
1949b Notes on Old Cahokia. *Journal of the Illinois State Historical Society* 42:7–29, 193–258, 313–84.
1965 The Houses of French St. Louis. In *The French in the Mississippi Valley,* ed. John F. McDermott, pp. 17–40. University of Illinois Press, Urbana.

Phillips, Richard
1975 The Missing Fort. *Illiniwek Magazine* 1:1–8.

Pittman, Philip
1770 *The Present State of the European Settlements on the Mississippi River.* Facsimile edition, Memphis State University, Memphis.

Price, Anna
1980 French Outpost on the Mississippi. *Historic Illinois* 3(1):1–4.
1986 Corporate Structures, Economic Development and Social Mobility in the Mid-Mississippi Valley during the 18th Century. Ms. on file, Department of Anthropology, University of Missouri, Columbia.

Price, Cynthia
1979 *19th Century Ceramics in the Eastern Ozark Border Region.* Center for Archaeological Research, Southwest Missouri State University, Springfield.

Purdue, James R., and Bonnie W. Styles
1986 *Dynamics of Mammalian Distribution in the Holocene of Illinois.* Reports of Investigations no. 41. Illinois State Museum, Springfield.

Quaife, Milo M. (editor)
1947 *The Western Country in the 17th Century.* Lakeside Press, Chicago.

Quimby, George I.
1966 *Indian Culture and European Trade Goods.* University of Wisconsin Press, Madison.

Rackerby, Frank E.
1970 Preliminary Report of the 1970 Archaeological Excavations at Fort Massac. Ms. on file, Center for Archaeological Investigations, Southern Illinois University, Carbondale.
1971 An Archaeological Site Survey of Fort Massac State Park. Ms. on file, Center for Archaeological Investigations, Southern Illinois University, Carbondale.

Ray, R. Craig
1976 Fort Toulouse of the Alabamas. *Periodical Journal of the Council on Abandoned Military Post* 8(1). Arlington, Virginia.

Rea, Robert R.
1973 *The Present State of the European Settlements on the Mississippi by Captain Philip Pittman.* University of Florida Press, Gainesville.

Reitz, Elizabeth J., Irvy R. Quitmyer, H. Stephen Hale, Sylvia J. Scudder, and Elizabeth S. Wing
1987 Application of Allometry to Zooarchaeology. *American Antiquity* 52:304–17.

Rennick, Percival
1934 The Peoria and Galena Trail and Coach Road and the Peoria Neighborhood. *Journal of the Illinois State Historical Society* 27:351–63.

Reynolds, John
1852 *A Pioneer History of Illinois.* N. A. Randall, Belleville, Ill.

Robinson, Gary
1986 A Report of Phase I Archaeological, Architectural, and Historical Investigations for the Franklin Street Bridge, Peoria and Tazewell Counties, Illinois. Ms. on file, Illinois Department of Transportation, Springfield.

Robinson, Willard B.
1977 *American Forts: Architectural Form and Function.* University of Illinois Press, Urbana.

Rogers, Karel
1975a Faunal Remains from the Zimmerman Site—1971. In *The Zimmerman Site*, by Margaret K. Brown, pp. 80–85. Reports of Investigations no. 32. Illinois State Musuem, Springfield.
1975b Faunal Remains from the Zimmerman Site—1972--Grid B. In *The Zimmerman Site*, by Margaret K. Brown, pp. 86–91. Reports of Investigations no. 32. Illinois State Museum, Springfield.

Rostlund, Erhard
  1952 *Freshwater Fish and Fishing in Native North America.* University of California Publications in Geography, vol. 9. University of California Press, Berkeley.

Roth, Rodris
  1961 *Tea Drinking in 18th Century America: Its Etiquette and Equipage.* The Smithsonian Institution Press, Washington, D.C.

Rowland, Dunbar, and A. G. Sanders
  1932 *Mississippi Provincial Archives 1704–1743: French Dominion.* Mississippi Department of Archives and History, Jackson.

Rubertone, Patricia E.
  1982 Urban Land Use and Artifact Deposition: An Archaeological Study of Change in Providence, Rhode Island. In *Archaeology of Urban America,* ed. Roy S. Dickens, pp. 117–41. Academic Press, New York.

Safiran, Edward T.
  1988 *Archaeological Investigations at the Louvier Site.* Master's thesis, Department of History, Illinois State University, Normal.

Saucier, Walter J., and Kathrine W. Seineke
  1969 Francois Saucier, Engineer of Fort de Chartres, Illinois. In *Frenchmen and Frenchways in the Mississippi Valley,* ed. John F. McDermott, pp. 199–230. University of Illinois Press, Urbana.

Sauer, Norman J., Samuel S. Dunlap, and Lawrence R. Simson
  1988 Medicolegal Investigation of an Eighteenth Century Homicide. *The American Journal of Forensic Medicine and Pathology* 9:66–73.

Schiffer, Michael B.
  1972 Archaeological Context and Systemic Context. *American Antiquity* 37:156–65.
  1976 *Behavioral Archaeology.* Academic Press, New York.

Schlarman, J. H.
  1929 *From Quebec to New Orleans.* Buechler Publishing, Belleville, Ill.

Schoolcraft, Henry R.
  1825 *Travels in the Central Portions of the Mississippi Valley.* New York.
  1918 A Journey up the Illinois River in 1821. In *Pictures of Illinois One Hundred Years Ago,* ed. M. Milo Quaife, pp. 85–160. Lakeside Press, Chicago.

Schultz, Christian
  1943 Travels on an Inland Voyage. *Journal of the Illinois State Historical Society* 36:322–23.

Scott, Elizabeth M.
  1985 *French Subsistence at Fort Michilimackinac, 1715–1781: The Clergy and the Traders.* Archaeological Completion Report Series no. 9. Mackinac Island State Park Commission, Mackinac City, Mich.
  1986 Diet and Status: The Case of Two French Traders at Fort-

Michilimackinac. Paper presented at the Nineteenth Annual Meeting of the Society for Historical Archaeology, Sacramento.

1987 Life on the Fur Trade Frontier: Work and Status in Northern Michigan, 1761–1815. Paper presented at the Twentieth Annual Meeting of the Society for Historical Archaeology, Savannah, Ga.

Sewell, W. H.

1982 *Work and Revolution in France: The Language of Labor from the Old Regime to 1848.* Cambridge University Press, Cambridge.

Shapiro, Gary

1978 Early British Subsistence Strategy at Fort Michilimackinac: An Analysis of Faunal Remains from the 1977 Excavation Season. In *Excavation at Fort Michilimackinac, 1977: House One of the South Southeast Row House,* by Donald P. Heldman, appendix 5. Archaeological Completion Report Series no. 2. Mackinac State Park Commission, Mackinac City, Mich.

Shay, C. Thomas

1985 Late Prehistoric Selection of Wild Ungulates in the Prairie-Forest Transition. *Reprints in Anthropology* 31:31–64. J and L Reprint Co., Lincoln, Neb.

Shea, John G.

1861 *Early Voyages up and down the Mississippi.* Joel Munson, Albany.

Shoemaker, Floyd C.

1927 *Missouri and Missourians.* Columbia, Missouri.

Snyder, John F.

1943 The Old French Towns of Illinois, a Reminiscence. *Journal of the Illinois State Historical Society* 36:356–68. Springfield.

South, Stanley

1968 Archaeological Evidence of Pottery Repairing. *The Conference on Historic Site Archaeology Papers* 2:62–71.

1977 *Method and Theory in Historical Archaeology.* Academic Press, New York.

1988 Whither Pattern? *Historical Archaeology* 22:25–28.

South, Stanley, and Randolph Widmer

1977 A Subsurface Sampling Strategy for Archaeological Reconnaissance. In *Research Strategies in Historical Archaeology,* ed. Stanley South, pp. 119–50. Academic Press, New York.

Stafford, Barbara D.

1989 *Central Illinois Expressway Archaeology: Floodplain Archaic Occupations of the Illinois Valley Crossing.* Center for American Archeology Technical Report no. 4. Kampsville, Illinois.

Stone, Lyle M.

1974 *Fort Michilimackinac, 1715–1781.* Michigan State University Anthropological Series, vol. 1. East Lansing.

Styles, Bonnie W., Terrance J. Martin, and Mary Carol Masulis
   1987   Middle Woodland and Historic Faunal Remains from the Naples-Abbott Site, Scott County, Illinois. In *Archaeological Testing of the Naples-Abbott Site,* by Barbara D. Stafford, pp. 62–86. St. Louis District Historic Properties Management Report no. 35, U.S. Army Corps of Engineers, St. Louis District.

Surrey, N. M. M.
   1916   *The Commerce of Louisiana During the French Regime.* Columbia University Press, New York.

Thompson, Erwin N.
   1969   *Grand Portage: A History of the Sites, People, and Fur Trade.* National Park Service, Washington, D.C.

Thurman, Melburn D.
   1984   *Building a House in 18th Century Ste. Genevieve.* Pendragon's Press, Ste. Genevieve, Mo.

Thwaites, Reuben Gold (editor)
   1903   *A New Discovery of a Vast Country in America by Father Louis Hennepin.* A. C. McClung, Chicago.

Tordoff, Judith D.
   1983   *An Archaeological Perspective on the Organization of the Fur Trade in Eighteenth Century New France.* Ph.D. dissertation, Michigan State University. University Microfilms, Ann Arbor.

Trask, Kerry A.
   1987   That Pleasant Reign: Life in the Metis Community of La Baye before the American Conquest. Paper presented at the Thirteenth Annual Great Lakes History Conference, Grand Rapids, Mich.

Trubowitz, Neal L.
   1987   Historical Archaeology Research by IU-Indianapolis, 1987. Paper presented at the Indiana Historical Society Conference, Indianapolis.

Tucker, Sara J.
   1941   Unpublished translation of La Salle ms. Ms. on file, Illinois State Museum, Springfield.
   1942   *Atlas of Indian Villages of the Illinois Country.* Scientific Papers no. 2. Illinois State Museum, Springfield.

Turner, Frederick J.
   1977   *The Character and Influence of the Indian Trade in Wisconsin.* University of Oklahoma Press, Norman.

Upham, Warren
   1884   Notes of Rock Outcrops in Central Minnesota. In *The Geological and Natural History Survey of Minnesota, Eleventh Annual Report,* ed. N. H. Winchell, pp. 86–136. Johnson, Smith, and Harrison, Minneapolis.

1969   *Minnesota Geographic Names, Their Origin and Historic Significance.* Minnesota Historical Society, St. Paul.

Usner, Daniel H.
1987   The Frontier Exchange Economy of the Lower Mississippi Valley in the Eighteenth Century. *The William and Mary Quarterly* 44:165–92.

Vauban, Sébastien Le Prestre de (Marquis)
1742   *Traite de L'attaque et de la Defense des Places.* The Hague.
1795   *Trait Des Sieges et de L'attaque des Places.* Paris.

von Frese, Ralph R. B.
1978   *Magnetic Exploration of Historical Midwestern Archaeological Sites as Exemplified by a Survey of Fort Ouiatenon.* Master's thesis, Department of Anthropology, Purdue University, West Lafayette, Ind.
1984   Archaeomagnetic Anomalies of Midcontinental North American Archaeological Sites. *Historical Archaeology* 18:4–19.

von Frese, Ralph R. B., and Vergil E. Noble
1984   Magnetometry for Archaeological Exploration of Historical Sites. *Historical Archaeology* 18:38–53.

Waddell, Jack O.
1985   The Ouia Post During the French Regime: Its Place in Canadian Strategy. Paper presented at the Annual Meeting of the American Society for Ethnohistory, Chicago.

Walitschek, David A., and Charles L. Rohrbaugh
1988   Report of 1986 and 1987 Archaeological Research on Historic Sites 28 and 29 at Argonne National Laboratory, Illinois. Ms. on file, Midwestern Archaeological Research Center, Illinois State University, Normal.

Wallerstein, Immanuel
1974   *The Modern World System: Capitalist Agriculture and the Origins of European World-Economy in the Sixteenth Century.* Academic Press, New York.

Walthall, John A.
1981   *Galena and Aboriginal Trade in Eastern North America.* Scientific Papers no. 17. Illinois State Museum, Springfield.
1991   Faience in French Colonial Illinois. *Historical Archaeology* 25 (1): 80–106.

Walthall, John A., and Elizabeth D. Benchley
1987   *The River L'Abbe Mission.* Studies in Illinois Archaeology no. 2. Illinois Historic Preservation Agency, Springfield.

Walthall, John A., and Bonnie L. Gums
1988   Historic Ceramics. In *Archaeology at French Colonial Cahokia* by Bonnie L. Gums, pp. 134–57. Studies in Illinois Archaeology no. 3. Illinois State Historic Preservation Agency, Springfield.

Warren, William
   1957   *History of the Ojibway Nation.* Ross and Haines, Minneapolis.

Westover, Allan R.
   1984   *A History of the Archaeological Investigations at Starved Rock.* Master's thesis, Department of History, Illinois State University, Normal.

Wheeler, Robert C. (editor)
   1975   *Voices from the Rapids.* Minnesota Historical Archaeology Series no. 3. Minnesota Historical Society, St. Paul.

Wild, J. C., and Lewis Thomas
   1841   *The Valley of the Mississippi Illustrated in a Series of Views.* Chambers and Knapp, St. Louis.

Wilford, Lloyd A., and John W. Brink
   1974   Hogback: A Protohistoric Oneota Burial Site. *Minnesota Archaeologist* 33:1–79.

Williams, J. Mark, and Gary Shapiro
   1982   *A Search for the Eighteenth Century Village at Michilimackinac: A Soil Resistivity Survey.* Archaeological Completion Report Series no. 4. Mackinac Island State Park Commission, Mackinac City, Mich.

Wilson, Samuel
   1965   Colonial Fortifications and Military Architecture in the Mississippi Valley. In *The French in the Mississippi Valley,* ed. John F. McDermott, pp. 103–22. University of Illinois Press, Urbana.

Wisconsin Historical Collections
   1906   *Collections of the State Historical Society of Wisconsin.* 21 vols. Madison.

Wood, W. Raymond
   1987   *Nicholas de Finiels: Mapping the Mississippi and Missouri Rivers 1797–1798.* The State Historical Society of Missouri, Columbia.

Wright, H. E.
   1974   The Environment of Early Man in the Great Lakes Region. In *Aspects of Upper Great Lakes Anthropology: Papers in Honor of Lloyd A. Wilford,* ed. Eldon Johnson, pp. 8–14. Minnesota Prehistoric Archaeology Series no. 11. Minnesota Historical Society, St. Paul.

Notes on the Contributors

DEAN L. ANDERSON received his B.A. from the University of Minnesota. After spending five years on the staff of the Archaeology Department of the Minnesota Historical Society, he obtained his M.A. from Michigan State University, where he is currently a doctoral candidate. His research interests lie primarily in the upper Great Lakes region, where he has conducted fieldwork in a number of areas, especially on sites of the Historic period. In addition, he has also carried out research on Historic period sites in Mississippi.

DOUGLAS A. BIRK is a cofounder and Senior Research Archaeologist at the Institute for Minnesota Archaeology. He has been involved in western Great Lakes archaeology for over thirty years and has done extensive research on prehistoric and French, British, and early American aspects of Minnesota-area history, including underwater investigations at the Grand Portage National Monument between 1972 and 1976. Birk received his training at the University of Minnesota and is currently working to promote and develop the Little Elk Heritage Preserve, a ninety-three-acre archaeological park that incorporates site Mo20.

THOMAS E. EMERSON is Chief Archaeologist for the Illinois Historic Preservation Agency. He has carried out fieldwork and published on numerous sites in the Midwest, as well as working in the Plains and Norway. Emerson received his M.A. from the University of Wisconsin at Madison, where he is currently a doctoral candidate.

BONNIE L. GUMS is the Coordinator of Historical Research, Contract Archaeology Program of Southern Illinois University at Edwardsville and a Research Associate with the Colonial Studies Program at the Illinois State Museum. Her M.A. degree from Southern Illinois University at Edwardsville focused on the French colonial village of Cahokia.

ROBERT L. HALL is a Professor of Anthropology at the University of Illinois-Chicago, where he began teaching in 1968 and served as departmental chairman for ten years. He received his B.A. and Ph.D. from the University of Wisconsin at Madison. His fieldwork activities have been conducted in Illinois, Wisconsin, Kentucky, South Dakota, North Dakota, and Venezuela.

DONALD P. HELDMAN received his Ph.D. from the University of London,

England, for research on Postclassic cultures along the northern mesoamerican frontier in San Luis Potosi, Mexico. He is currently Director of Archaeology for the Mackinac Island State Park Commission in Michigan, where he is engaged in research on French and British colonial archaeology at the Straits of Mackinac.

WILLIAM ISEMINGER is employed by the Illinois Historic Preservation Agency at Cahokia Mounds State Historic Site, where he is in charge of public relations and coordinating temporary exhibits. He received his B.A. in Anthropology from the University of Oklahoma and his M.A. from Southern Illinois University at Carbondale.

DAVID KEENE received his M.A. from the University of Wisconsin at Madison. He is currently completing his Ph.D. dissertation on Fort de Chartres, where he directed excavations between 1985 and 1989. He has been a member of the Anthropology Department faculty at Loyola University in Chicago for a number of years.

MARGARET KIMBALL-BROWN received her Ph.D. from Michigan State University in anthropology for a systems model study of the Illinois tribe. She has done fieldwork on a variety of historic French and Indian sites and extensive archival research in French colonial documents. She was District Historian and Chief Staff Archaeologist for the Illinois Department of Conservation for several years and is currently Site Manager of Cahokia Mounds State Historic Site.

TERESITA MAJEWSKI received her Ph.D. in anthropology from the University of Missouri-Columbia in 1987 and currently works at the University of Arizona as managing editor of *American Antiquity* and *Latin American Antiquity*. Her specialties include historical archaeology, ceramic analysis, and the archaeology of the Euro-American frontier.

FLOYD MANSBERGER currently is the Director of Fever River Research in Springfield, Illinois. He received his B.A. in anthropology from the University of Illinois and his M.A. at Illinois State University. Some of Mansberger's research interests include early housing in the Midwest and nineteenth-century Illinois pottery.

TERRANCE J. MARTIN received his M.A. in Anthropology from Western Michigan University (1976) and his Ph.D. from Michigan State University (1986). He is Associate Curator of Anthropology at the Illinois State Museum, where he is responsible for management of archaeological and ethnographic collections. His research has focused on archaeozoology in the Midwest with an emphasis on Historic period sites.

MOLLY E. McKENZIE is Site Manager for the Cahokia Courthouse and Jarrot Mansion State Historic Sites in Cahokia, Illinois. Her research interests include French colonial and Illinois territorial architecture, frontier material culture, preservation of historic structures, historiography, and public interpretation. She is completing a M.B.A. at Southern Illinois University at Edwardsville.

F
543
.F74
1991

French colonial
archaeology

112027

SAUK VALLEY COMMUNITY COLLEGE
LIBRARY
DIXON, IL 61021